AF574325

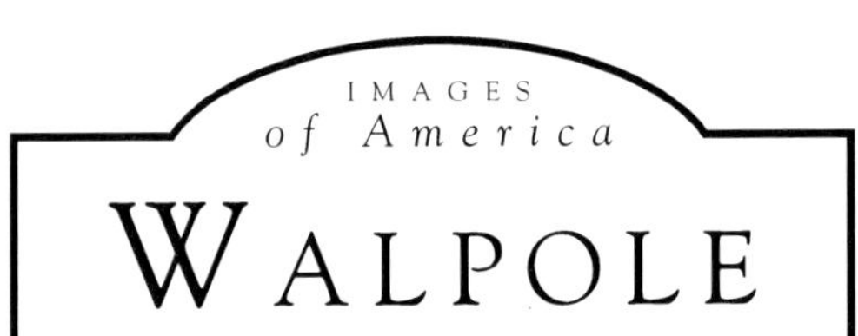
IMAGES
of America
WALPOLE

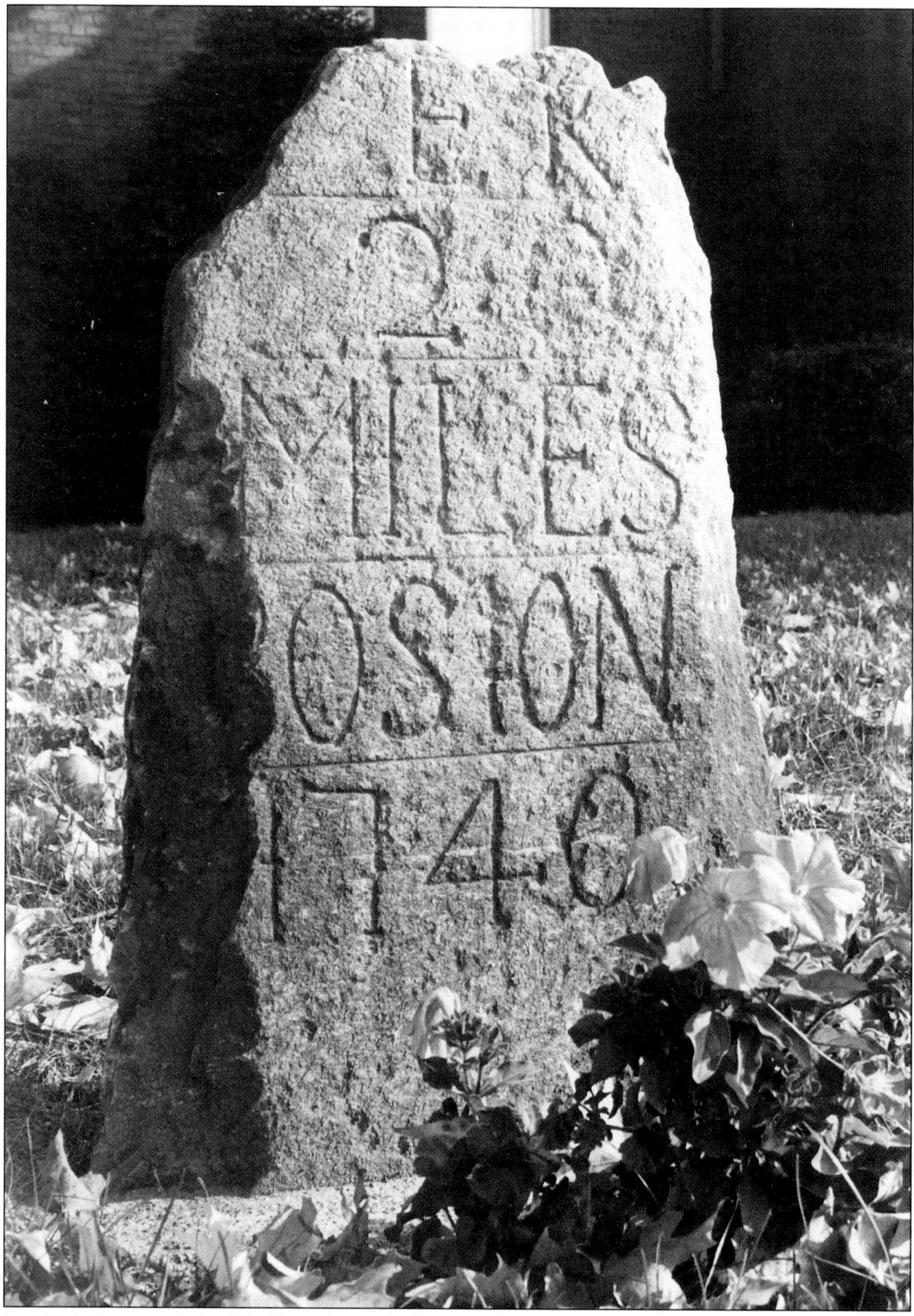

In 1724, Deacon Ezekiel Robbins kept the Brass Ball Tavern, on West Street. Robbins set this milestone marker a short distance beyond his house toward Wrentham, marking the 20 mile point from Boston, as then reckoned. The milestone, a historic reminder of the past, now sits on the lawn of "old" Town Hall.

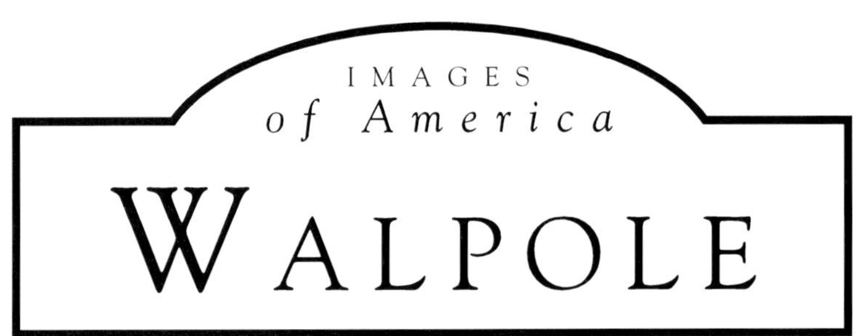

Walpole Historical Society

Deborah Ranaldi
Guy Ciannavei
Barbara Parker
Jeff Mattson
Roberta McCormack

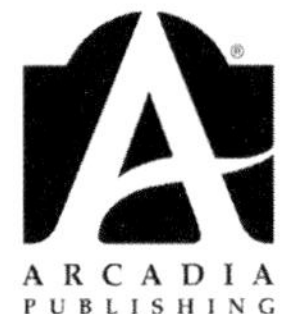

ISBN 978-0-7385-6481-4

Published by Arcadia Publishing
Charleston, South Carolina

Printed in the United States of America

Library of Congress Catalog Card Number: 2008938095

For all general information contact Arcadia Publishing at:
Telephone 843-853-2070
Fax 843-853-0044
E-mail sales@arcadiapublishing.com
For customer service and orders:
Toll-Free 1-888-313-2665

Visit us on the Internet at www.arcadiapublishing.com

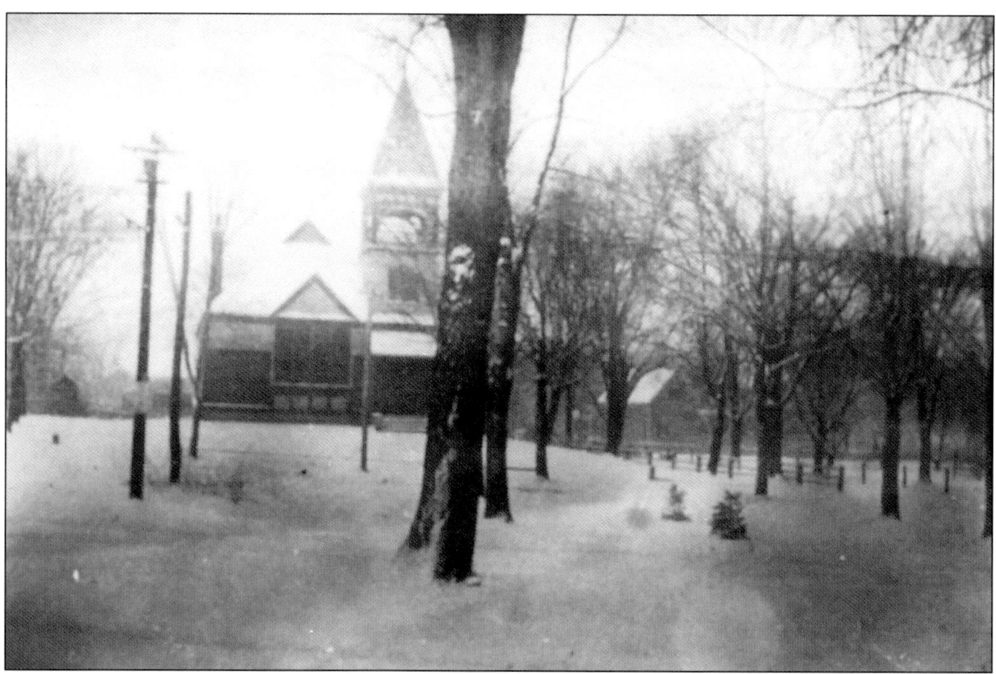

Night descends on a snow-covered church in the quiet town of Walpole, 1916.

Contents

Acknowledgments

The Walpole Historical Society would like to acknowledge and thank all who in any way have contributed to this book. Many people have put in many hours searching for pictures, researching, cataloging, and writing. Many citizens have searched their house over, donated images, and helped to identify events, dates, places, and people. Our journey back in time would not have been possible without their support. Thank you!

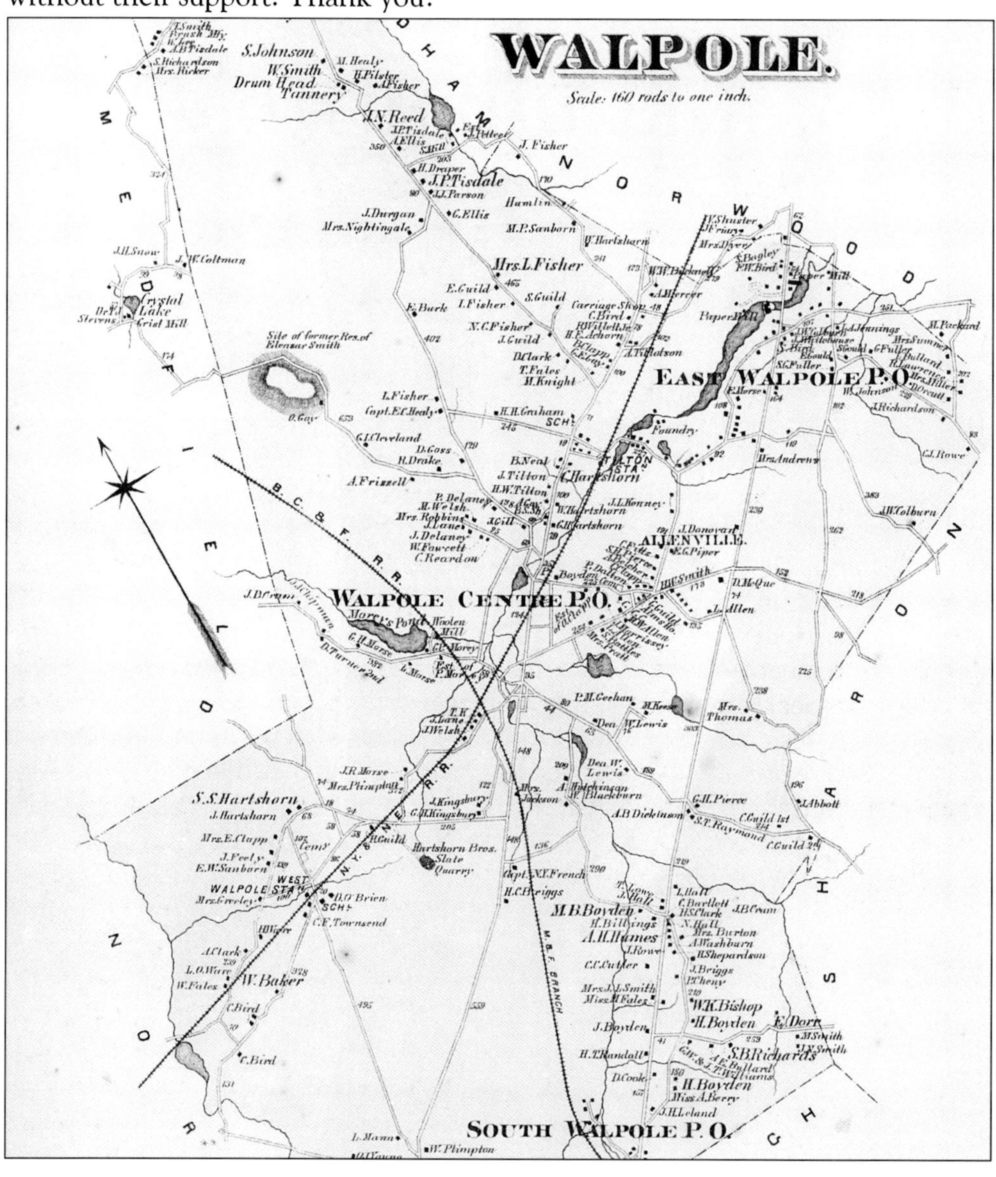

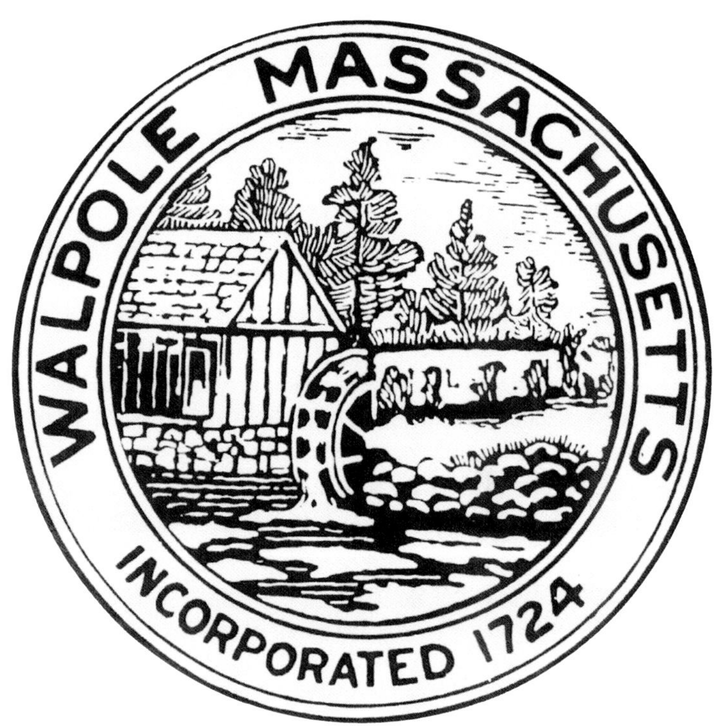

The original town seal of Walpole had only the date of incorporation, with a blank space in the center and, to a stranger, it would appear that the incorporation was about all that the town could boast of. To correct this impression, a committee was appointed on March 4, 1912, "To receive designs for a new town seal, said designs to be submitted by the inhabitants of Walpole." The committee consisted of Harry A. Whiting, originator of the motion; Henry M. Stowell, chairman of the board of selectmen; Harry L. Howard, town clerk; Frank O. Pillsbury, town treasurer; and Henry P. Plimpton, chairman of water commissioners.

At a town meeting held on April 7, 1913, it was voted "that the Committee on the Town Seal be authorized to expend a sum of money not exceeding $25.00 in securing a design for a Town Seal."

Notices were published offering a prize of $25 for the best design of a town seal, to be submitted on or before January 1, 1914. Several drawings were received by the committee, and on January 6, 1914, the committee met and accepted the design submitted by Miss Edna Buck of High Street, Walpole, a pupil attending Walpole High School. There are four parts to the design, each of which vividly represents part of the history of Walpole.

The first is the Neponset River, the very foundation of the early industrial life of Walpole. From its source in North Foxborough to the Fowl Meadows, there were a dozen water privileges where the river turned wheels, ground the corn for the early settlers, and sawed logs to build their houses. Walpole became famous in later years for the diversity of the industries located along the river's banks.

The second aspect, the wheel, signified the industry for which Walpole has been known far and wide from the time when the old mill was erected in 1650 to the present time, when our mills continue to produce products worth many millions of dollars.

The third image, the trees in the background, represents the cedars, one of the many gifts from the "Giver of All" to the early settlers of the New World. Their value was so appreciated that a road, called the "Saw Mill Road," was built from Dedham to the Great Cedar Swamp, so that citizens of Walpole might have access to this raw material to build their homes and meetinghouses. Owing to the cedar's great height and straight grain, entire buildings were built of them, as they were used to make shingles, clapboards, boards, and framing. Nearly all of the old houses of this town contain the cedar frames, etc., in their construction. Many of the best trees were carted by oxen to Boston to be used as masts for the "Yankee Ships" which sailed on every sea.

The fourth image in the design, the "Old Saw Mill," depicts one of the most significant landmarks of the original town. All the records of Dedham that mention anything regarding our part of the original town read "at or near the Old Saw Mill." The last record is as follows in part: "May 14, 1722, This day the inhabitants of the South part of the Town, at or near the Old Saw Mill, presented a petition to the Town desiring to be set off from this Town as a township or precinct, etc."

So it was that the "river" turned the "wheel," allowing the "cedars," so tall, straight, and perfect of grain, to be prepared by the "Old Saw Mill" to build the homes of our ancestors. These were the foundations of our industrial greatness and are a fitting design for our permanent town seal.

Harry A. Whiting
1919

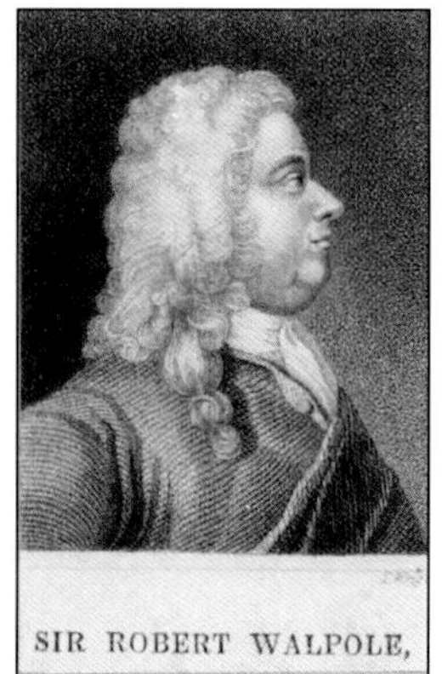

Let this Order be Executed as to the Residual Sum payable thereupon Whitehall Treasury Chambers 4 July 1721
Walpole

Walpole takes its name from Sir Robert Walpole, the prime minister of England from 1721 to 1742. He showed himself to be a friend of the colonists by refusing to levy heavy taxes; successors to Sir Walpole, however, insisted on these burdensome taxes, and the result was the American Revolution. It appears that the leaders in Boston decided to honor Walpole by naming a town after him.

One

Hearth and Home

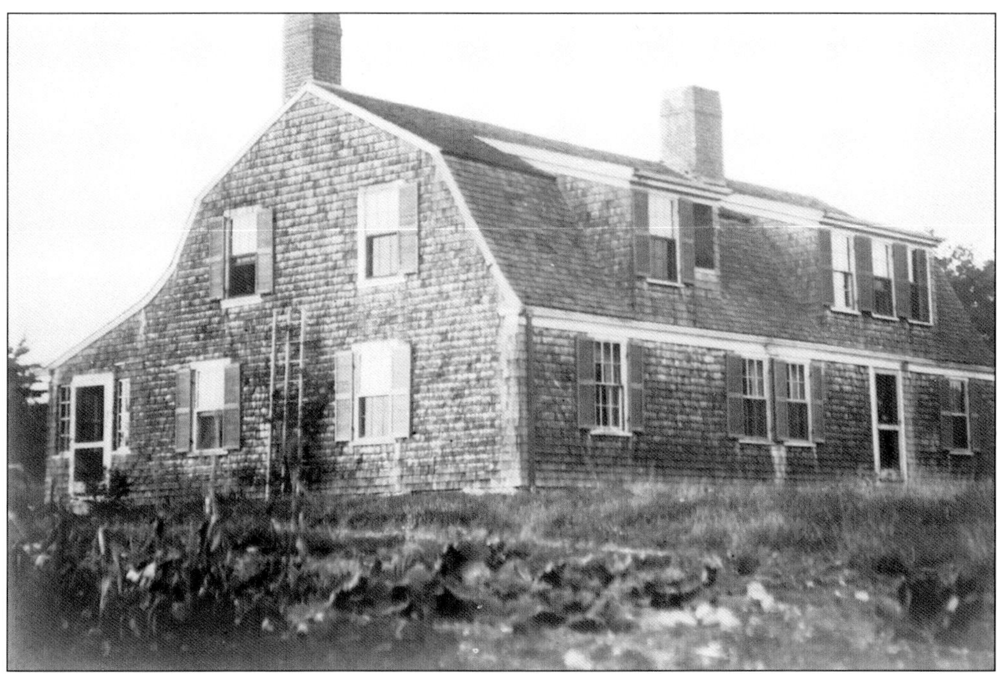

Early maps and property records indicate that Ebenezer Robbins built his *c.* 1700 home on what is now South Street when that area was referred to as "the uplands of Dorchester." The Dedham-Dorchester town line approximately followed present-day Washington Street. Walpole's eastern boundary line was redrawn in 1755. George and Francene Burnett acquired the property in 1945 and resided there for many years.

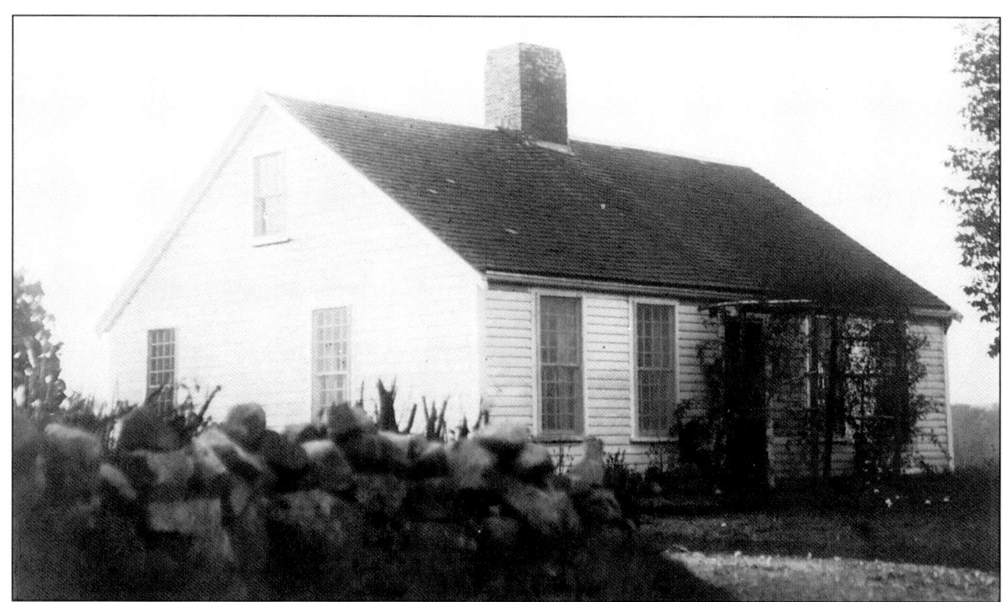

One of the very early houses that is still in existence is the Clap/Goss home, located on North Street. It was built in 1712, when North Street was one of the two original paths into the area from Dedham. In 1734, Thomas Clap (Clapp) is noted on town records as a blacksmith who made nails, hinges, and latches. A young German immigrant, Daniel Goss, became the owner of record in 1866.

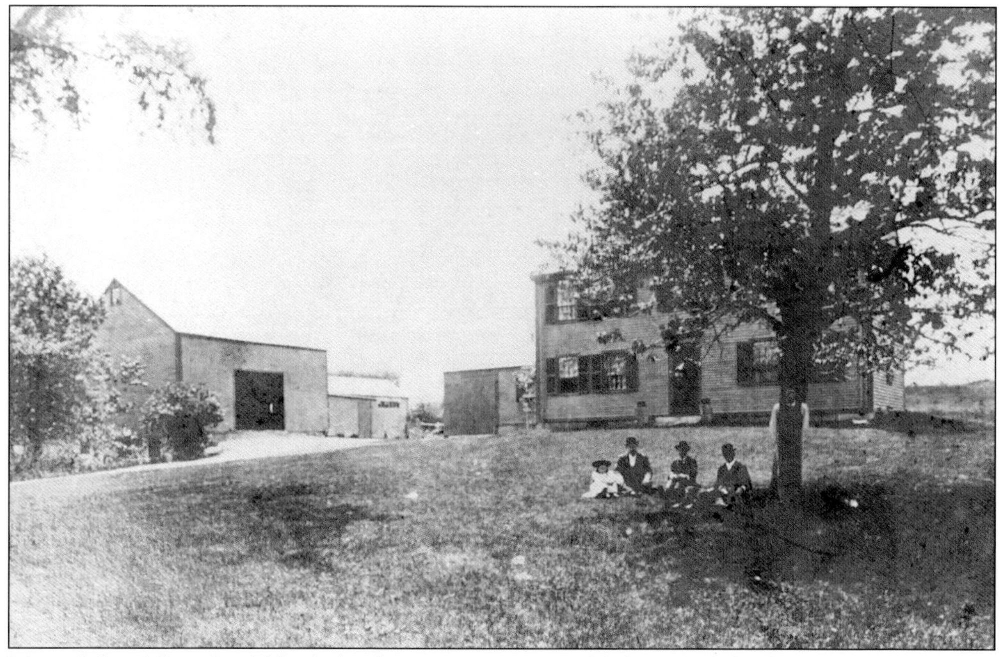

Major John Allen Gould built his home in 1811. Gould described the location of his North Street house as being "On the road leading from the house formerly the residence of John Hall, to Bubbling Brook." Active in town affairs, Gould served as a selectman, tax collector, and school committeeman. In 1846, Gould was an incorporator of the Walpole Railroad Co., which established the first rail line from Walpole to Dedham. Gould Street was named for him.

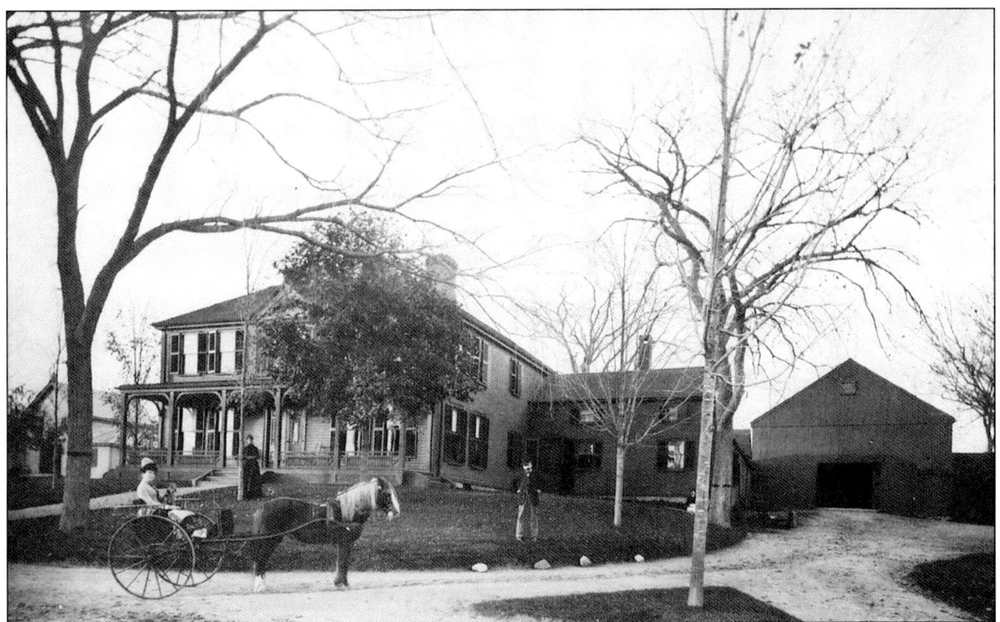

The back parts of this East Street house date to 1810–20 and the main part to 1833. Charles Henry Hartshorn, owner of Hartshorn's Market located for many years at the corner of East and Main Streets, bought this property at auction in 1884. The Hartshorns moved to a new home, the present Delaney Funeral Home, in 1900, but ownership of the house remained in the Hartshorn family until the mid-1980s.

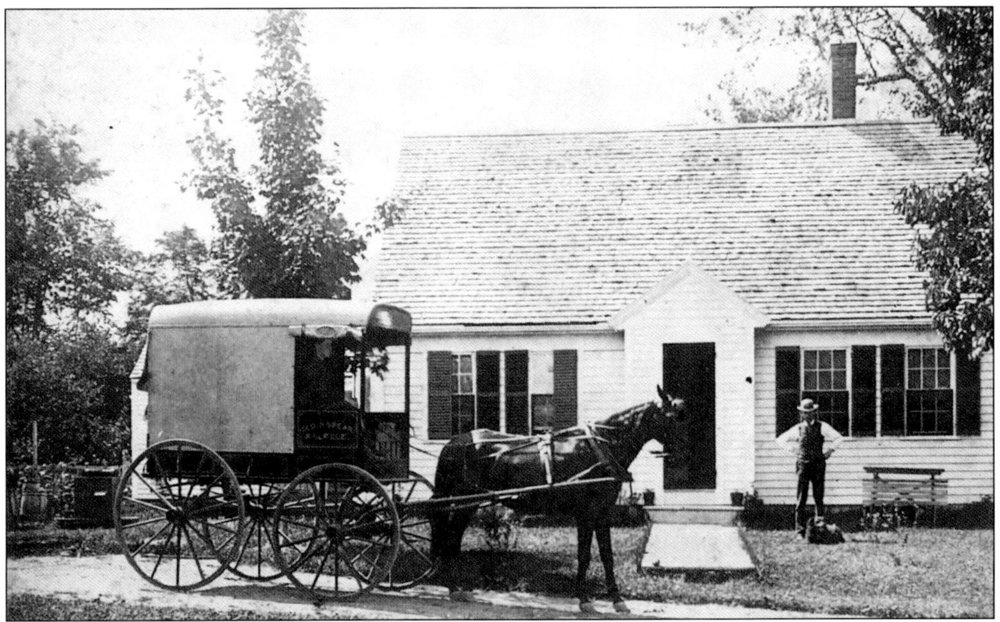

Sometime prior to 1858, George Prescott Spear bought this home which is tucked away on Kendall Street near the corner of School Street. With his son Frank, barely visible in the handsome wagon, Spear was an early "door-to-door" salesman who carried his dry goods to homes around town and as far away as Canton. He also served in town government as the "Collector of taxes and water rates."

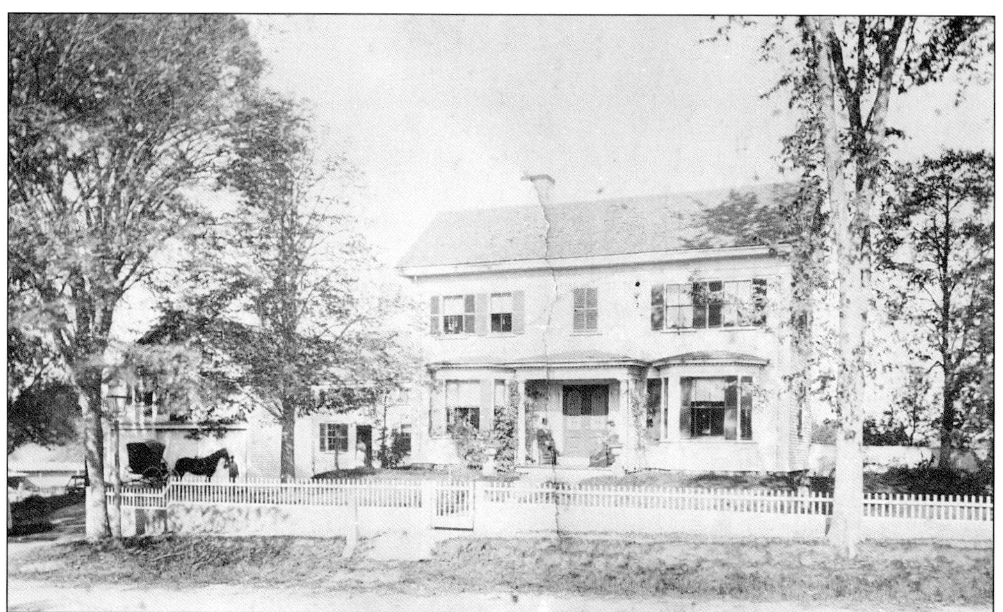

Built in 1826 by Horatio Wood, this house is known today as the Deacon Willard Lewis House and is the home of the Walpole Historical Society. Deacon Willard Lewis was one of the town's early mill owners. Located adjacent to his home, the company, which later became Kendall Mills, produced a wide variety of cotton products. In the 1950s, when occupied by a local realtor, it was known as "the big red house on the Common."

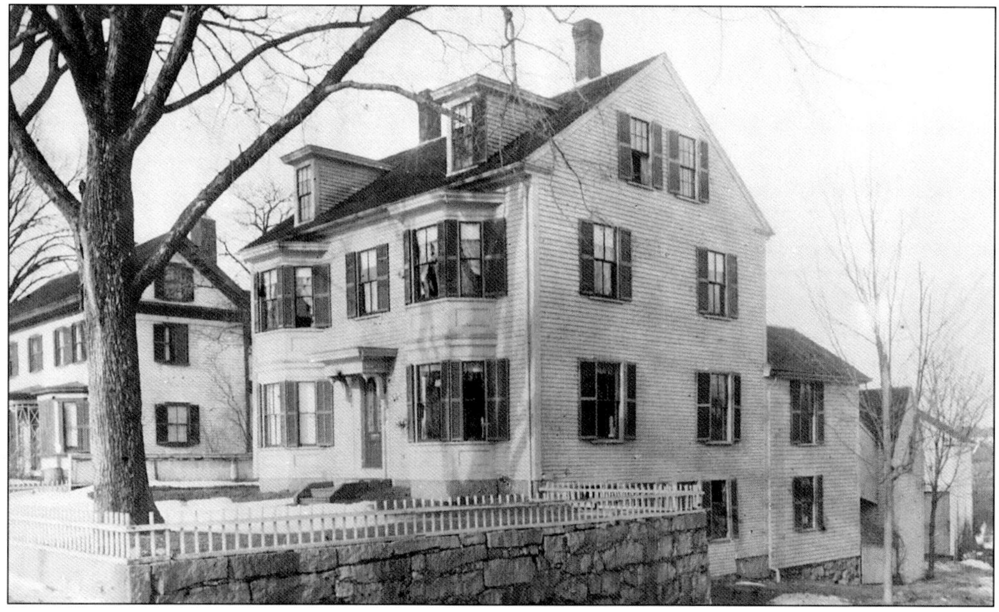

Walpole's first schoolhouse was built in 1757–58 at the corner of West and Elm Streets. In 1820, it was replaced with a larger school building. The second schoolhouse was renovated and enlarged by Dr. Andrew J. Runnells in the 1880s and was used as his home and office. His daughter, Susie Runnells Hartshorn, resided here until 1949. The house was dismantled in 1973. Today this historic school site, at the side of the Deacon Willard Lewis House, is marked with a commemorative stone.

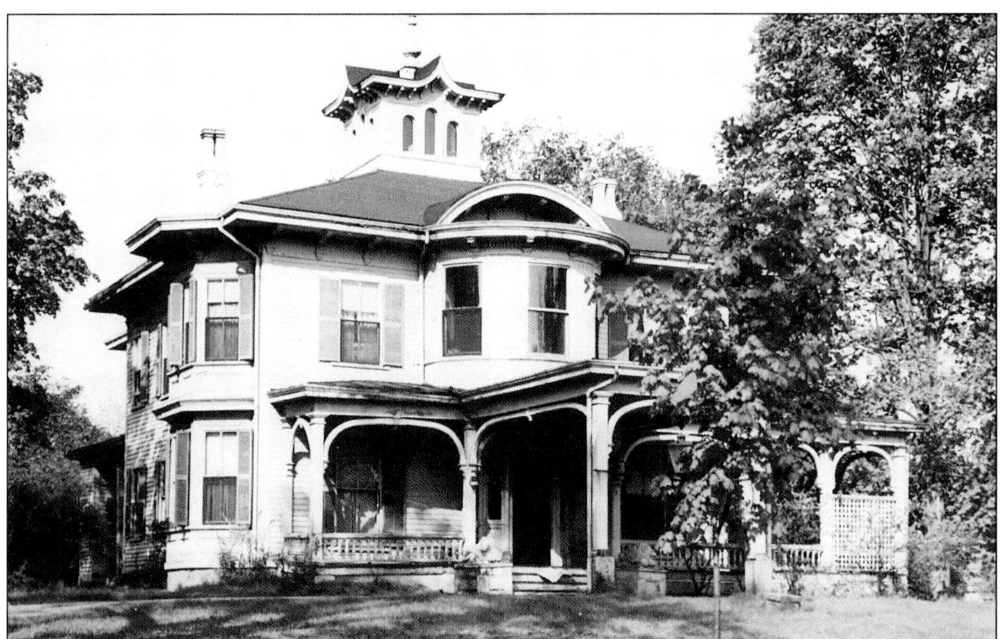

Lionhurst, the home of Col. William Moore on Common Street, was built in 1876. It reflects the popular Italianate style of that period. Lionhurst derived its name from the two stone lions that adorned the front entrance. The home remained in the Moore family until the 1940s. Today it is the Keeling-Tracy Funeral Home.

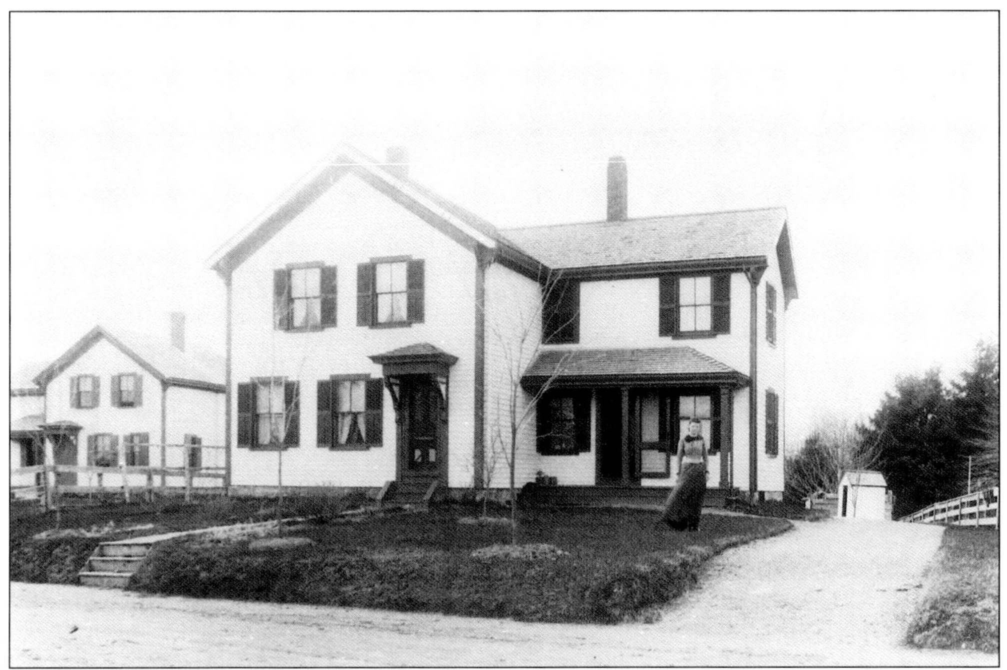

The Higgins home is one of several "look-alike" houses that were built on Diamond Street in the 1880s. Katherine Higgins, shown in this photograph, served as Walpole's town clerk for many years. Note that the home of John Flynn, in the background, is the same plan reversed.

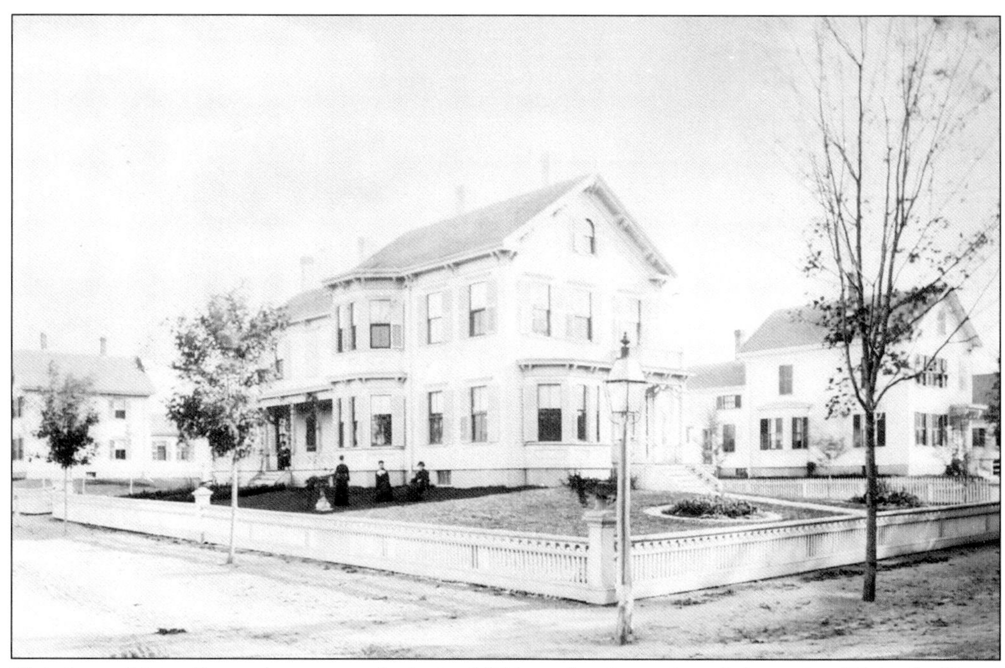

This large Main Street house was built in 1874 on land purchased from the Walpole Hotel Company. The Greenwood and Haney families have lived here since 1906. Joseph Greenwood was the owner of Greenwood's Garage, also on Main Street. His son-in-law, Charles Haney, a pharmacist, was the proprietor of Haney's Drug Store in Walpole center. At right in this photograph is the John Campbell residence, once the home of Fred O. Pilsbury, a pharmacy owner in Walpole during the 1800s.

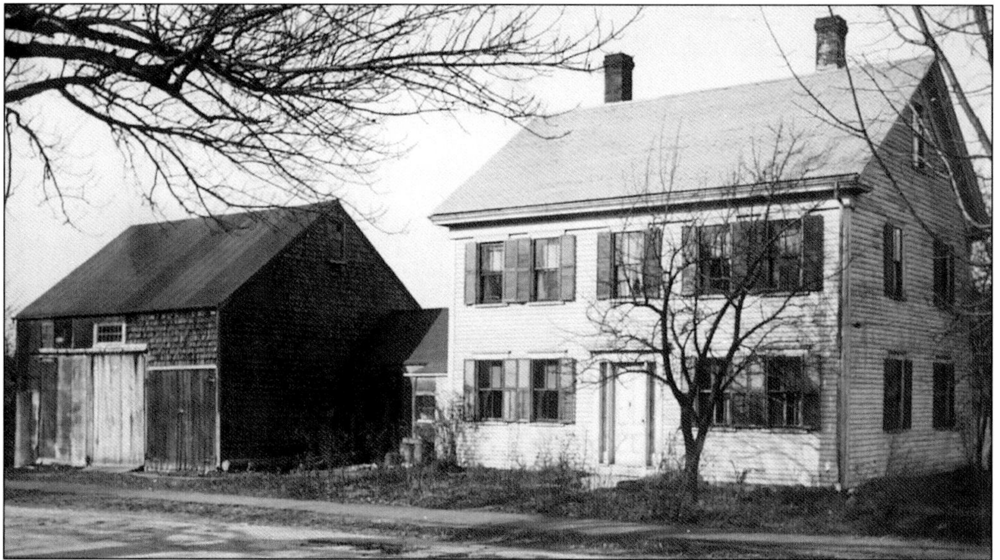

Family records indicate that Deacon William W. Rhoads (Rhoades) built his East Walpole home in 1841. The original one-story house faced old Union Street. A boot maker by trade, Rhoads used as his shop (not shown here) a building that was moved from Washington Street that had earlier housed the town's first department store. It has been said that some of Bird and Co.'s early paper shingles were used on Deacon Rhoads's barn.

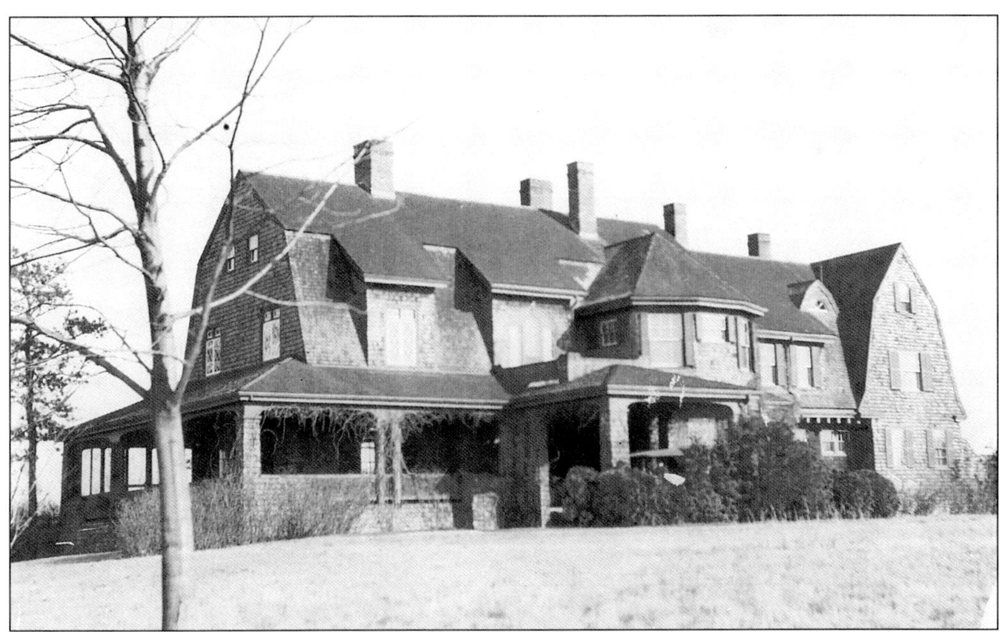

Soon after forming a partnership with Zachary Hollingsworth in 1881, Charles Vose constructed this 19-room home off Woodland Road. In 1920, the property was purchased by Bird and Son and became a social club for company employees. Burgess Read, president of the L.F. Fales Machine Company, later resided here. The house has recently become visible from the street.

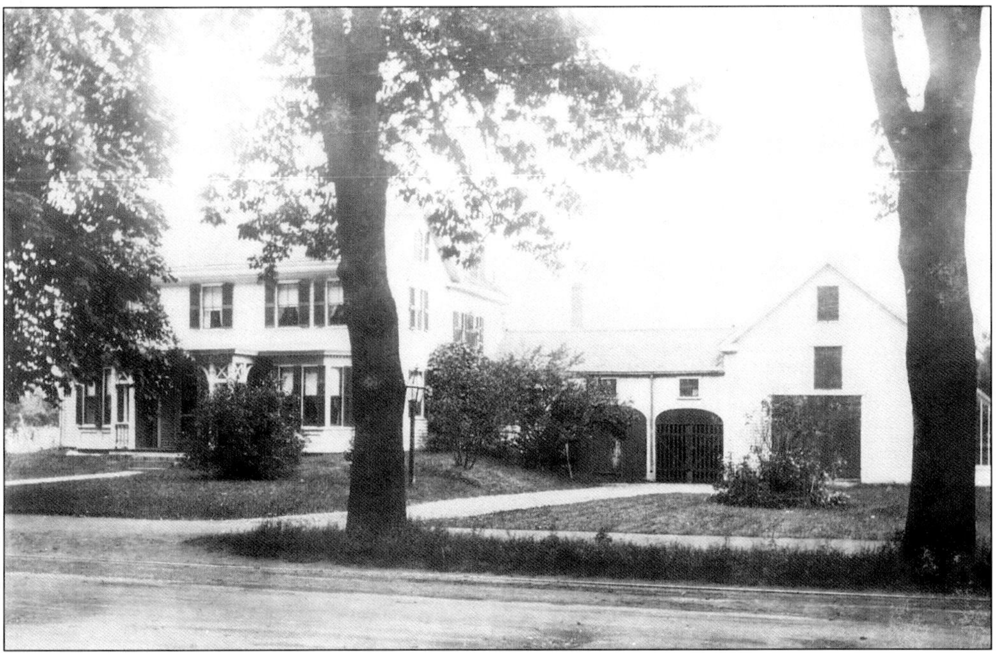

Calvin Hartshorn built his Common Street home in 1827. As did most large property owners of his day, he farmed and raised cows, horses, pigs, and chickens. In 1874, the bay windows and entrance shown in this picture were added to "update" the house. The property remained in the Hartshorn family until it was purchased by Edward and Louise Hawkins in 1944.

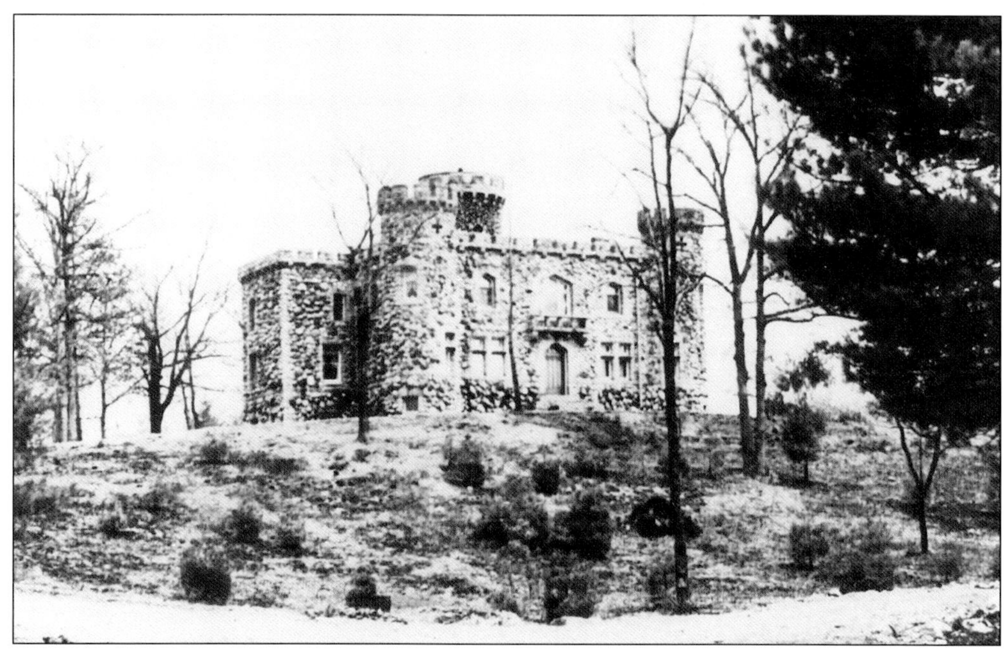

Lewis Castle, located in East Walpole, was built in 1879 by Isaac Newton Lewis on land that had been in his family since 1742. Constructed of local fieldstone and trimmed with granite from Quincy and Cape Ann, the house walls are 2.5 feet thick. Ownership of the castle has never left the Lewis family.

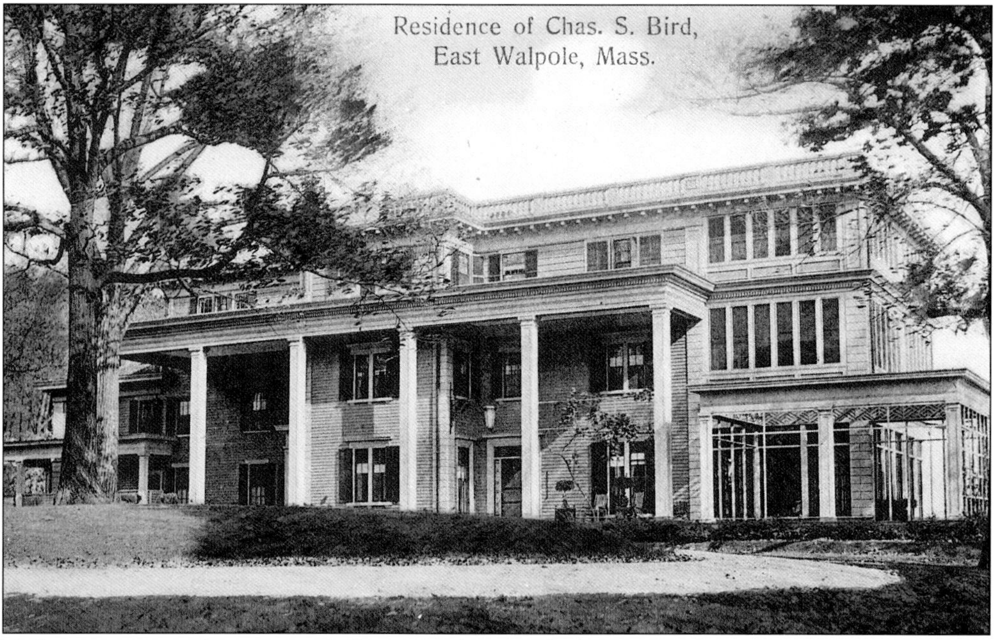

Endean, meaning "house on a hill" in Gaelic, was built in 1839 by Francis William Bird. In the early 1800s, his father, George Bird, started a paper-making business in East Walpole. Succeeding generations continued the business, now Bird Inc., and extensively added to the original home, eventually creating an early Walpole mansion. Endean has been unoccupied since 1983. The mansion was the Junior League of Boston's Decorator Show House in 1987.

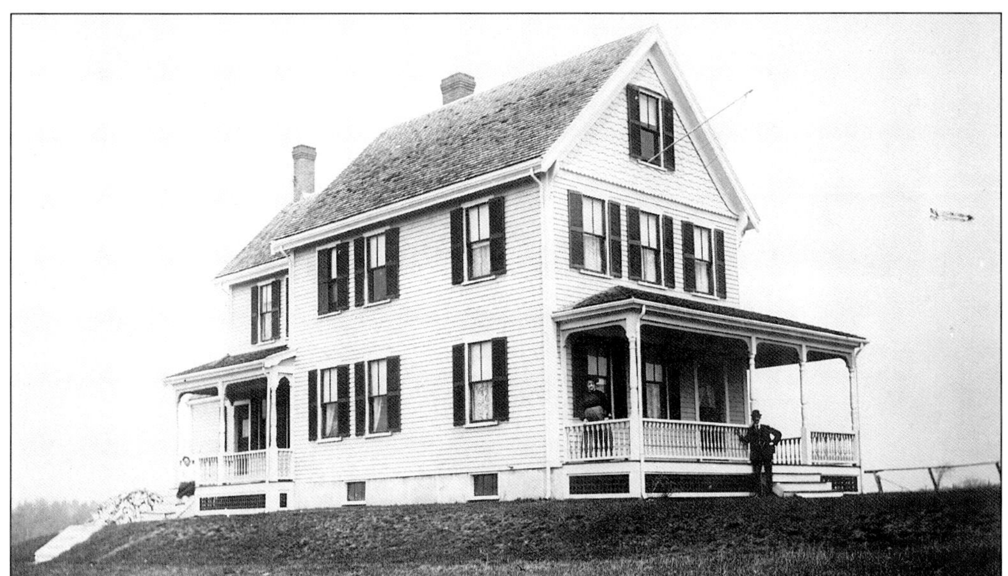

The Edwin Cobb House, located on the corner of Gould and Main Streets, was built in 1897. "Corn Cobb Farm," as the property was known when operating as a dairy farm in its early years, encompassed 54 acres. Following the 1938 hurricane, Cobb's Pond was the scene of an emergency logging operation. Thousands of board feet of lumber were salvaged. In the early 1960s, most of the land around the house was sold, and the "new" Fisher School was built on a large portion of the old farm. The home remained in the Cobb family until 1993.

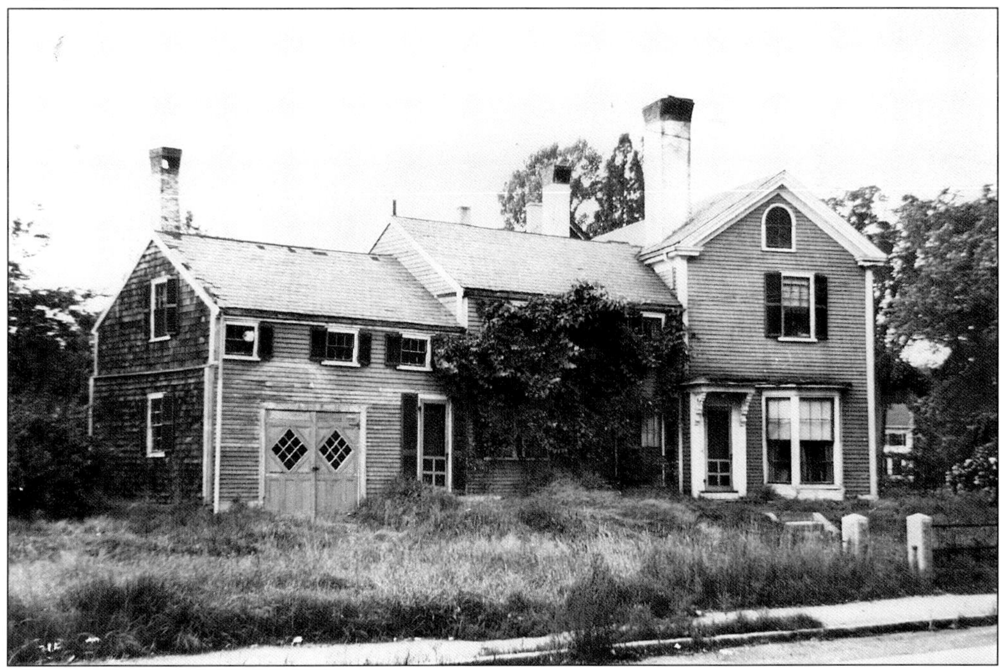

This undated photograph shows the Henry Craig House on Front Street at the corner of Main Street. According to an 1897 Walpole directory of businesses and residences, Craig was a member of the board of assessors and made his living as an undertaker. It is not known if he conducted the business in his home. Today this corner is occupied by a Sunoco Gas Station.

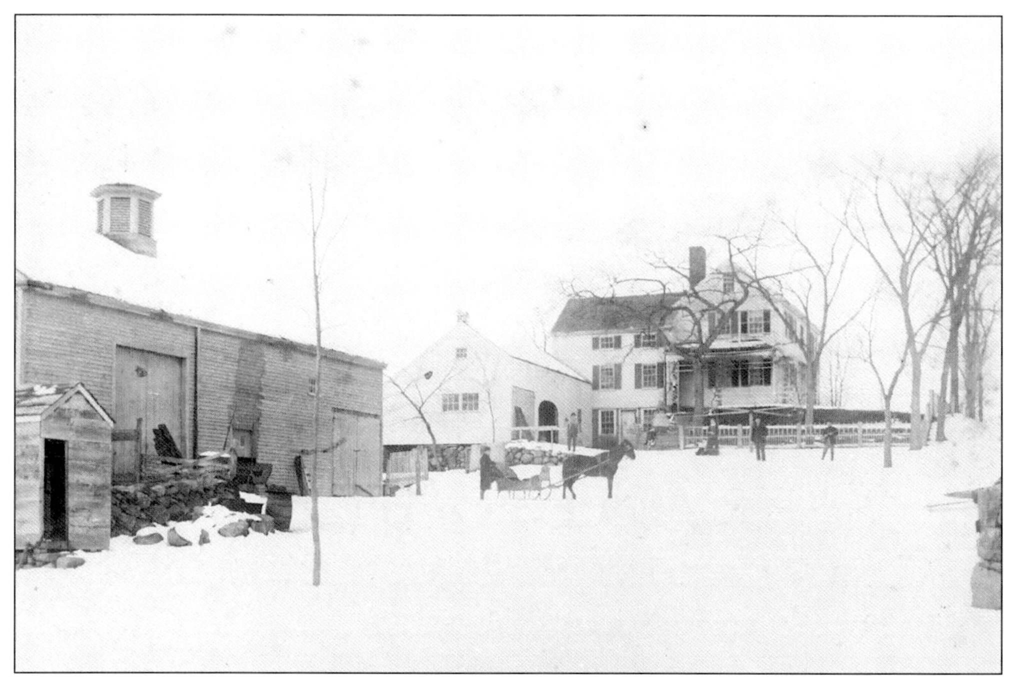

Looking like a Currier and Ives scene, this undated winter photograph is of Philip Allen's Spring Brook Farm on Baker Street. Allen, once president of Bird and Son, was also active in Walpole town affairs. This extensive acreage was originally part of Stoughtonham (Sharon). Following the successful petitioning of the town and the state legislature by then-owner Ebenezer Baker, it was annexed to Walpole in 1803. Today the Walpole Country Club is located on the Baker-Allen property.

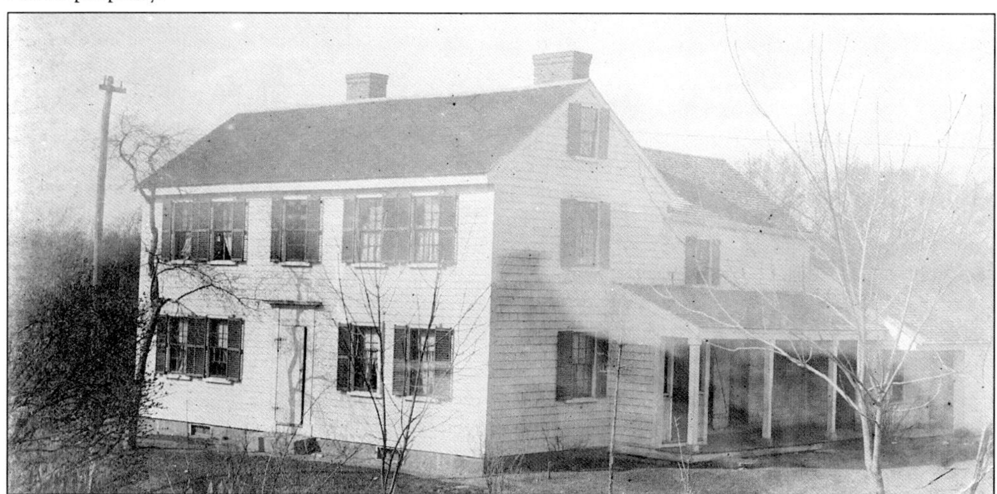

Deacon Henry Plimpton's *c.* 1816 home sits high on Plimpton Street overlooking the Neponset River. Following the organization of the Orthodox Congregational Church in 1826, Plimpton was appointed as its first deacon. A devoted church member, the deacon personally transported visiting clergy from Boston to Walpole and back by horse and carriage. Henry Plimpton was a brother-in-law of John Allen Gould and later became the father-in-law of Deacon Willard Lewis. Attorney Joseph Welch, known for his role in the McCarthy Hearings, owned the home in the 1940s.

Two

School Days

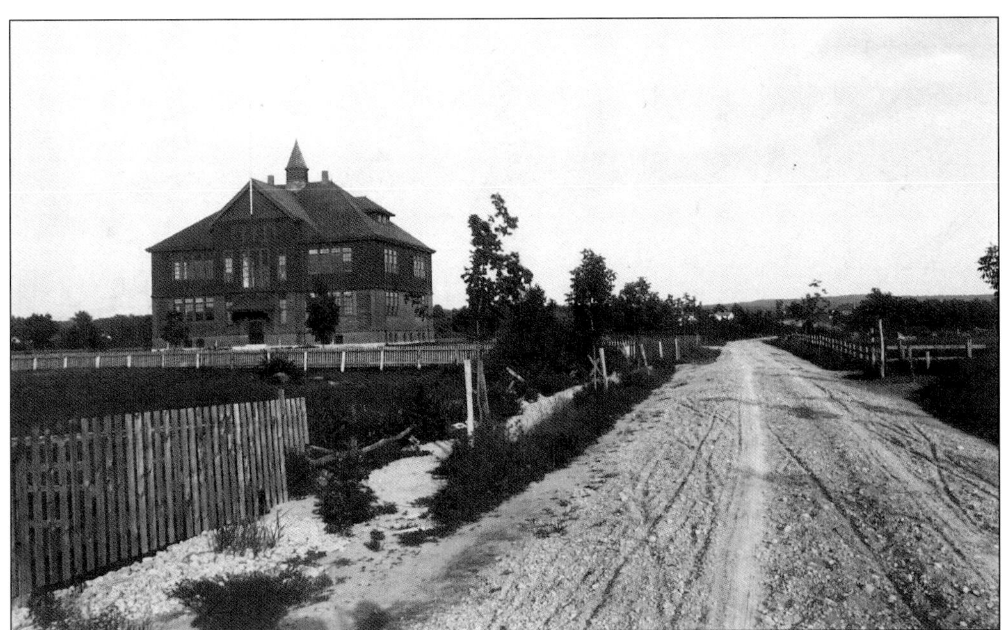

The old Stone School stood on the corner of School and Stone Streets. Architect J. William Beal designed the 1886 structure using Queen Anne Revival and Shingle styles, which were popular at the time. The school was closed in 1950, but the town's growing population necessitated its reopening in the 1960s. After many years of service, the school was finally razed in 1981.

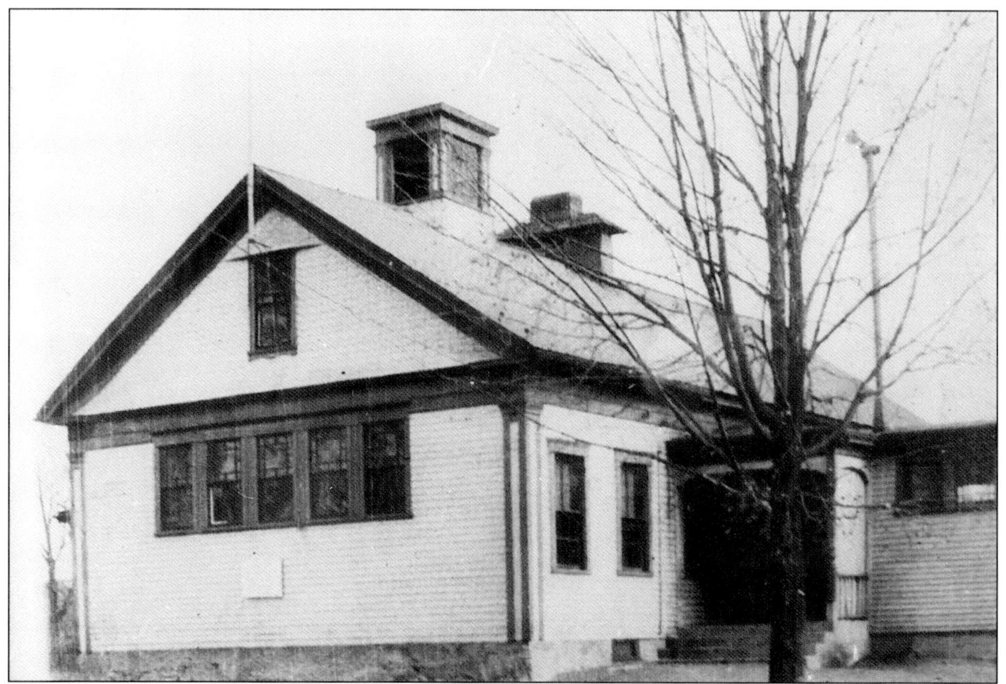

The South Walpole School (later named the Boyden School) was built on a patch of land 85 by 85 feet. The total cost of the land and building in 1855 was $3,643. By 1876, two rooms were added. In November 1930, Josiah Hall, having paid the town $145 for the school, had it dismantled and moved to a new location.

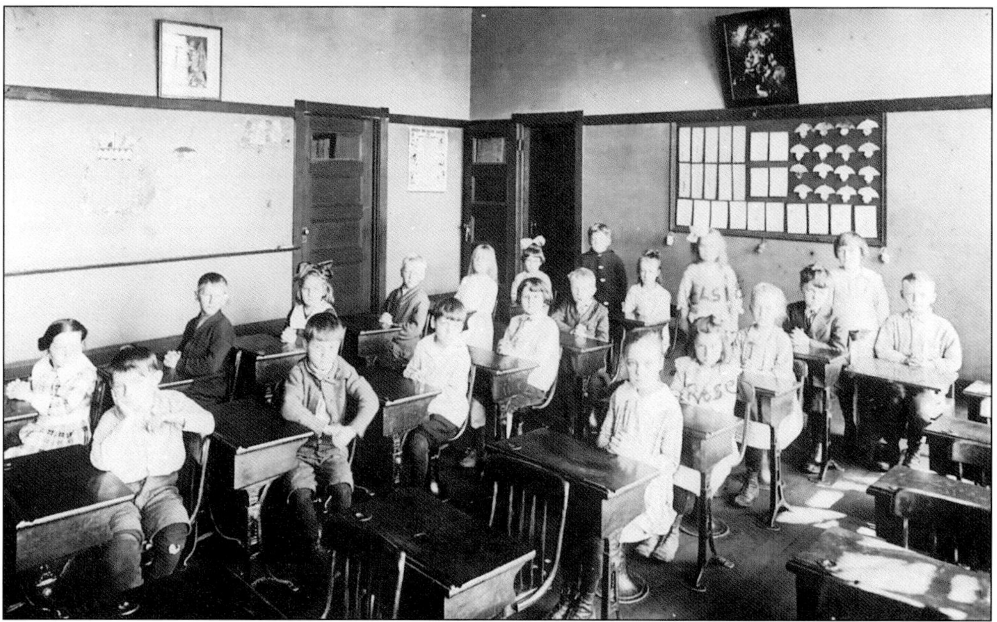

The South Walpole School was heated by a wood stove. Records state the school averaged 52 students, although 72 students were registered. Overcrowded conditions in the two-room building meant that some students sat less than 3 feet from the stove, while others were near doorways that opened to cold drafty halls.

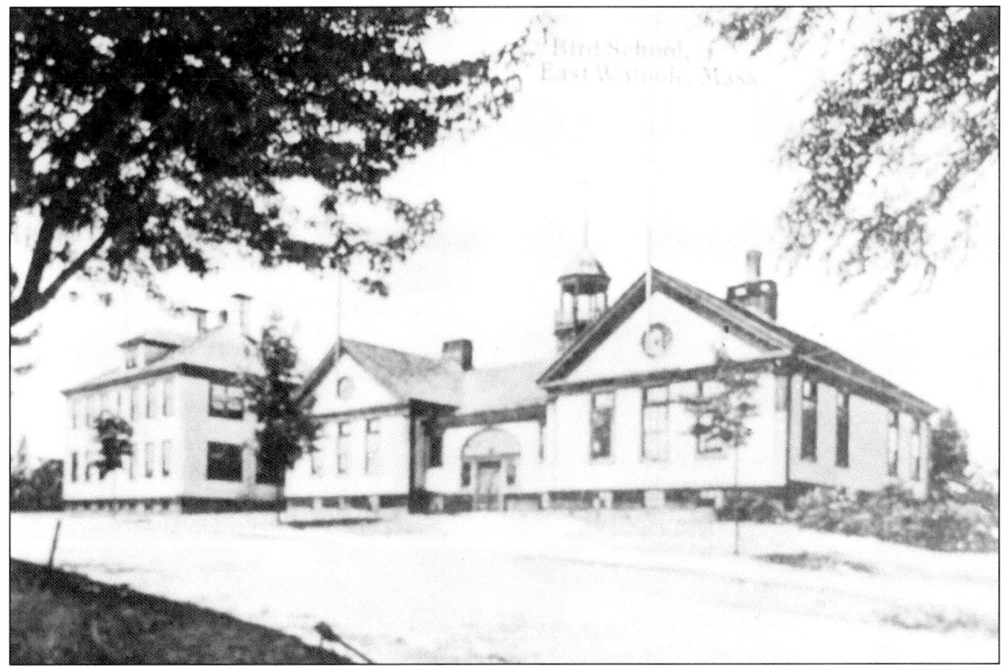

According to locals, the original Bird School Building, shown here, was moved to its Washington Street site in 1892. By 1910, two additions had been built. The building next door was a private home.

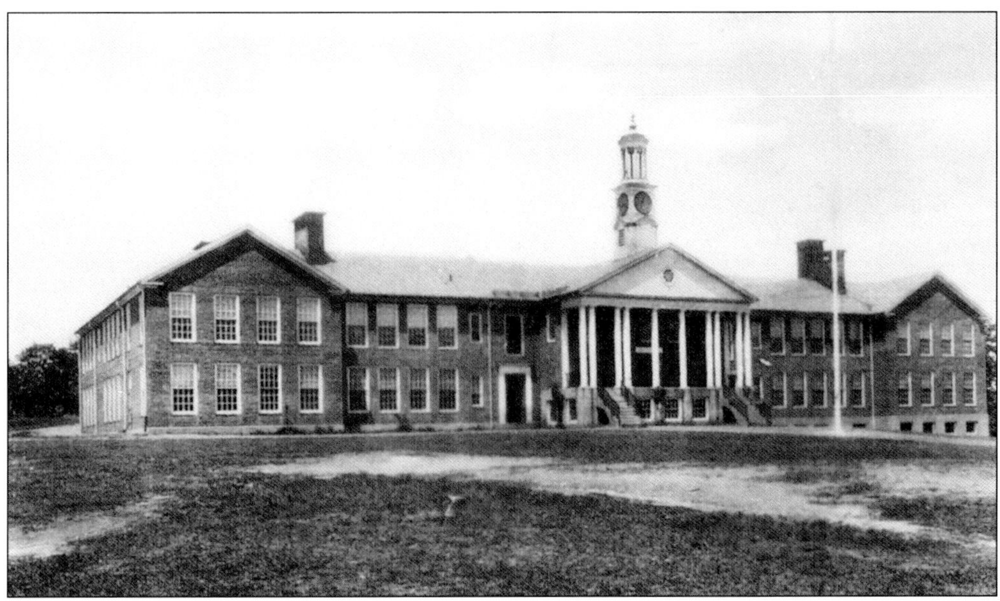

Built in 1920, the Georgian Revival style Bird School was able to accommodate four hundred students. The first dental clinic for schoolchildren, which was run by Dr. Maguire, was located in this new school. In 1981, the Bird School was sold and converted into condominiums.

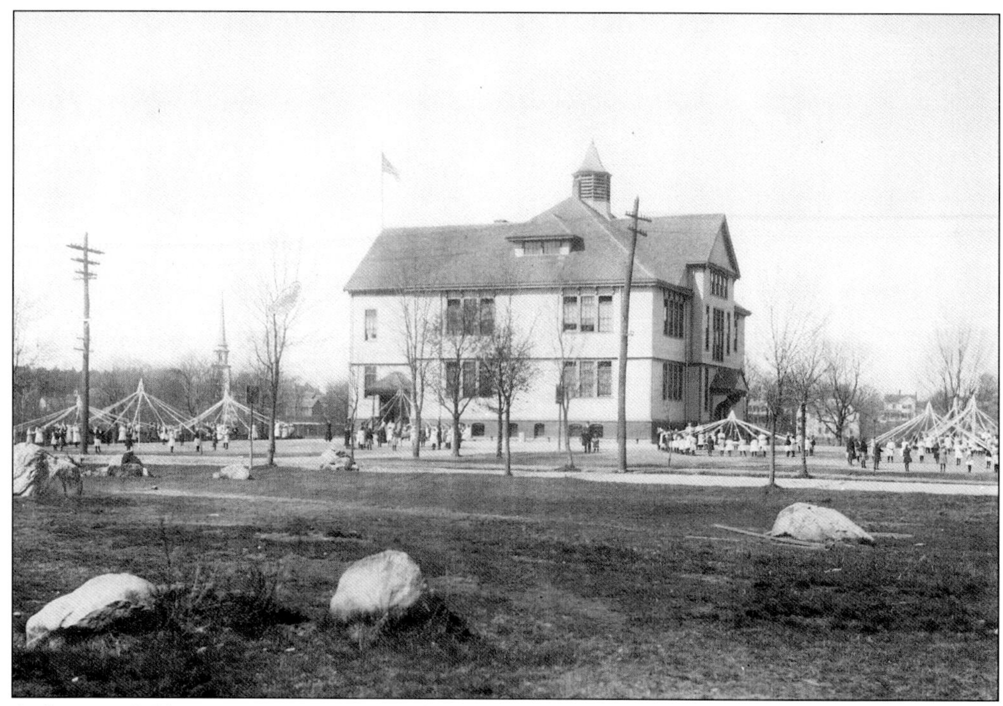

A favorite "old-time activity" was to dance around the maypoles at the Stone School. The church spire to the left of the school belonged to the Orthodox Congregational Church, located where Gallo's flower shop is today.

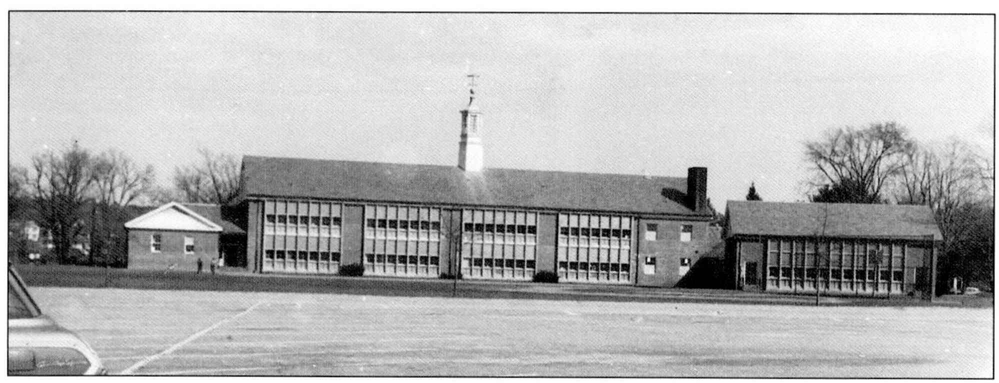

The "new" Stone School was built in 1950 to replace the aging school next door. Closed for school use in 1981, the building now functions as Walpole's town hall.

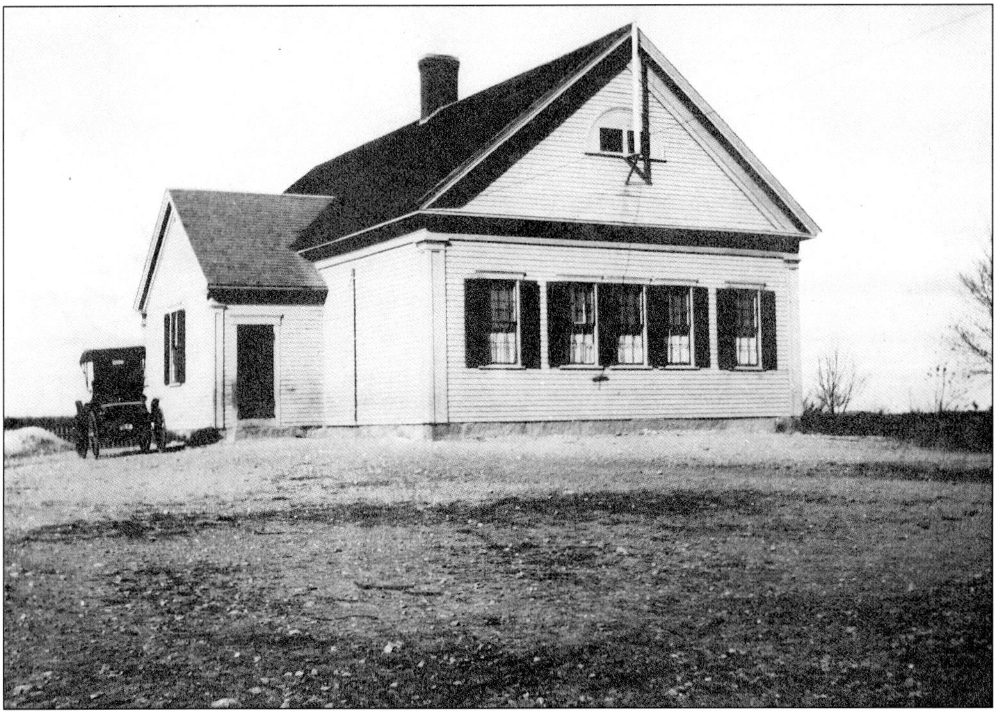

The North District School, dedicated in 1853 (photograph, early 1900), was located next to today's Norfolk County Agricultural School. To make way for the "old" Fisher School in 1913, local carpenter Carl Thomas dismantled and rebuilt this school for use as a barn in East Walpole.

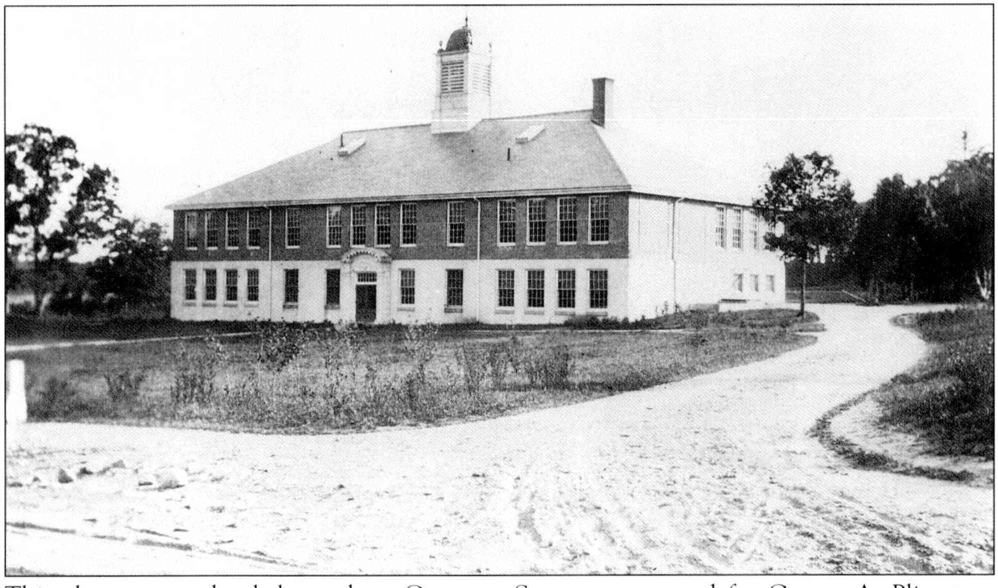

This elementary school, located on Common Street, was named for George A. Plimpton, who donated 30 acres of land for school use. Also on this property are Walpole High School, several athletic fields, playgrounds, and forestry land. In 1913, the school had 550 children in its 16 rooms.

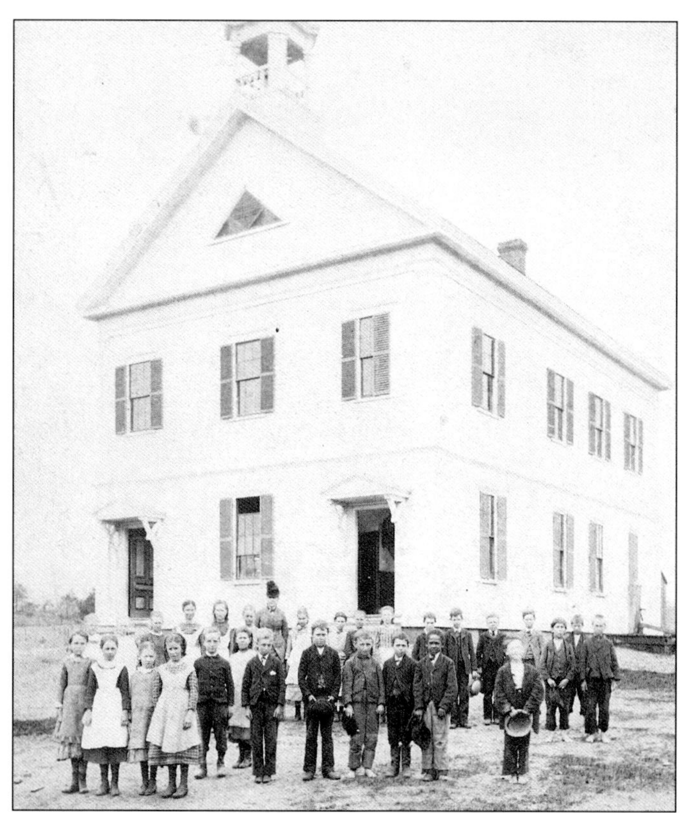

You would never know that this school is still standing on School Street. Thirty students and teacher Miss Morse posed for this 1878 photograph. The school was remodeled and occupied as the high school from 1898 to 1908. The classes were then moved to the new high school. In the late 1920s, Mr. Hill purchased the old building for use as a machine shop. Building expansion around the school continued until only the peak of the school can be seen above the roof line of the Ingersoll-Dresser plant today. (See page 33.)

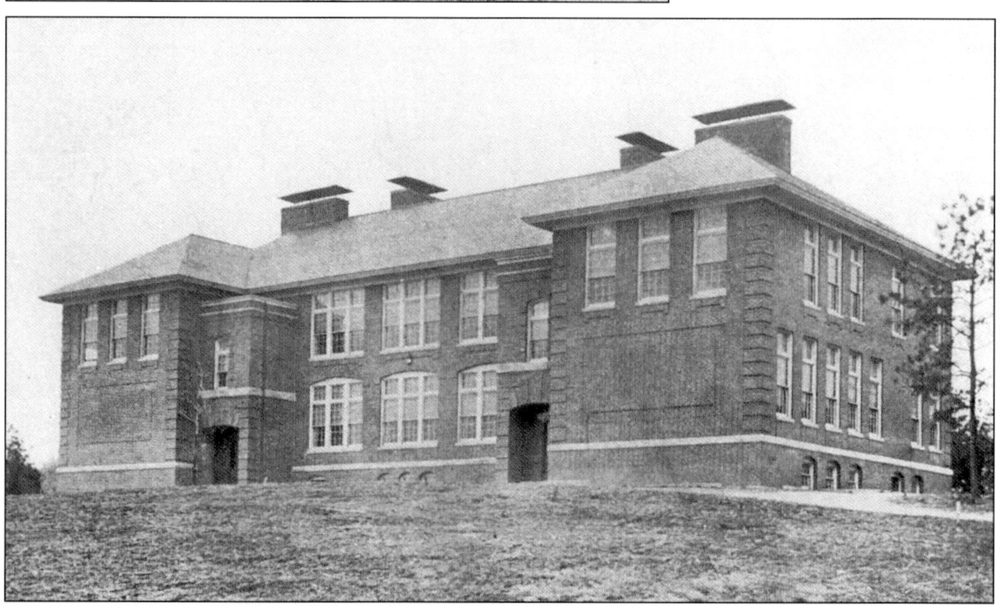

One of the *Boston Sunday Herald* headlines in 1908 was "Structure on Butcher Hill is modern and convenient, cost $50,000." The first floor of the high school measured 125 by 56 feet. It accommodated five classrooms, laboratories, and an assembly hall. The offices were on the second floor. The gymnasium was located in the basement. Situated on 13 acres of land, the school had additions constructed in 1927 and again in 1954.

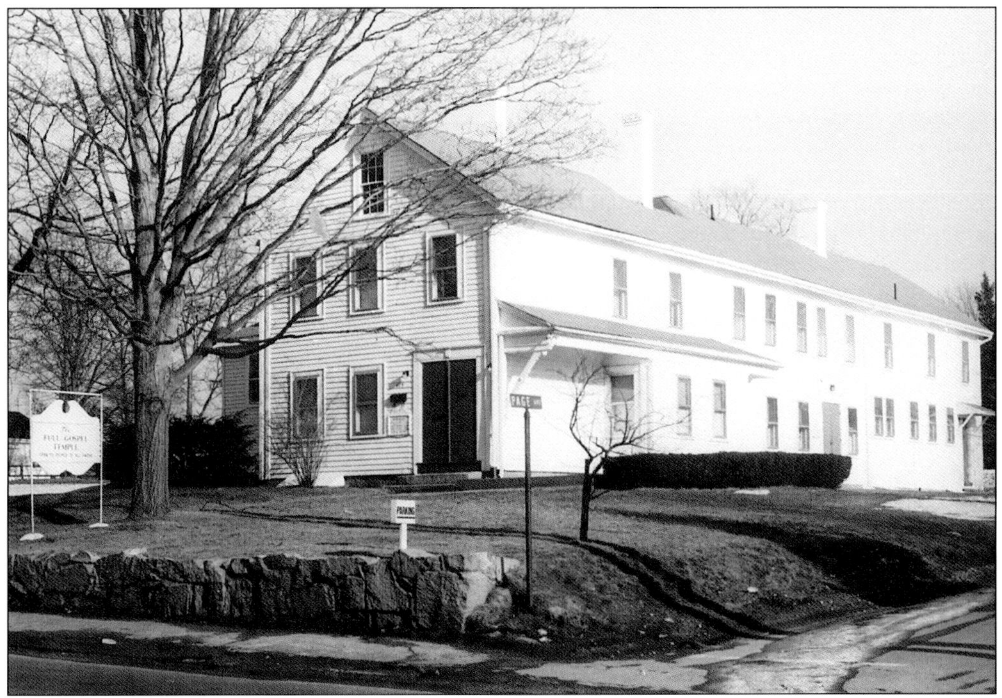

In 1916, Norfolk County purchased 40 acres of land for the purpose of building a vocational school. Pictured is the original classroom building of the Norfolk County Agricultural School. Known as the Bullard House, it was located on Main Street and is now occupied by the Full Gospel Church.

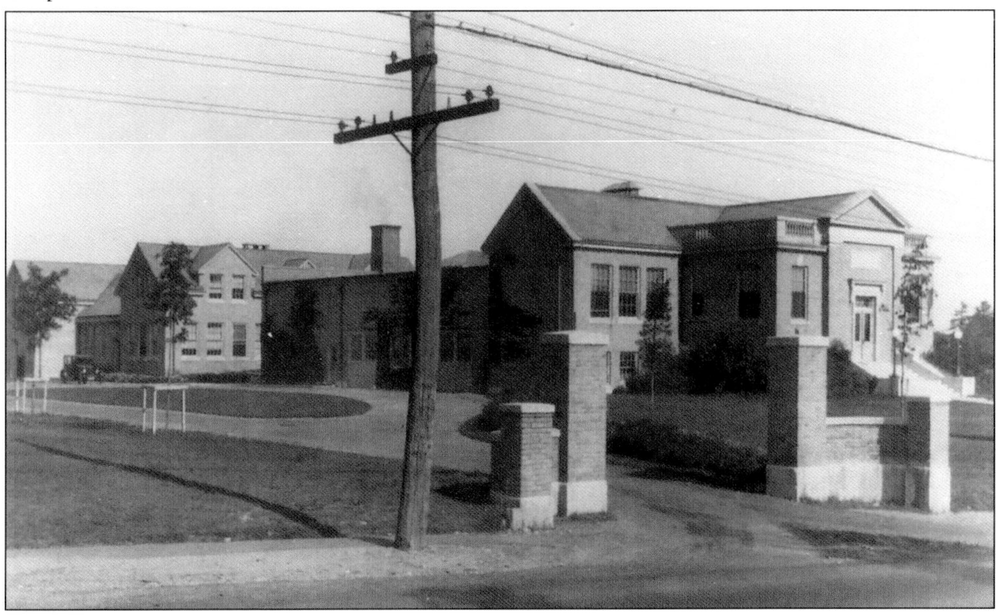

By 1917, the new brick school building containing classrooms and labs was completed. The Bullard House then became a dormitory. As enrollment increased, new programs were introduced. By 1927, accreditation enabled graduates to enroll in the Massachusetts Agricultural College in Amherst.

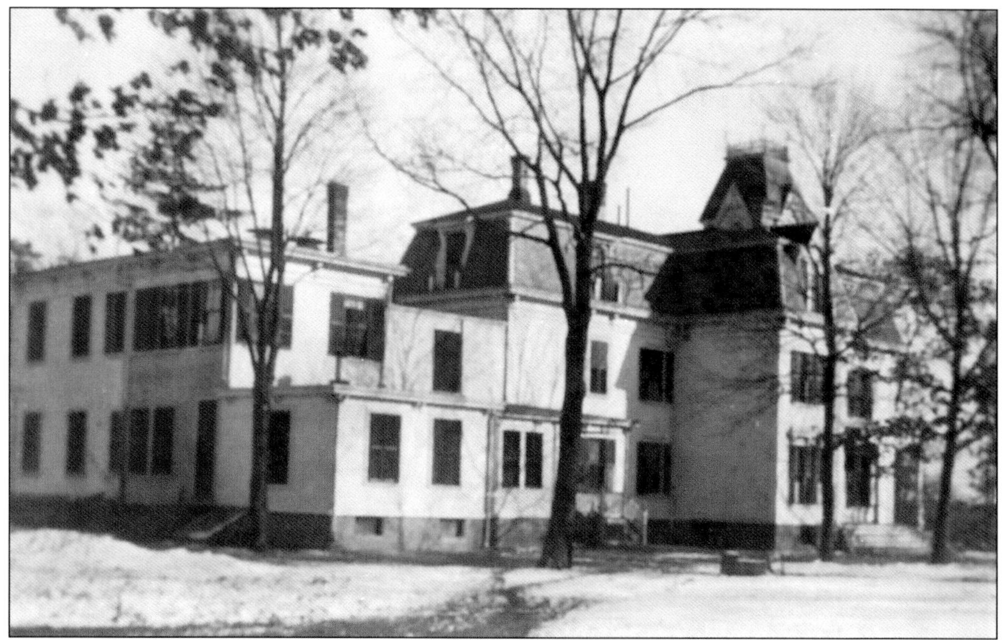

Powder House Hill, Spring Street, was the location of the Union Training School. It was also known as the "Truant School" from the late 1800s to 1933. This was not a reform school as we might think today, but a self-contained farm/campus for runaways and boys unwilling to attend school. Forty-five to fifty boys, whose average age was 13 years old, stayed 25 days to a year to learn a trade.

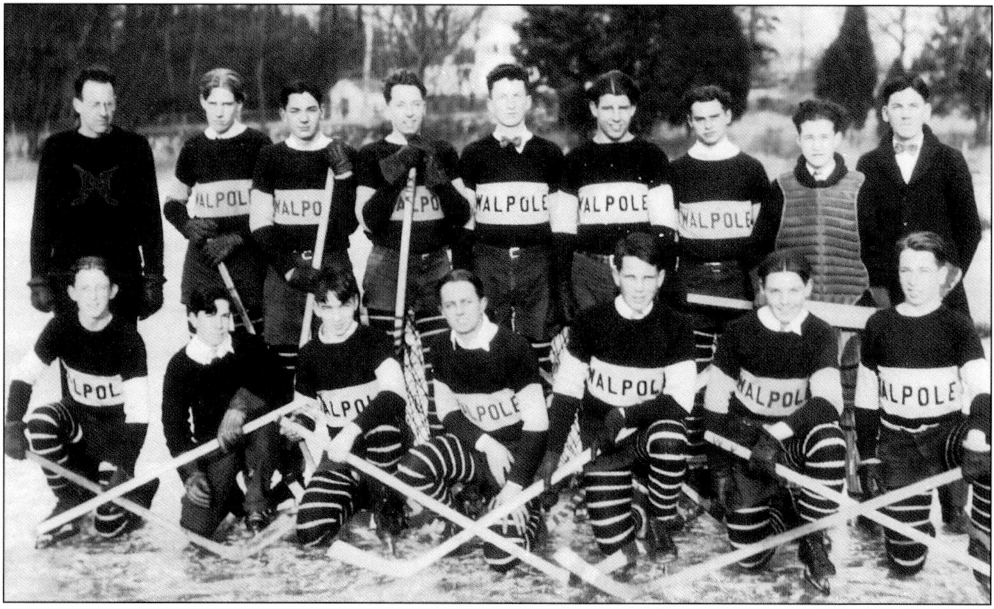

An important part of school life has always been extracurricular activities, and Walpole has led the sports scene in all phases for many years. Long before skating arenas, helmets, and gloves, the hockey team practiced on Allen's Pond, on East Street, across from the Walpole Woodworkers. Pictured here is the first official hockey team. Captained by Charles Gould, the 1927–28 team had a winning season.

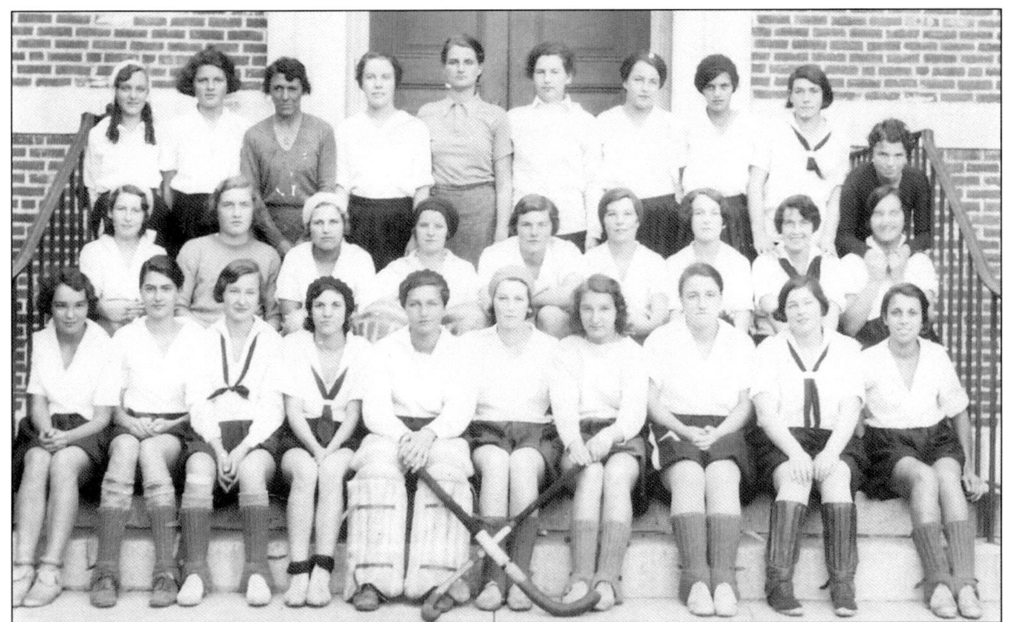

The girls field hockey team is an important sport today as it was in 1932. Under the direction of Coach Wallace (top row, third from left) and captained by Barbara Cole Fitzpatrick (top row, fifth from left), the team had a victorious 1931–32 season.

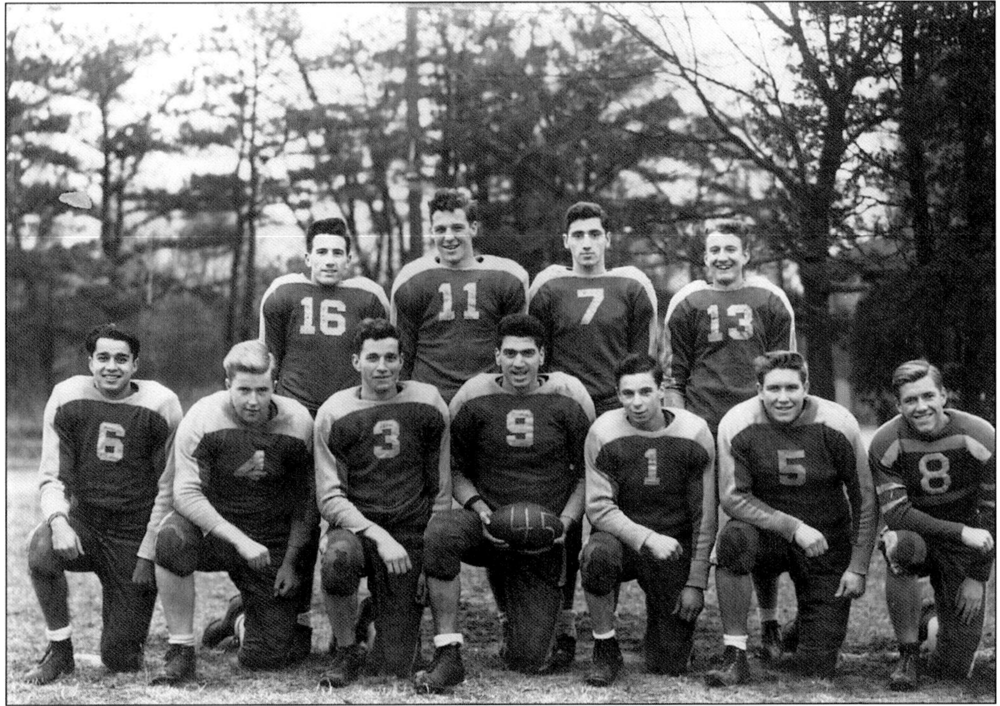

These members of the 1945–46 football team are, from left to right, as follows: (front row) Emil Petrovick, William Egan, Martin Coyne, Anthony Campagna, Francis Sansone, Nils Idman, and Bill Murphy; (back row) Patsy Marino, Harold Songin, Mario Presentato, and John Turco. The varsity football team finished its season with a record of three wins and five losses.

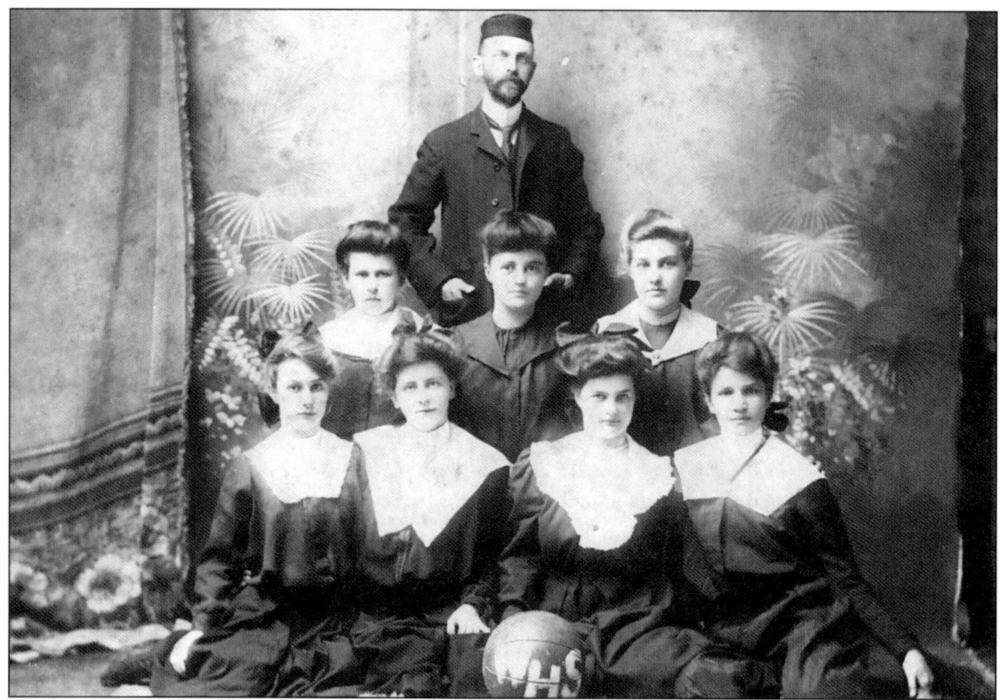

Basketball was introduced to Walpole High School girls in 1909. Miss Guild was the first coach. Mr. Colton (principal) took over the instructor duties in 1913. The following year the team played neighboring schools and won their first game, beating Wrentham 10-0.

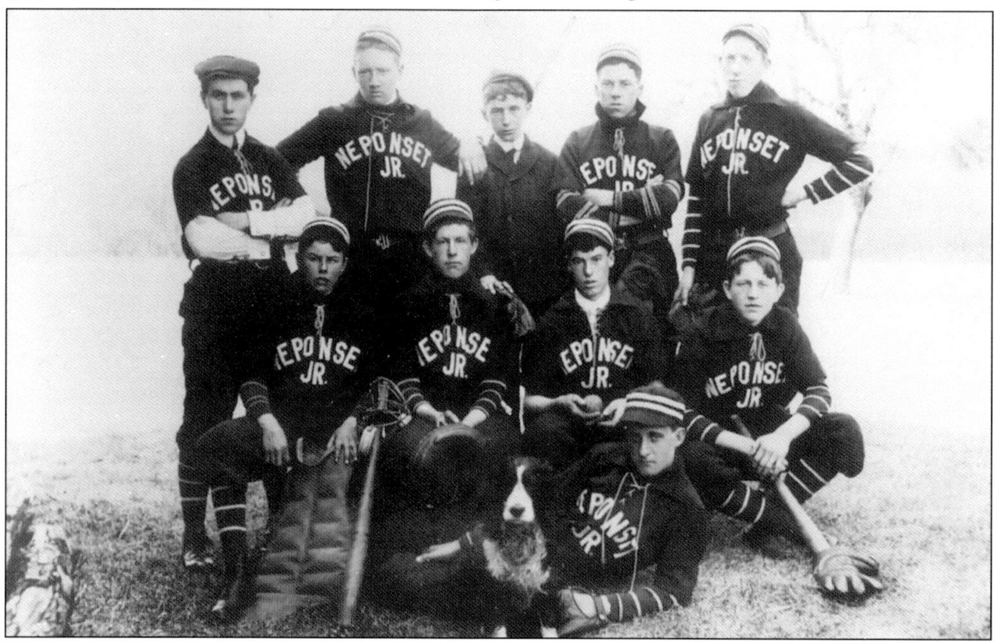

Bird and Son Company sponsored many league teams through the years. Pictured is the Neponset Junior Baseball Team. The senior team might have been the fathers to these boys. In the second row, fourth from the left, is Edward Burns. This photograph was taken between 1890 and 1900.

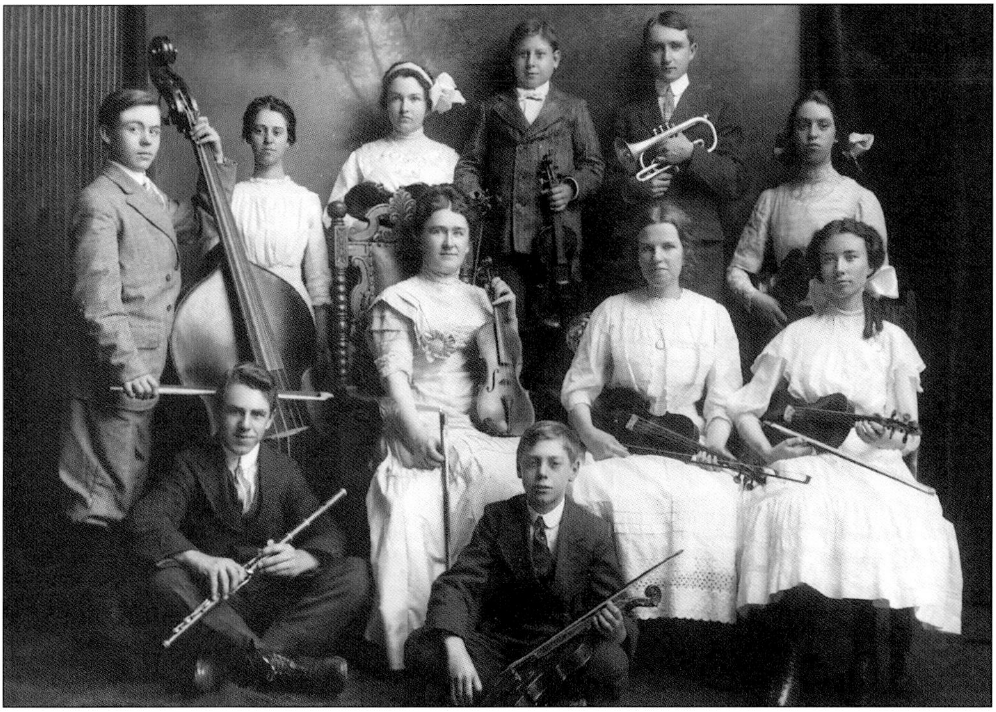

The Walpole High School Orchestra was organized in 1912 by Miss Dagget. They are, from left to right, as follows: (front row) Dana Spear and James Gardner; (middle row) Miss Dagget, Catherine Donnally, and Alice Ahern; (back row) Herbert Davis, Elizabeth French, Alice Maguire, Chester Milliken, Rueben Fliegelman, and Elizabeth Urquhart.

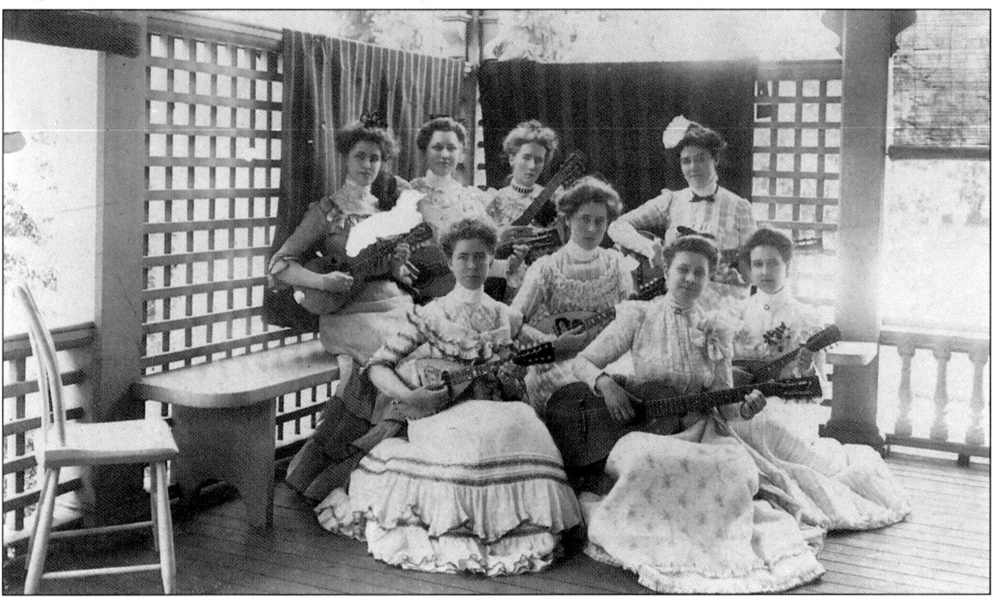

Much interest was expressed in the mandolin, the favored instrument in 1913. Miss Wilson organized the Mandolin Club for girls. From left to right, they are as follows: (front row) Ella Hartshorn, Betty Vose, Bertha Gardner, and Jessie Bentley; (back row) Marion Harper, Edith Kelbourne, Rebecca Bent, and Treby Moore.

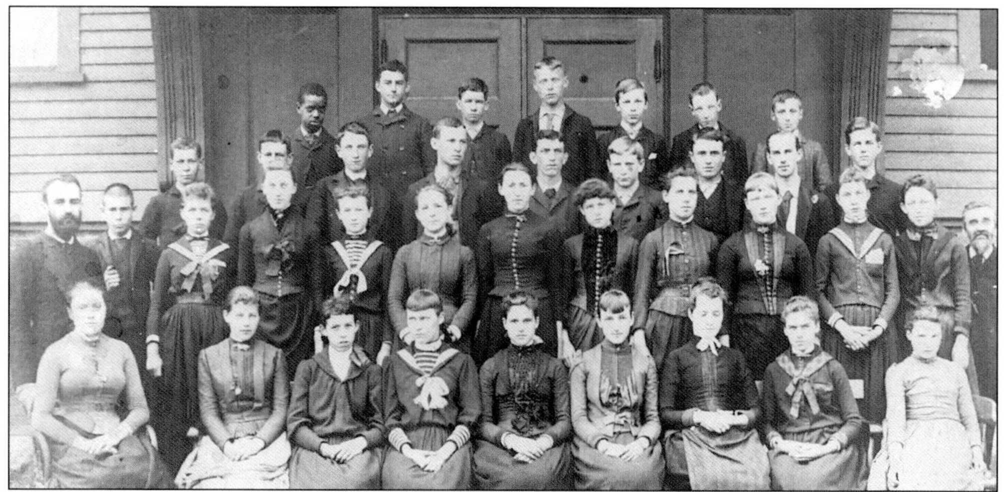

Teachers of the 1889 classes at the Stone School included Miss Hutchinson (seated), Mr. Kendall (left), and Mr. Willard (right). They appear here dressed in their finest for their June class picture. The colors are dark, and the clothes are stiff and long sleeved.

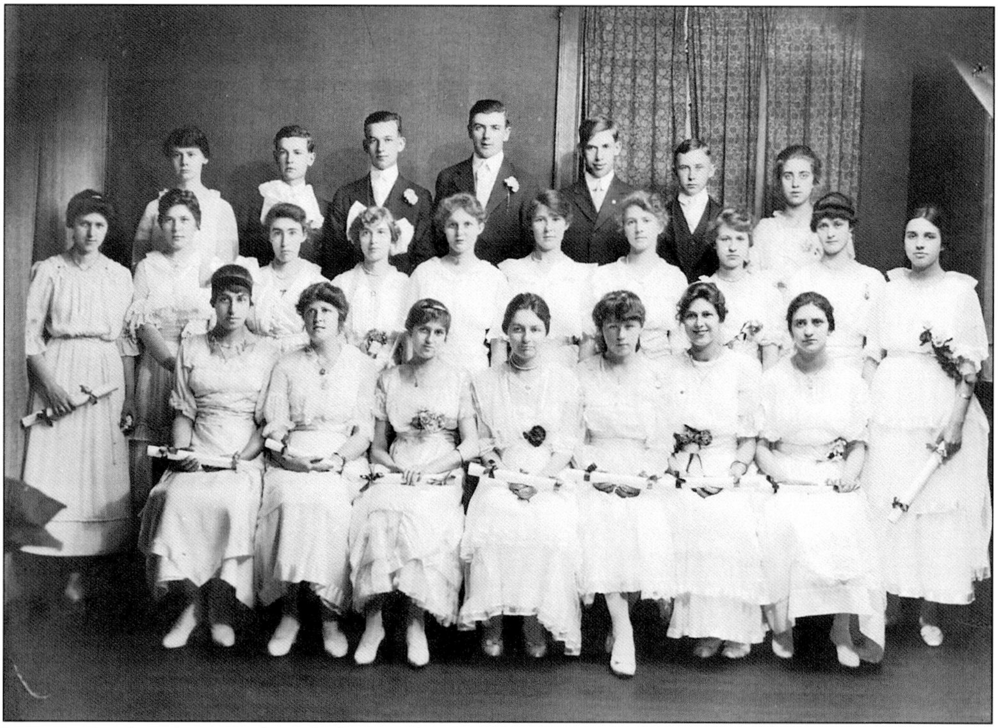

By 1916, the dress style of the graduation class had become light colors, gauzy, with short sleeves. The program for seniors in 1916 was much the same as today, and consisted of class day exercises, graduation (with a reception), the senior promenade, and a class trip to Provincetown.

Three

Industry—Walpole's Backbone

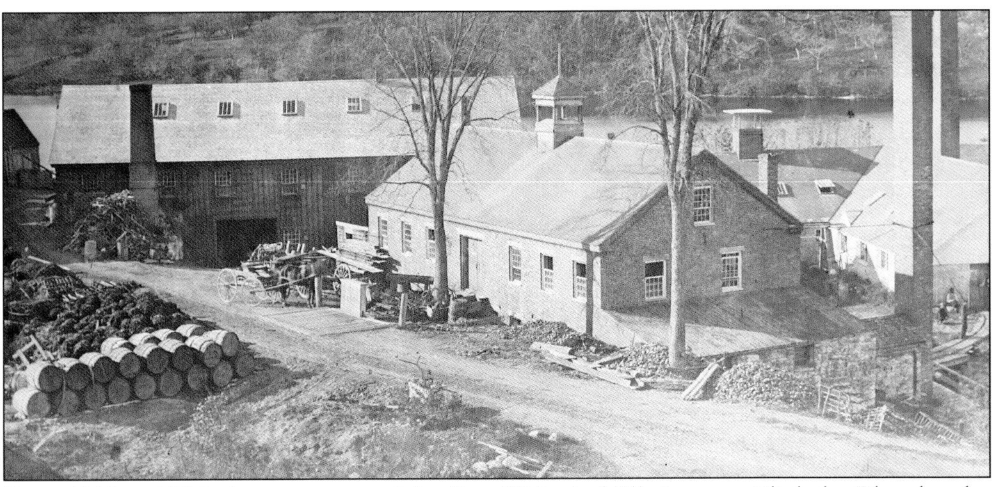

From 1817 to 1836, the occupants of the East Walpole Mill site were Eliphalet Rhoads, who owned a small gristmill; Webb's cotton mill; and then Silas Smith and Jabez Coney Jr., who became the owners of the Neponset Paper Mill Company. Coney, who became sole owner in 1836, sold the mill site to Francis W. Bird on November 8, 1838. Charles S. Bird joined his father in 1876. The mill was destroyed by fire in 1880 and rebuilt. In 1913, Charles S. Bird Jr. and Philip Allen joined as partners, the Bird and Son name was adopted, and expansive growth of products and production capacity began. In 1917, Bird and Son became incorporated, and by 1924, there were more than 2,000 employees. Additional factories were owned in Norwood, Massachusetts; Phillipsdale, Rhode Island; and Chicago, Illinois. There were also two factories in Canada.

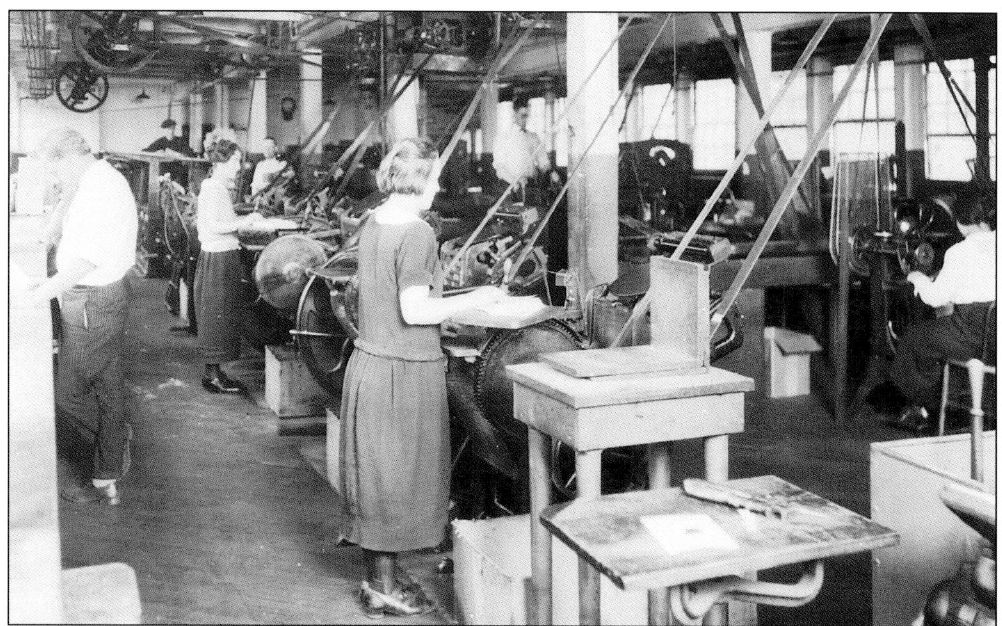

Women are shown here working in the printing department at the Bird and Son factory in East Walpole. Readers may guess the date by using as clues the hair styles, fashions, and equipment. It is to be hoped that the two unidentified standing women did not have to remain in that position for the entire workday. It appears that they are feeding sheets of paper into belt-driven printing presses. The presence of exposed drive belts and moving flywheels may have added an uncomfortable noise level to what, by today's standards, might be considered an unacceptable work place.

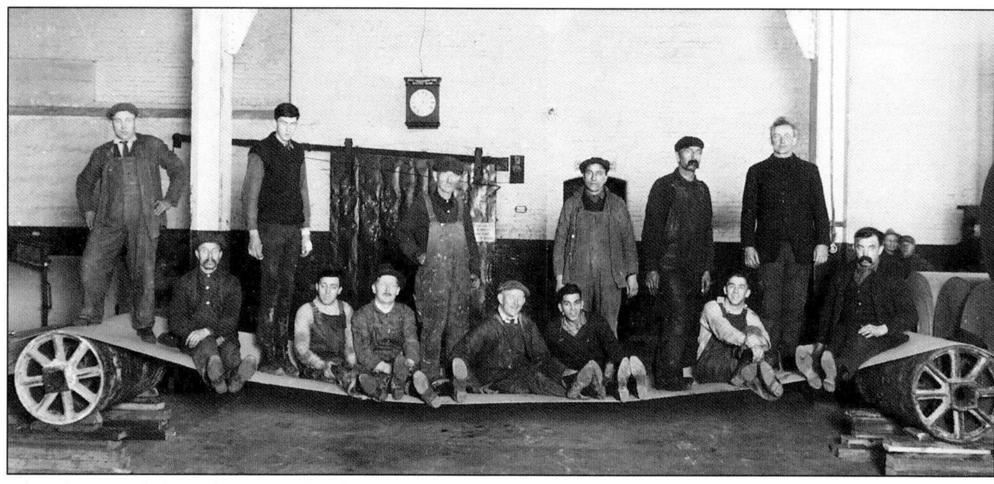

The donor of this photograph identified the site as Bird and Son. Shown is a 20-foot panel of unidentified non-rigid material supporting 13 unnamed men in 1921. The image may have been a Bird product advertisement. Bird started in 1817 as a newsprint paper mill (the panel was probably not newsprint). By 1938, Bird had grown into a large enterprise with at least five separate divisions. The faces and clothing of the 13 men suggest a diversity of ethnic origin. Bird's need for a large supply of menial labor exceeded Walpole's supply. Recent immigrants, willing to work for low wages, came to the rescue. Their presence would have a significant influence on Walpole's future profile of ethnic demographics.

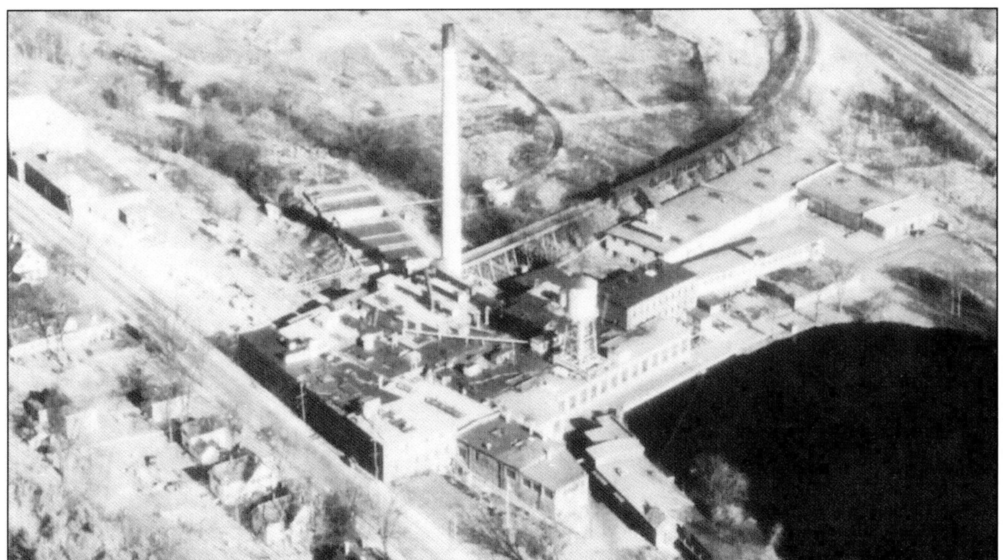

Hollingsworth & Vose Co., located at 112 Washington Street, East Walpole, is shown here as it appeared in the late 1940s. George Bird (father of Francis W.) built a paper mill at this location in 1812 and made newsprint. He sold the mill to Zachary T. Hollingsworth in 1871. In 1873, the original mill was destroyed by fire and was immediately rebuilt. Charles Vose became a full partner in 1881. In 1875, the mill had seven employees, but by 1924, the number had grown to 250 who produced—daily—30 tons of "strong" paper for cable insulation, sand paper, and tag papers from jute, manila fiber, and unbleached sulfate wood pulp.

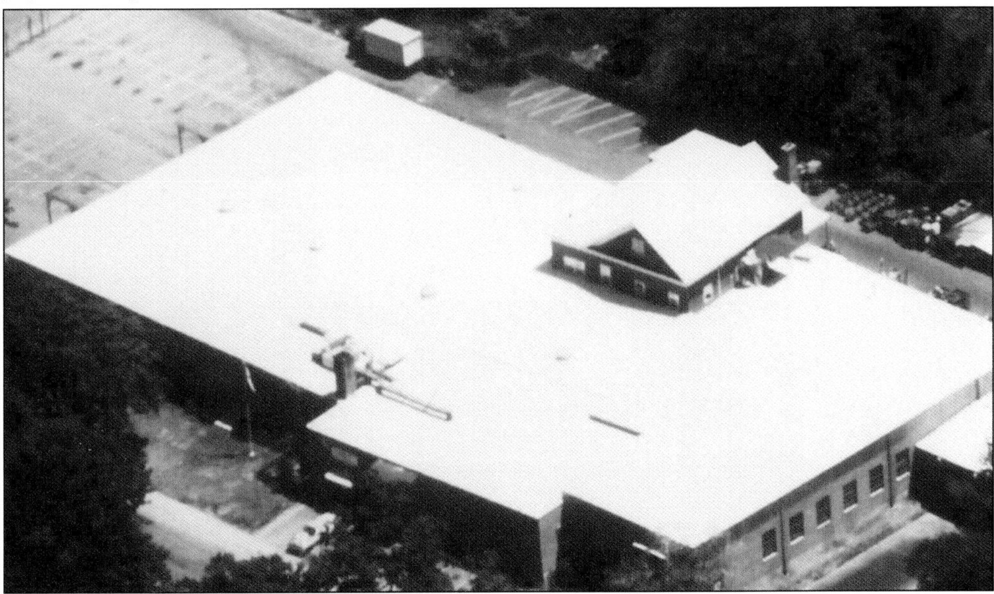

Aerial view of the Frank M. Hill Machine Shop in 1939, located on School Street on the site of the first high school. Hill started his business in 1928 with his sons, Arthur, Ralph, and Fred. Growth of the shop accelerated in the late 1930s with the production of "bullet presses" for the English and U.S. governments. This photograph was taken after the first addition to the front of the "schoolhouse," the peak of which can still be seen from certain viewpoints on School Street.

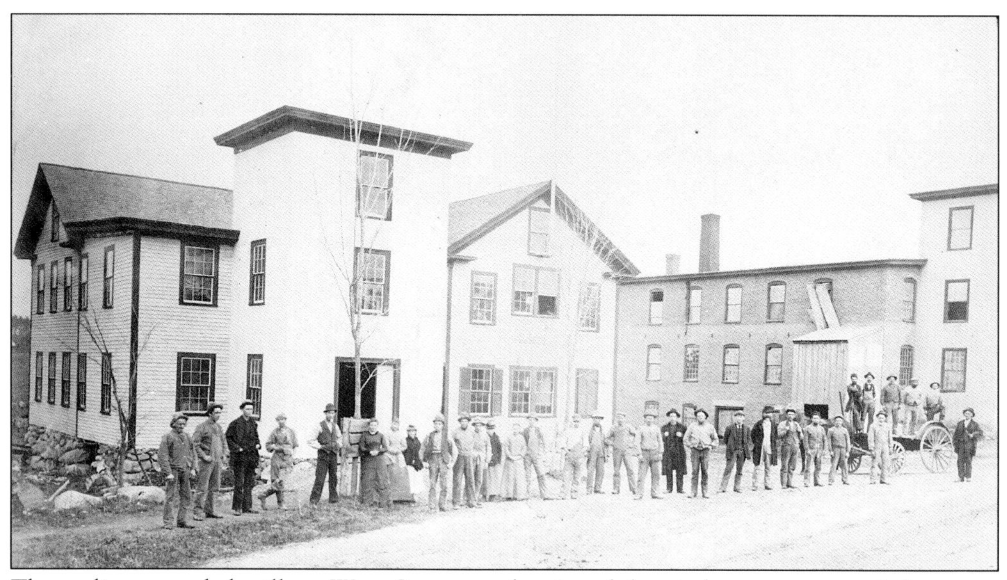

The earliest recorded mill on West Street, or the site of the sixth waterpower privilege, was Daniel Clap's "Fulling Mill" (1812), which manufactured cloth. In 1821, Harlow Lawrence, an ex-employee of Clap's mill, bought the property and built a mill (complete with a bell tower) to produce cotton thread. In 1863, the mill was bought by Deacon Willard Lewis, who was making "lint" bandages for the Civil War at a hired mill on Morey Pond. In addition to lint, later products included carpet lining, cotton batting, and cotton percolator (used in the South for straining rosin). This photograph shows 32 employees in front of the wooden factory, which was later destroyed by fire.

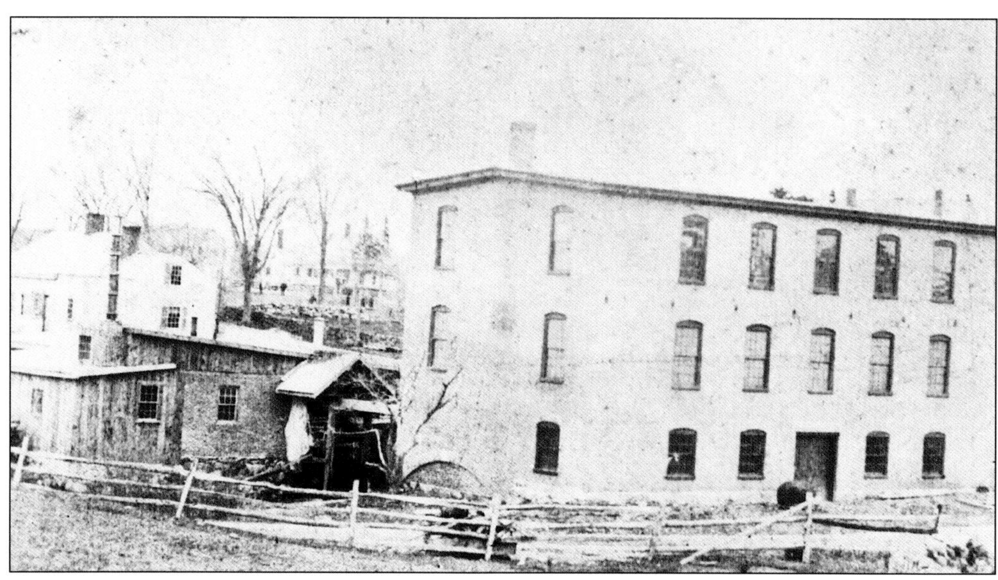

Deacon Lewis rebuilt the factory and employed 70 workers. Lewis died in 1892, and the business was continued by his son, W.I. Lewis, for many years. George A. Plimpton later purchased and operated the mill as the Lewis Batting Company.

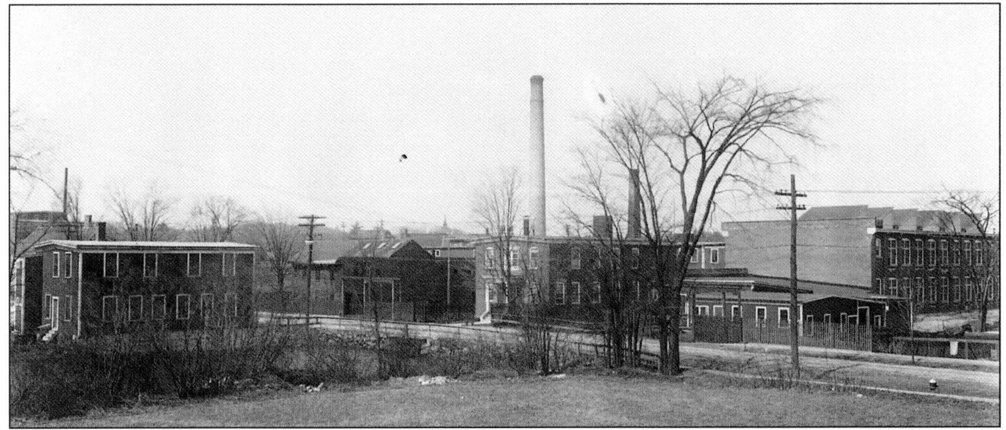

By 1903, there were only 75 employees working at the Lewis mill, and the company became insolvent. In 1905, Henry Plimpton Kendall, who had worked at the Plimpton Press, took charge of the mill. He turned the insolvent "Shoddy Mill" into the multi-million-dollar Kendall Company. Expansion began in 1915 with the acquisition of the Slatersville, Rhode Island plant. By 1953, there were 8,000 employees in 16 North American plants.

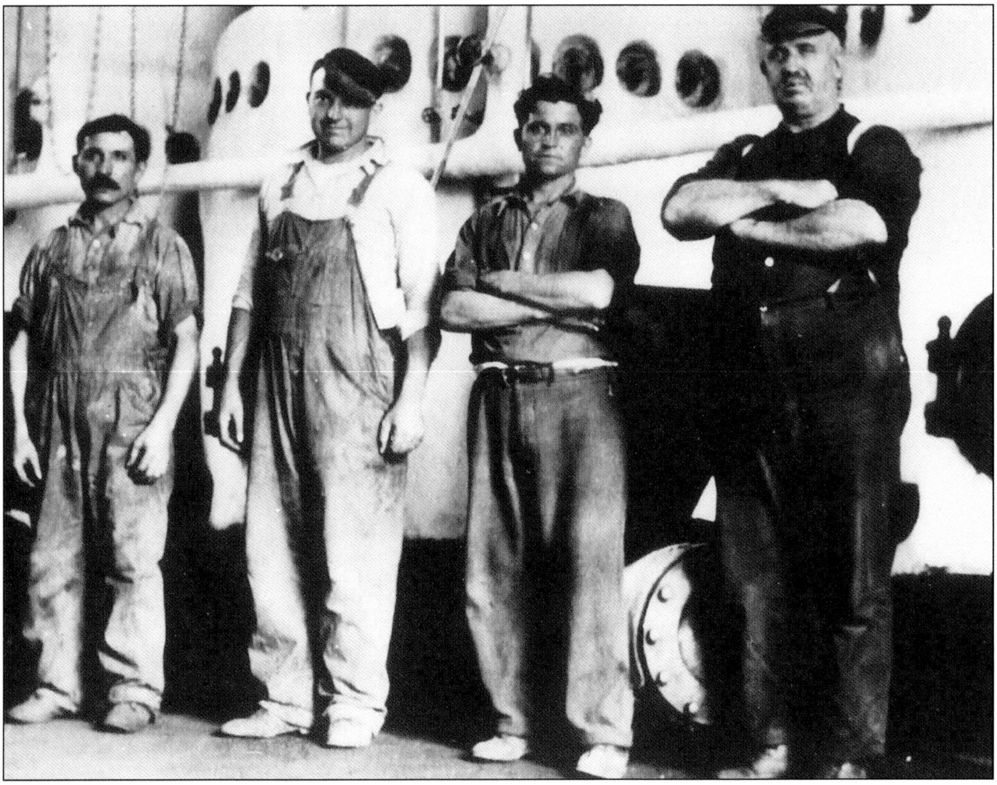

Posing in 1931 in the Kendall Company boiler room are, from left to right, Jake Silvi, Joe Ciannavei, John Silvi, and Harry Giles (supervisor). Steam from the coal-fired boilers was used to bleach cotton and to sterilize hospital dressings. The boiler room was hot, strenuous, and septic. "Big Joe" Ciannavei and the Silvi brothers emigrated from Italy to Walpole because of promised jobs at Kendall. The plant operated continuously through the Great Depression of the 1930s, and assured jobs for many residents of Walpole and nearby towns.

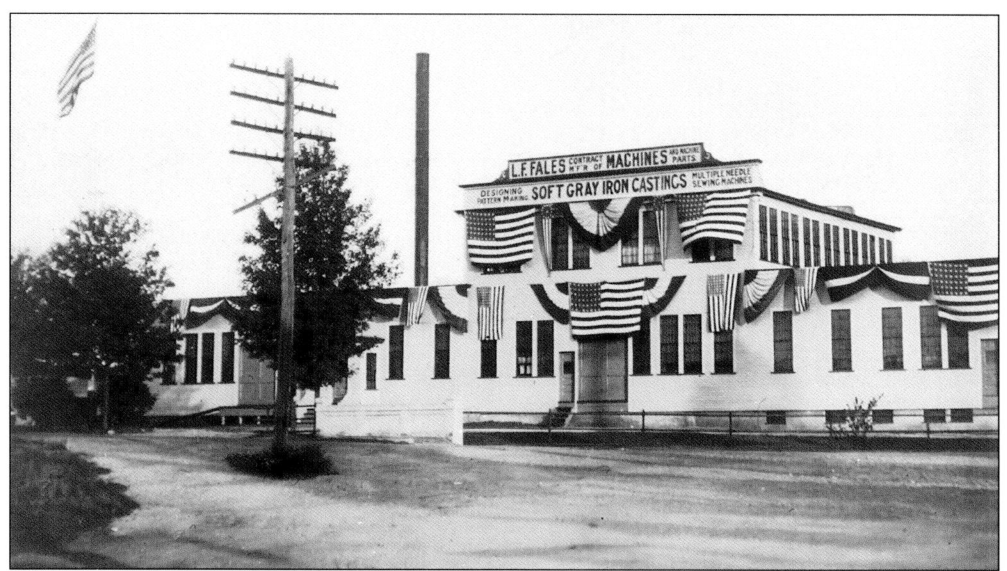

L.F. Fales was founded in 1894 in a room at the Lewis Mill. Later a small machine shop was built in 1898 at the corner of East and Elm Streets. Multiple expansions took place, including a foundry in 1907. The industrial sewing machine was invented by Charles Fales, the father of L.F. Fales. The sign reads, "L.F. Fales contract mfg. of machines and machine parts. Designing Pattern Making / Soft Gray Iron Casting / Multiple Needle Sewing Machines." The decorations suggest this photograph was taken at the time of Walpole's bicentennial.

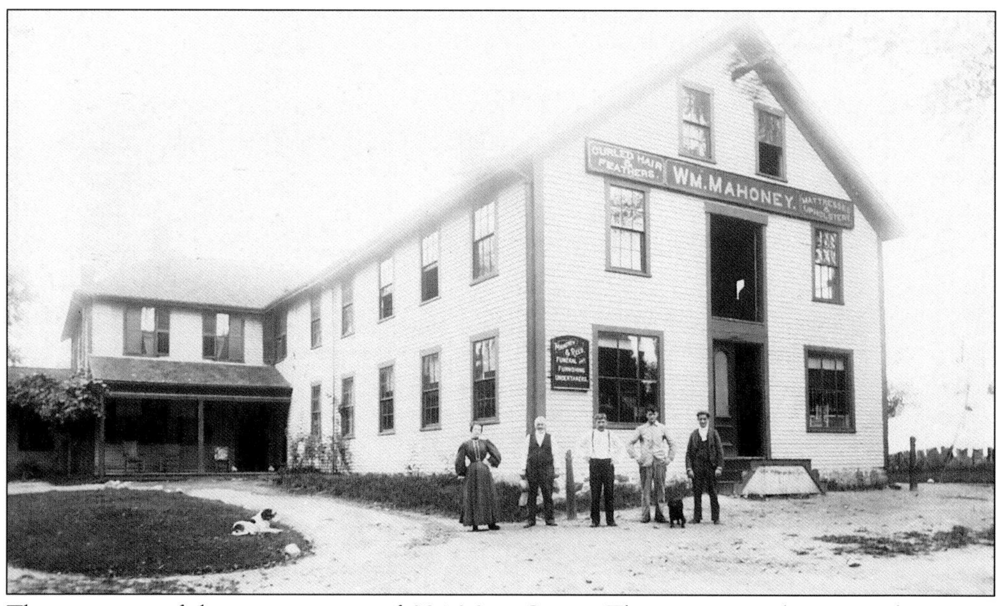

This is a turn-of-the-century view of 904 Main Street. The tiny-waisted woman, four men, and two dogs are probably the entire family and/or staff of Mahoney's Mattress Works. The Mahoney family lived in the ell at the rear. The building was previously a hoopskirt factory and for a time hosted Methodist church services. The building was razed in 1965. The large sign reads, "Curled Hair & Feathers / Wm. Mahoney / Mattress & Upholstery." The small sign reads, "Mahoney & Reed Funeral & Furnishings Undertakers."

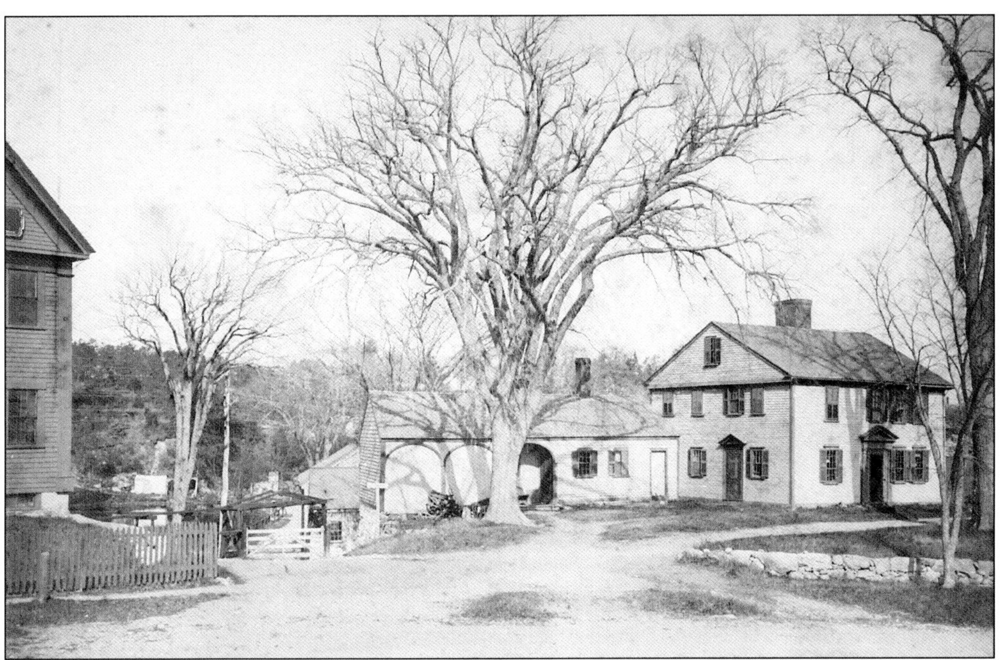

The Stetson Homestead was located at 761 Main Street, currently the site of Hydralign Inc. At left is the corner of the Stetson Mill, now the home of Allied Auto Parts. The path between the buildings was Old Mill Street, which ran across the bridge over the 12-foot waterfall at Stetson Dam. It then turned right, meeting North Street. The neighborhood was a beehive of industrial activity. Some of the industries included John Hall's sawmill (1754); John Cleveland's forge (1779); Ebenezar Hartshorn's gristmill (1794); Joshua Stetson's forge and toolworks (1796); Mr. Roberts, Rand & Hooper and Ira Gill's hat shop until 1855; Joshua Stetson Jr.'s cotton factory (1830); and Plimpton Manufacturing (1925). Oliver Ames, who apprenticed at the Stetson Tool Works, later became wealthy supplying shovels for the railroads.

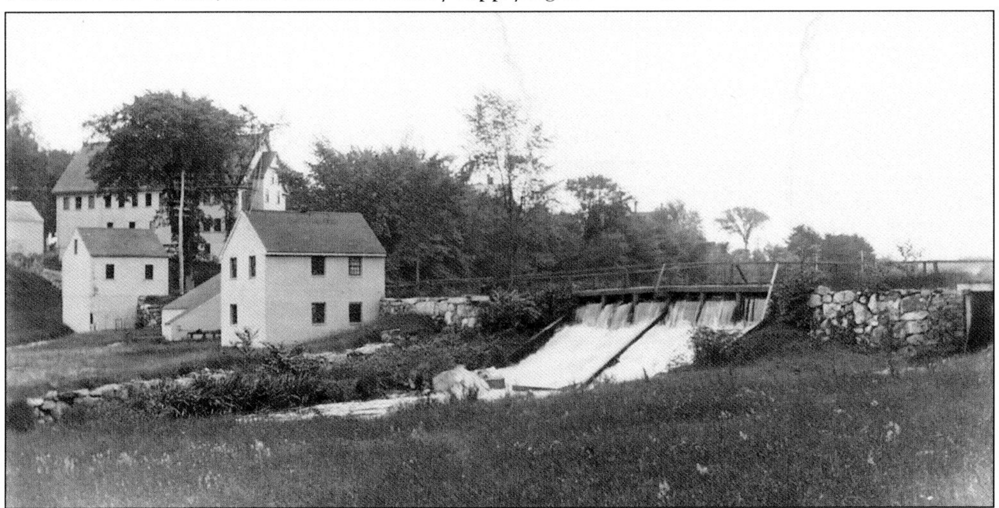

The Stetson Privilege has one of the longest histories of industrial occupation in Walpole or the surrounding area. Archaeological digs have yielded a variety of industrial materials pertaining to factory and mill products. A foot path from 761 Main Street, behind Hydralign, leads to the old dam site.

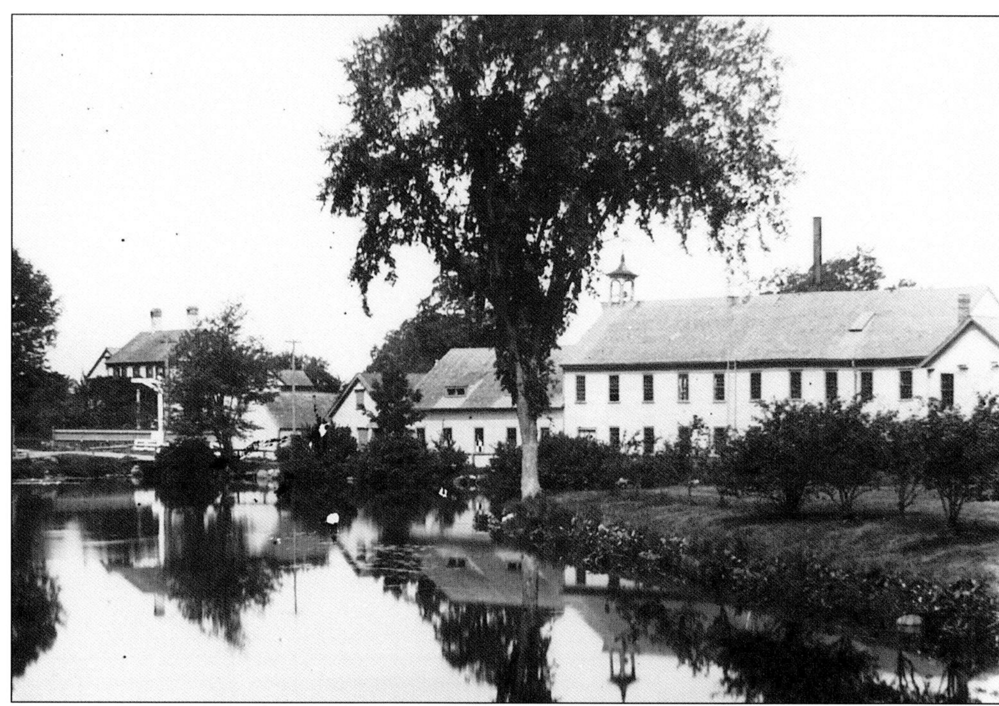

Clarke's Mill, *c.* 1895, was located on Summer Street in South Walpole at the site of the second water privilege, which included a 21-foot waterfall. As early as 1720, Theodore Mann operated a "fulling" mill here. It was continued by his son, Col. Timothy Mann, and, in turn, his grandson, Timothy Mann Jr. The latter's son-in-law, Trueman Clarke, took over in 1825 and produced woolen goods, broadcloths, and "cassimeres." Trueman was a local civic leader and was elected to the Massachusetts Senate. Ultimately, the last proprietor was Trueman's grandson, W.H. Clarke. In 1875, there were 18 employees. By 1905, W.H. Clarke sold the building to the Norfolk & Bristol Electric Street Railway, and it was used as a car barn until it was abandoned in 1919, when the railway operations ceased.

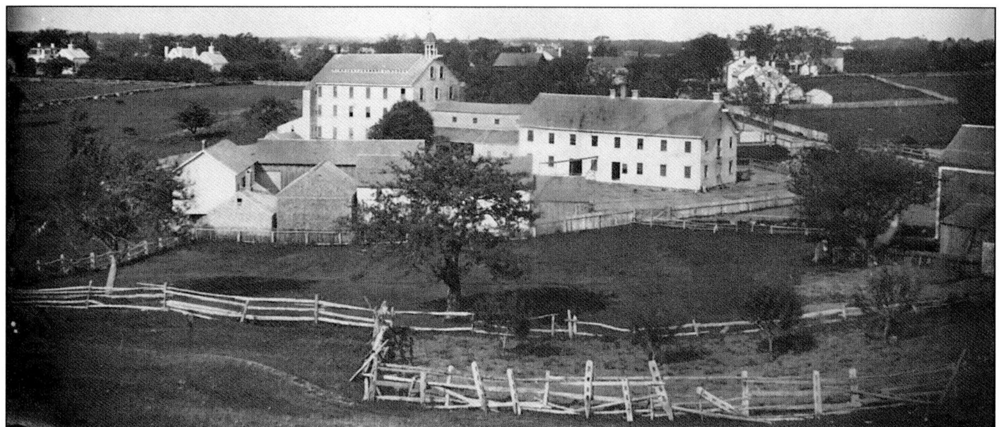

The Manning, Glover & Co. Curled Hair Factory was located on South Street. In 1812, Samuel Fales owned a snuff factory on this property. Cotton and textiles were produced at the Walpole Union Manufacturing building of 1813. After many transfers, Charles Manning, Henry R. Glover, and Jerome B. Cram became Manning, Glover & Co., producing curled hair mattresses, cotton batting, and wicking. In 1875, there were 24 employees.

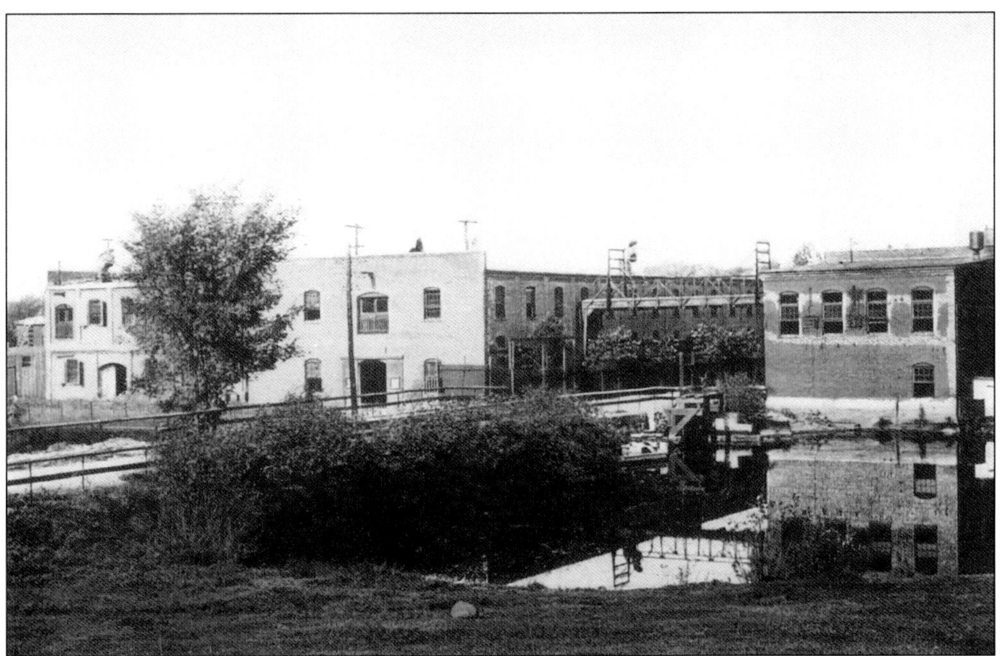

Many small factories operated at the Union Dam site on South Street. One of note was the Union Carpet Lining Company, owned by Mr. Pember until his death in 1891. The property was then sold to the Massachusetts Chemical Company.

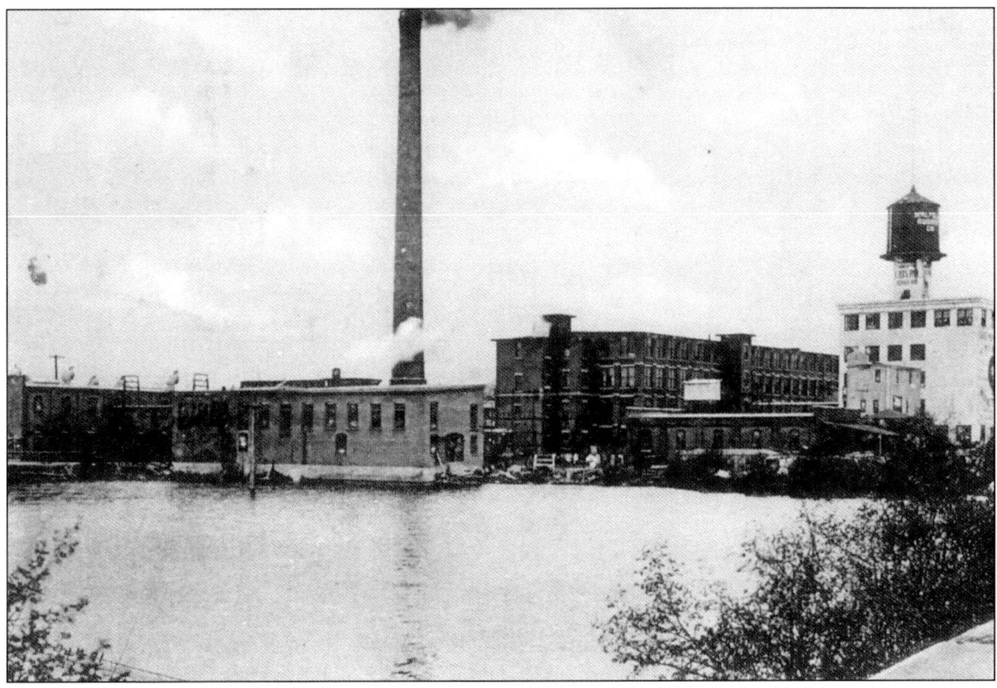

When the Massachusetts Chemical Company became the Walpole Rubber Company is unknown. Many additions were made to the original structure, located to the left in this 1914 photograph. The company was later purchased by the Multibestos Company, a manufacturer of asbestos brake linings.

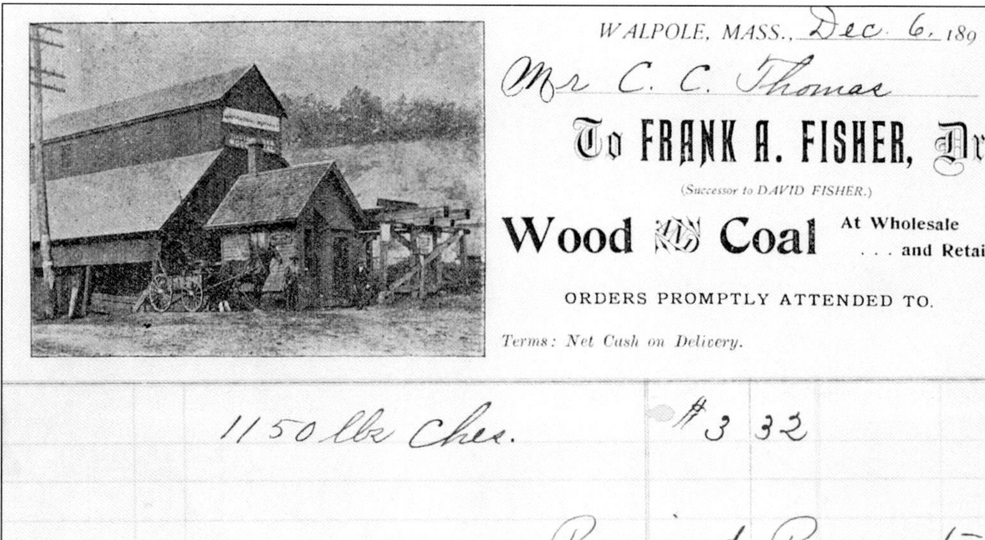

WALPOLE, MASS., Dec. 6, 189

Mr C. C. Thomas

To FRANK A. FISHER, Dr

(Successor to DAVID FISHER.)

Wood and Coal At Wholesale . . . and Retai

ORDERS PROMPTLY ATTENDED TO.

Terms: Net Cash on Delivery.

1150 lbs Ches. $3 32

Received Payment

F. A. Fisher

This image is from a receipt dated December 6, 1894. The billhead identifies the enterprise as "Frank A. Fisher, Wood & Coal (successor to David Fisher)." The receipt was for a payment of $3.32 for "1,150 lbs. ches. [?]" Between 1905 and 1910, Walpole's report of polls and estates shows that Fisher's wood and coal business was augmented by the ownership of several two-family houses on Riverview Place. Fisher's assessed valuation was $1,075 in 1905, $10,875 in 1910, and $40,505 in 1930. Many Italian immigrants lived in one of Frank Fisher's houses (Casa di Franga Faysha) and worked nearby at Lewis's Shoddy Mill (Shoddameel).

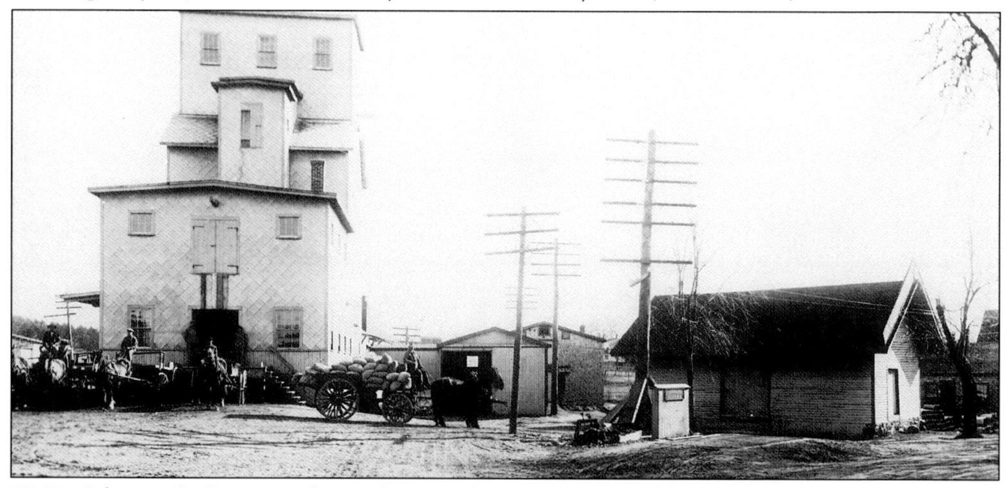

W.K. Gilmore & Sons was located at 1015 East Street. Willard DeLue's 1924 *The Story of Walpole* reports the following: "The business of W.K. Gilmore & Sons Inc., coal, grain, hay and cement was founded by Mr. Gilmore in 1870 in Wrentham, Mass." The Walpole branch was purchased in 1890 from the Gould Estate and incorporated in October 1904. In 1911, a grain elevator was built at Walpole and modern machinery was installed. All milling and mixing for the Franklin, Norfolk, and Wrentham stores was done at Walpole. About 1,400 cars were handled at Walpole and the various branches.

Four

All around Town

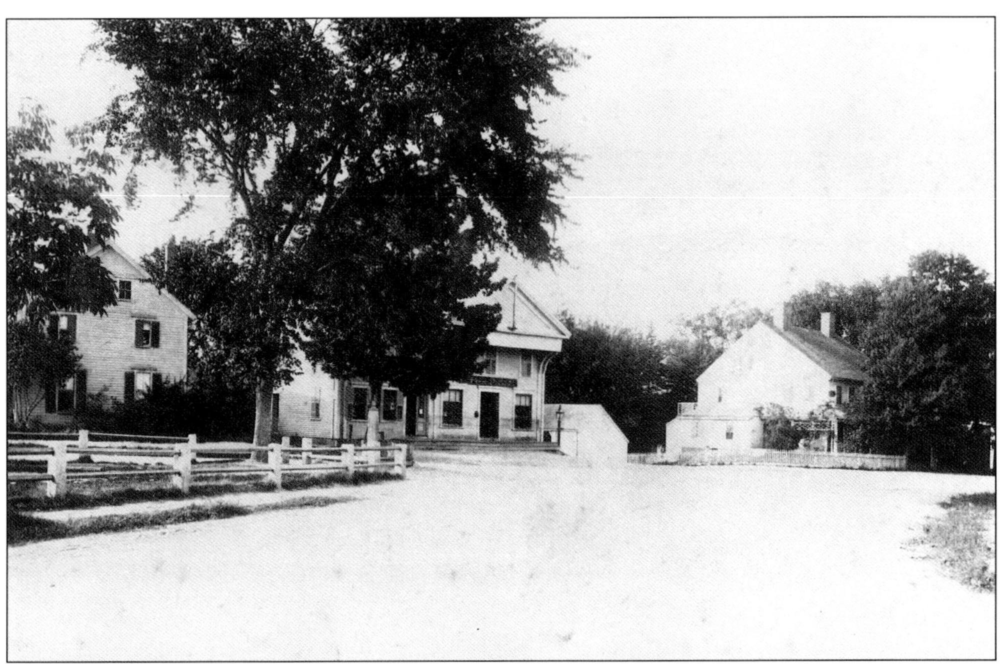

Downtown Walpole, in the 1890s, was a quiet place. The town pump and trough are located at the north end of the common. The middle building housed the first telephone office (on the left) and Craig's store (on the right). The Odd Fellows Building is on this site today. During the summer months, water would be sprayed on the road to keep the dust down.

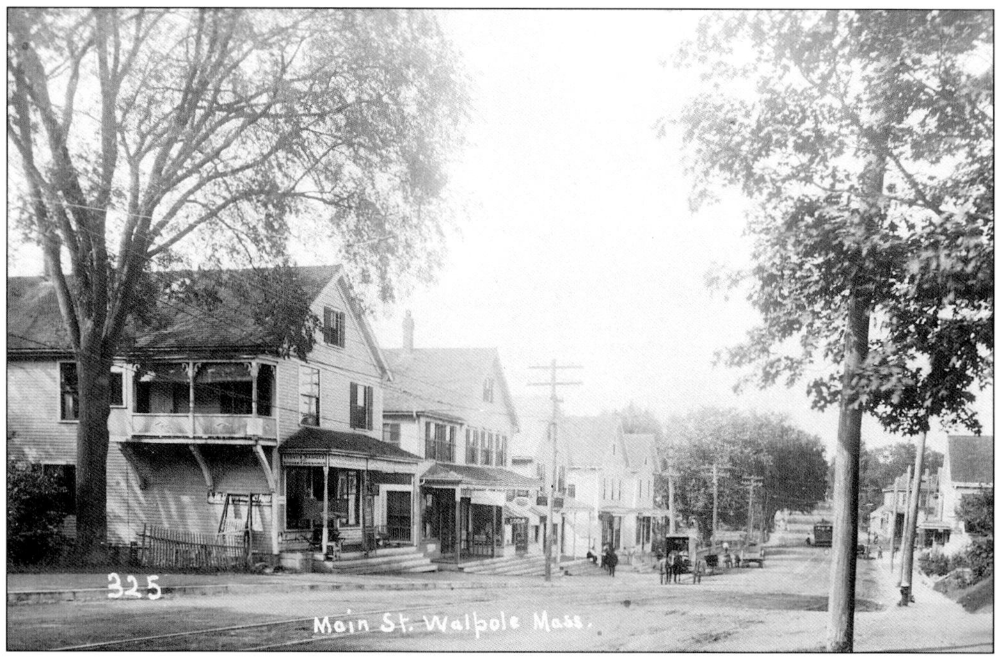

This is Main Street looking north from Town Hall. The high steps to the stores were necessary because of the steep road pitch. Later the street was lowered 5 feet, and the fill was put at the bottom of the hill to flatten the incline.

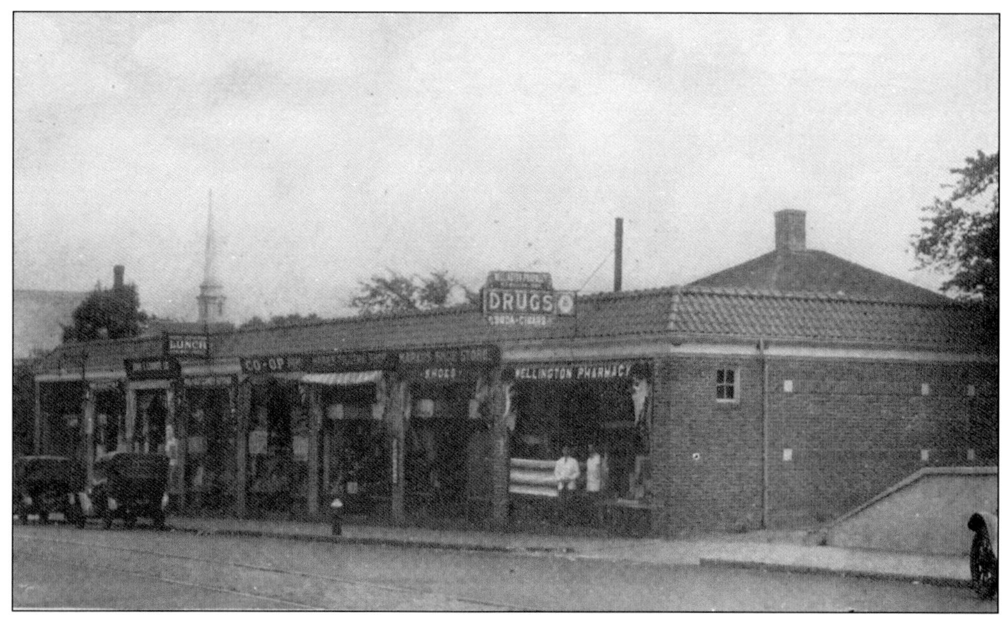

This is the right side of Main Street starting next to Town Hall. The brick building has held many businesses over the years. One of the businesses was Wellington Pharmacy, which later moved up the street to the building that is now Watson's Candies.

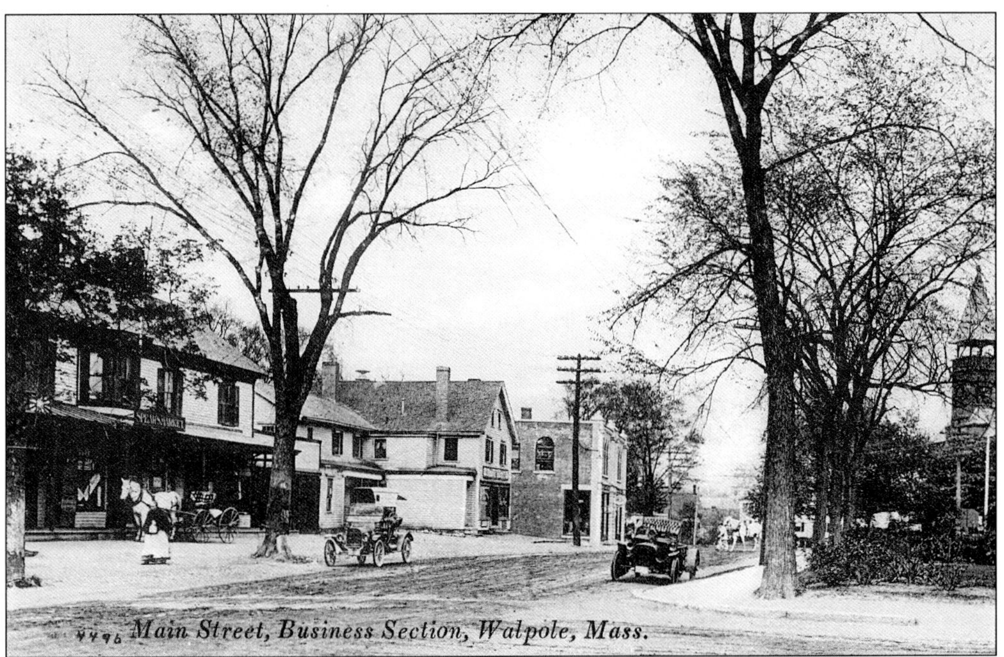

Early in the 1900s, a change to the town was in the making. This view looks up West Street toward unpaved Main Street. Horse-drawn buggies were still being used, but the automobile had made its appearance on the streets of Walpole.

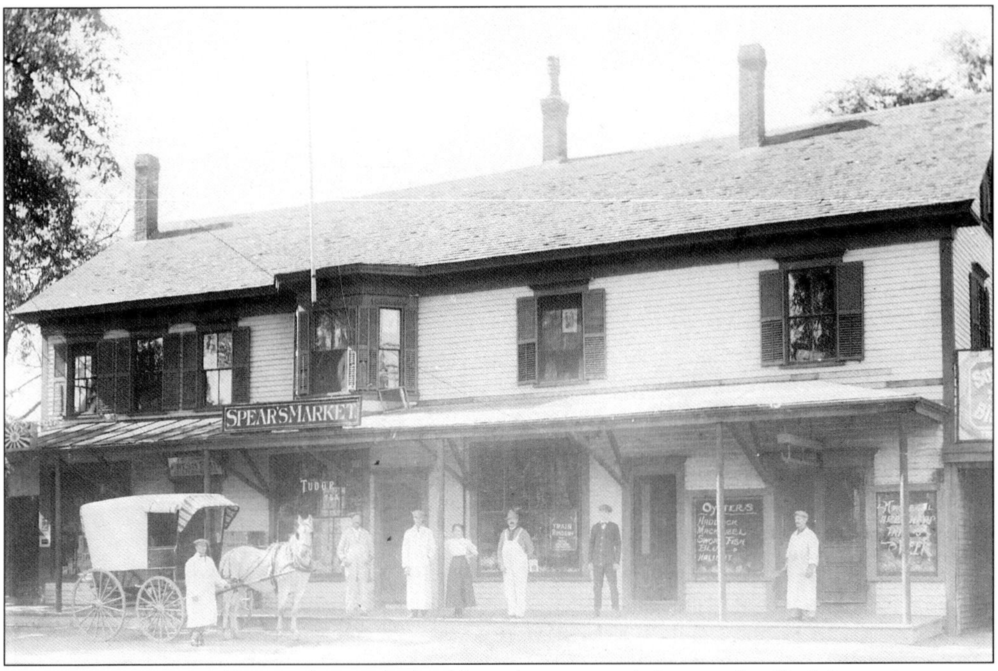

Elmer Spear operated his market in the building that currently houses the Herb Lewis Insurance Agency (at the corner of Elm and West Streets). The size of his market indicates that he was quite a prosperous businessman. In later years, Gove Hardware and a funeral parlor occupied the building.

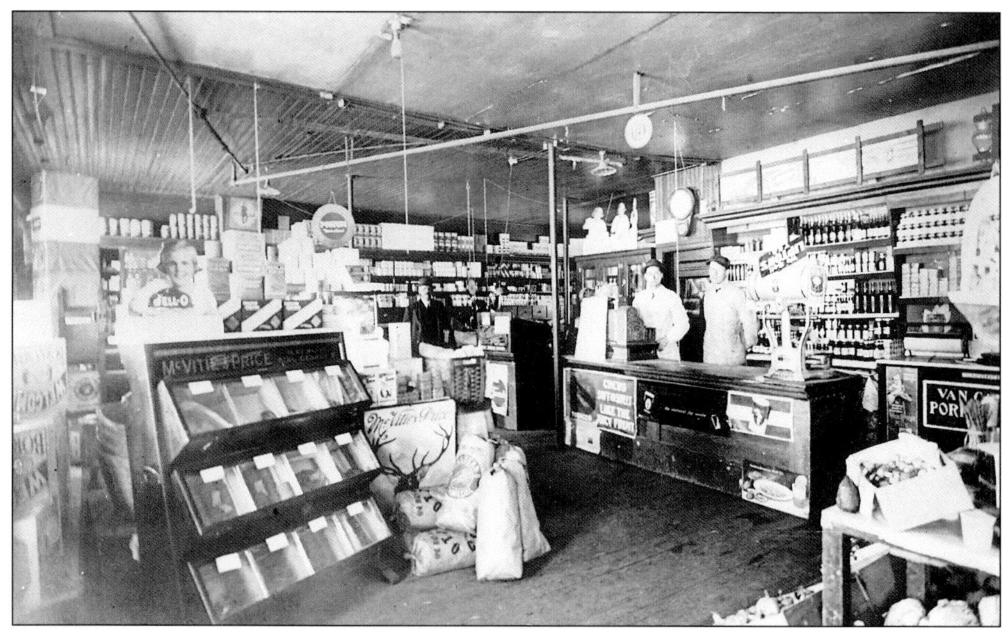

The interior of Elmer Spear's Market was typical of early markets in the area. Just about anything a family might need is displayed under large advertising signs. Canned goods, biscuits, boxes of Borax, and sacks of potatoes were all neatly arranged. Manning the store are George Shepard and Bernie "Bunny" Splaine. The display ad below the cash register reads, "Chews soft and sweet like the juicy fruit. The name of the fruit-tobacco."

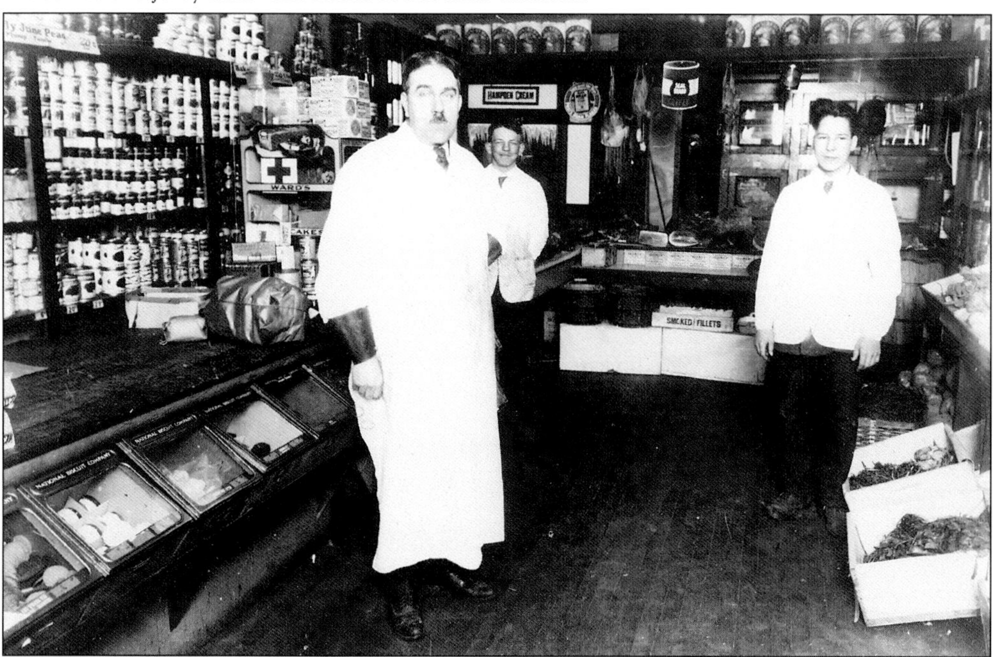

The Spear family had many relatives in the market business. Frank Newell Spear was the owner of this market located at 998 Main Street. Mr. Spear is pictured with his two clerks. One is Albert "Gussy" Nagle. The usual array of fresh produce is displayed, and hanging in the back doorway is the "fresh" poultry.

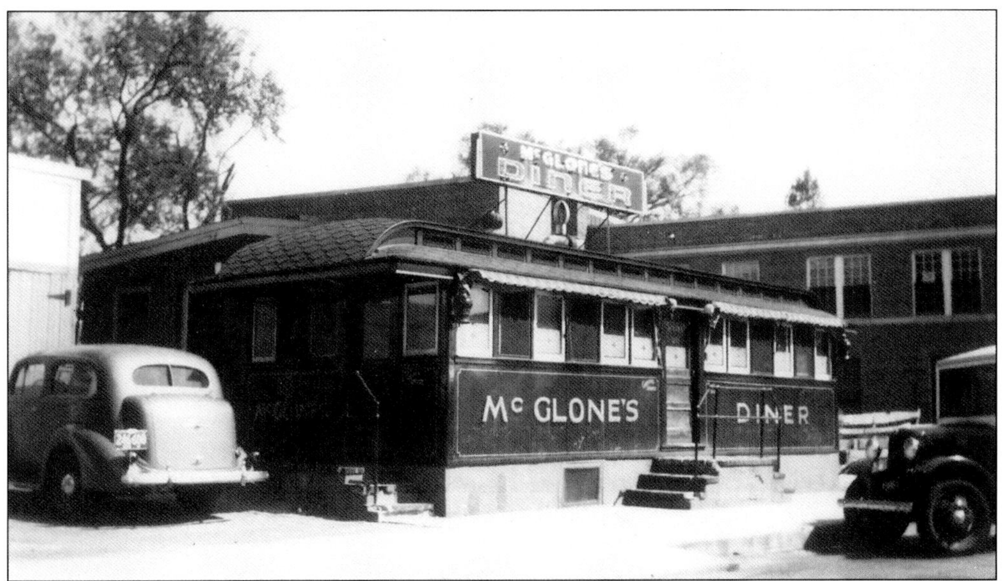

McGlone's Diner, seen here in 1938, was open 24 hours a day to serve the Route 1A truck route, mill workers, and the townspeople. Bill and Mamie McGlone's first diner was at the corner of East and Main Streets. In 1923, a new diner was purchased in Worcester and located on this West Street site, between the Odd Fellows Building and the Herb Lewis Insurance Agency.

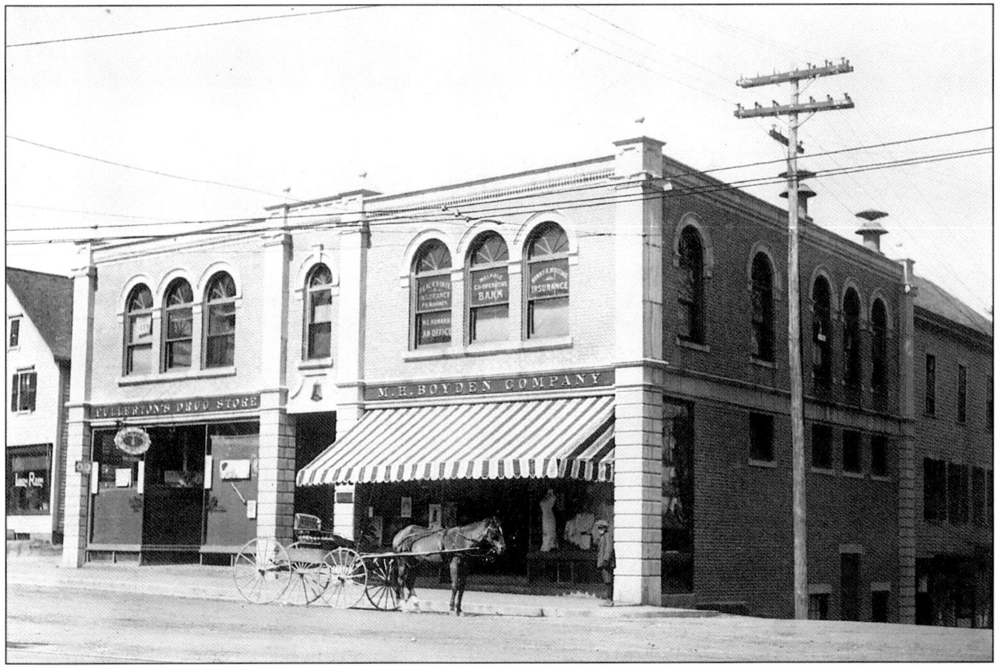

Craig's store is a memory and in its place is the "Business Block." Located on the ground floor was the Fullerton Drug Store and M.H. Boyden. The Walpole Cooperative Bank, the Whiting Insurance Company, Mahoney Real Estate, and the law office of A.W. Howard were located on the second floor. The building was demolished after a fire in the drugstore. At left in this photograph is the Lunch Room Restaurant.

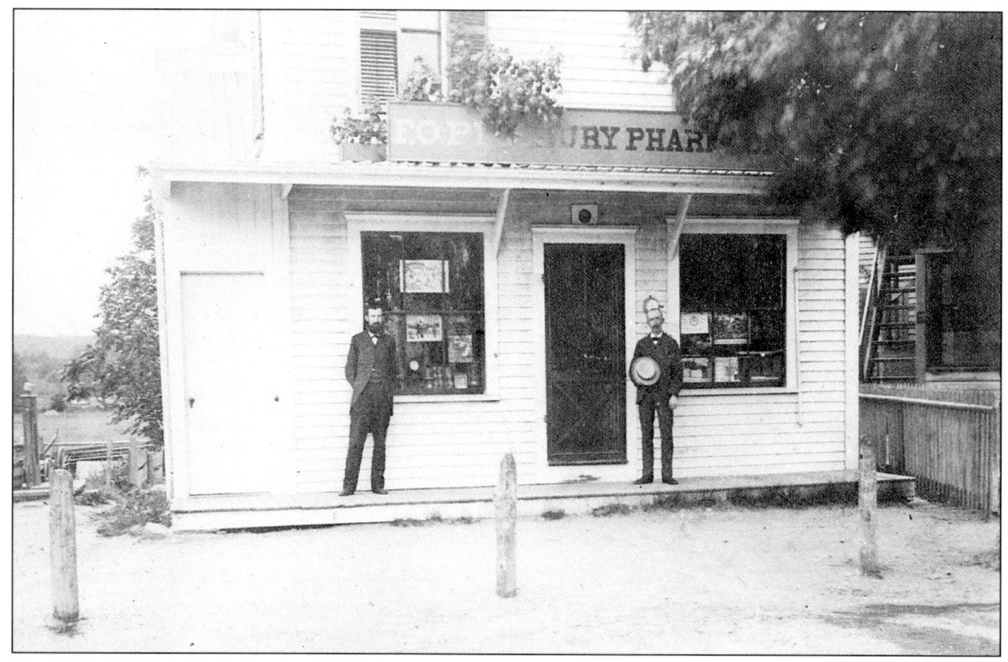

Fred O. Pilsbury had two professions, one as a pharmacist and the other as town librarian. The public library, formed in East Walpole by Miss Mary Bird in 1872, was later transferred to Pilsbury's Pharmacy in Walpole Center. Books were available for the townspeople in a corner of the store. In 1881, the library was moved again to the newly completed town hall. This photograph was taken in 1880.

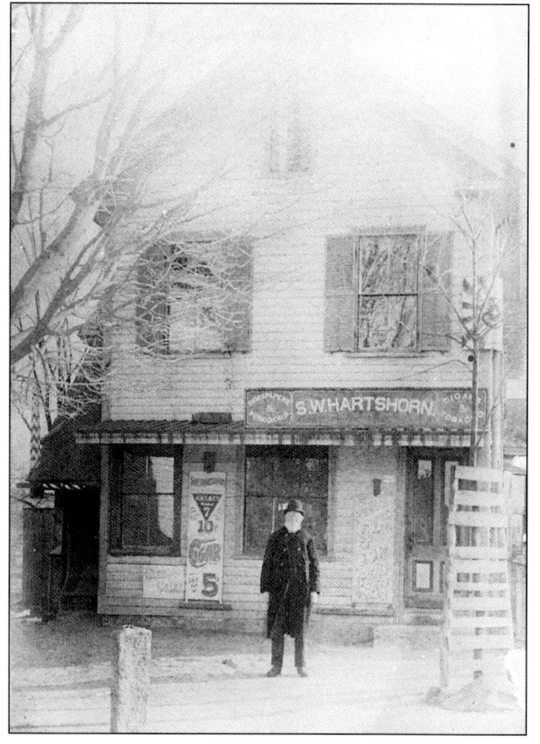

Sylvanus Hartshorn is standing in front of his store located at the corner of Common and Main Streets (the site of Mimi's Variety). A 1927 modernization of the Main Street area removed all the old wooden buildings and replaced them with a one-story brick complex.

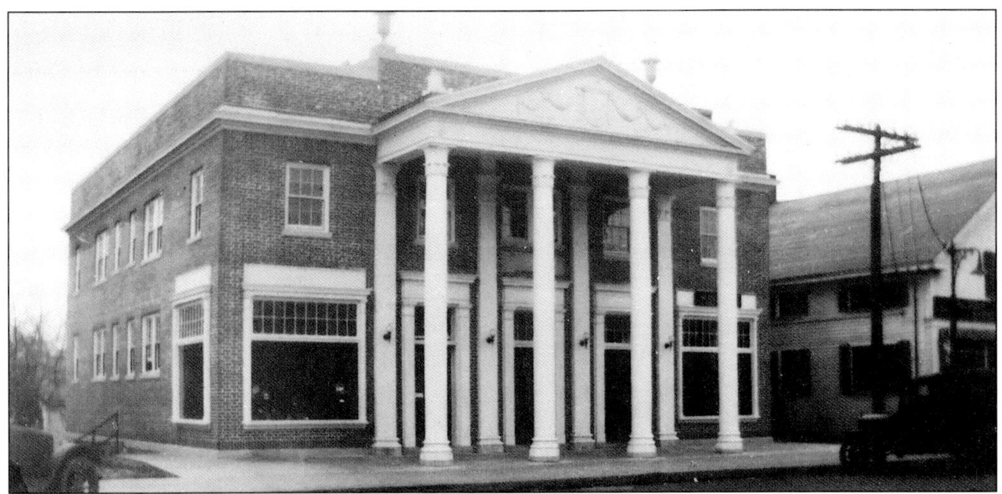

This fine Georgian Revival style building was built in 1934. The upper floor contained professional offices. The street floor housed a variety of businesses over the years, including the post office, a Boston Edison showroom, and Swenson's Mens Store. Men remember Ryan's Barber Shop on the first floor, but smile remembering Ryan's Pool Hall in the basement. Pictured to the right in this 1937 photograph is Watson's first store.

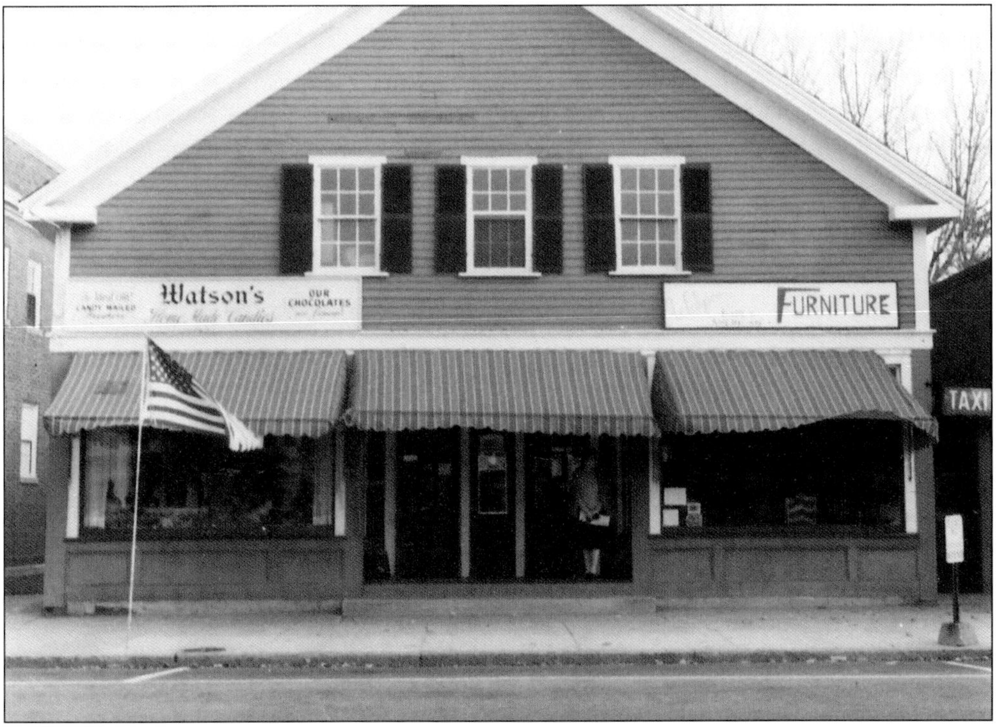

As time marched on so did the businesses housed in this building (seen here in 1969). The town's first taxi service was conducted here when it was Briggs Stable. The automobile took the place of the horse, and the stable was converted into I.T. Snow's Chevrolet Show Room. In 1932, Watson's Candies shared the building with Parker's Newstand, later known as Fowle's Newspaper. During the early 1930s, the American Legion used the second floor for their meeting hall. In 1974, the building was razed. The site is currently a small park.

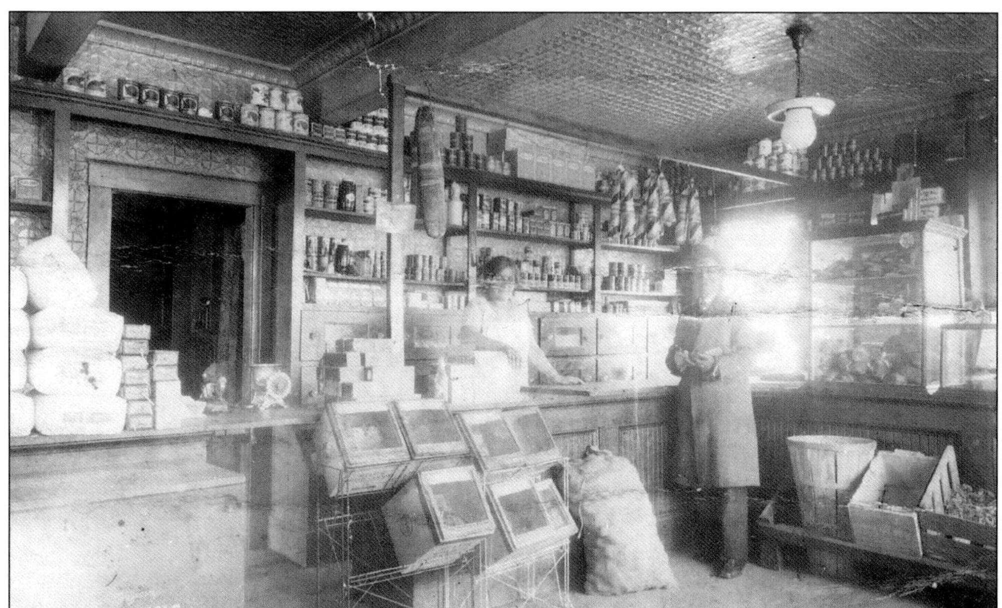

Emidia Civita Procaccini and a La Touraine Coffee salesman posed for this 1929 photograph in her market at 940 East Street. Of interest is the tin ceiling and walls of the market.

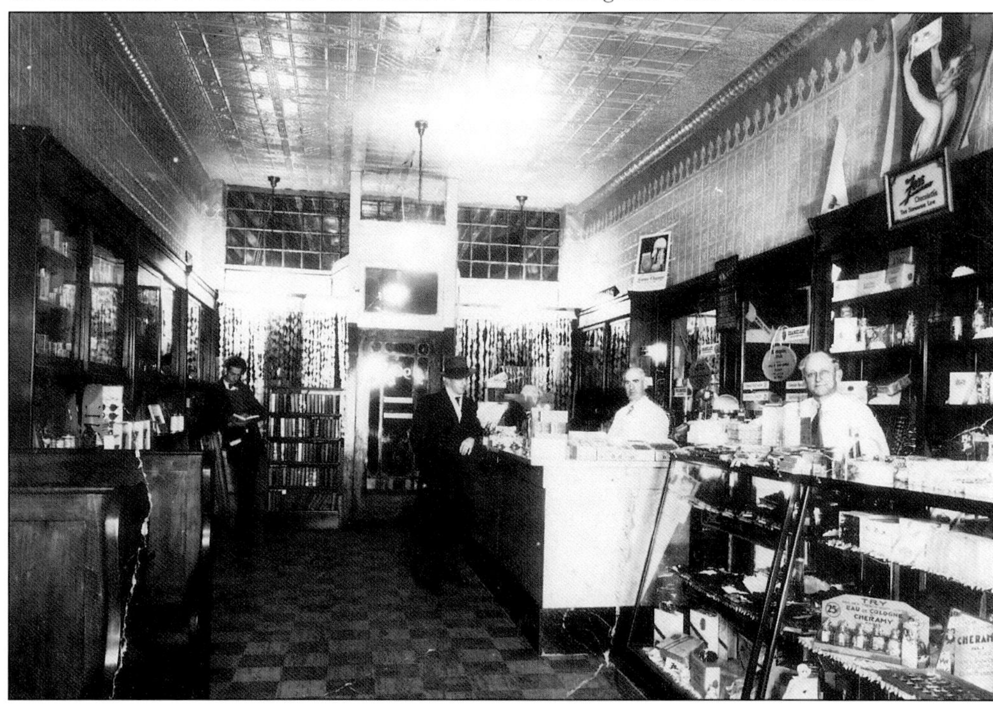

Haney Pharmacy was located at 960 Main Street, and it appeared small and uninteresting situated between the A.L. Morse Company and the First National Store. Once inside, however, there was a wide variety of merchandise. Charles Haney, the proprietor, is second from the right. Among the usual items for sale were sunglasses, Fors chocolates, books, and perfumes. In 1935, customers would purchase these items, visit the soda fountain to choose an ice cream treat, and relax in the wooden booths.

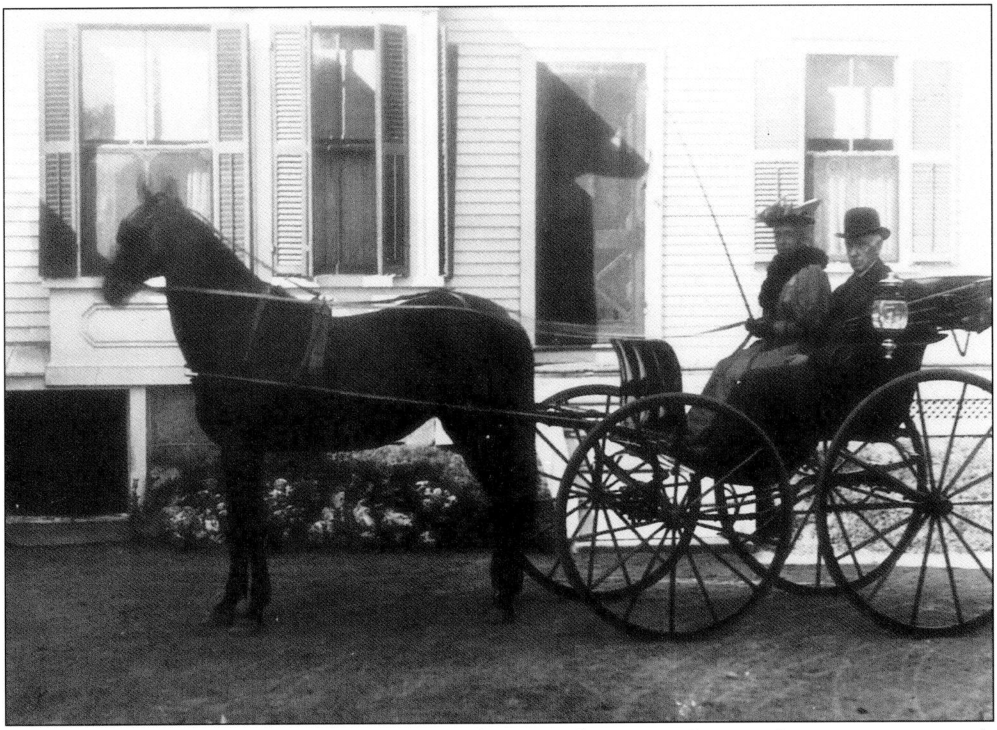

Miss Florence Lewis holds the reins to this horse and carriage for an afternoon outing with Bradford Lewis. Horse and carriage was the mode of transportation in 1892.

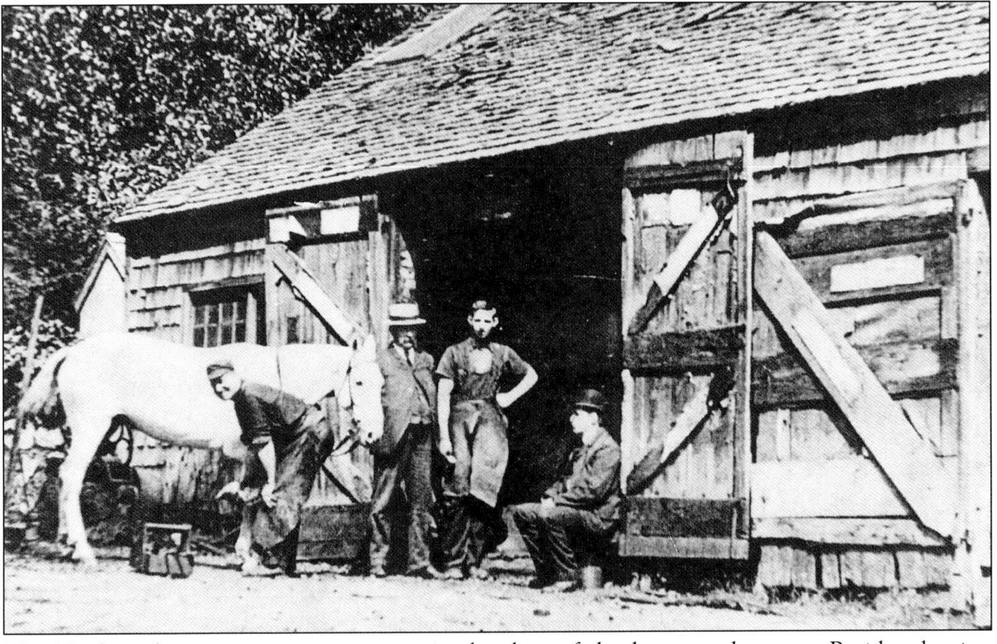

The blacksmith was an important man in the days of the horse and wagon. Besides shoeing horses and fixing wagons, the blacksmith also performed other forge-related jobs. T. Carlisle built his shop in 1828 (it is now Danom Forge) on Washington Street in East Walpole. Pictured in this early 1900 photograph is Arthur MacLean (to the left). The other men are unknown.

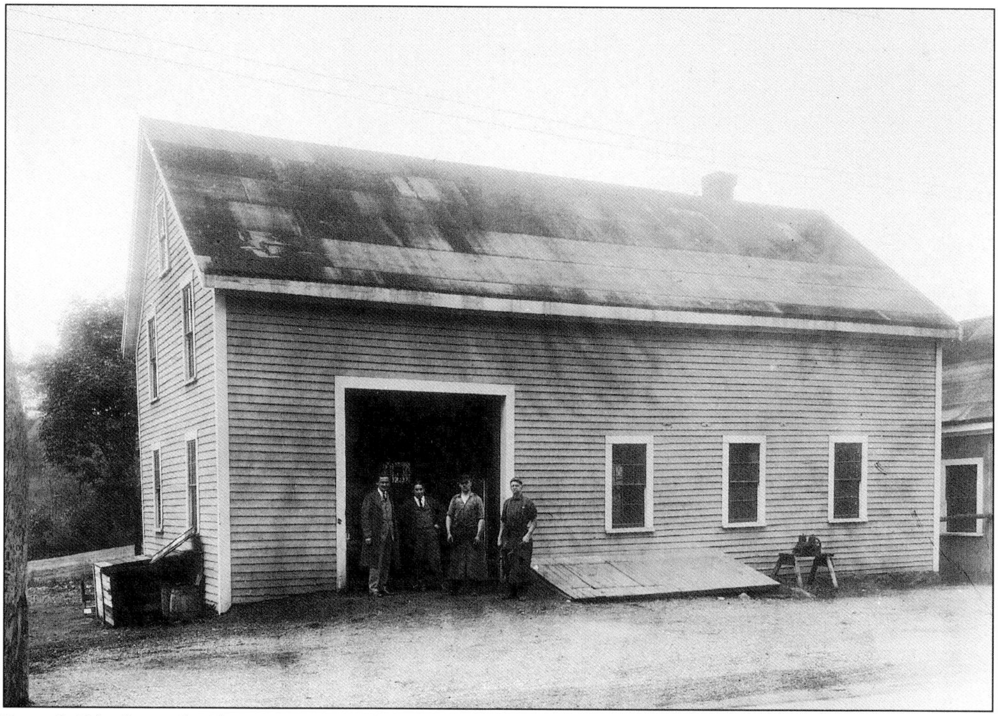

Ryan's Blacksmith Shop was moved to the corner of North and Main Streets in 1902. The art of the blacksmith faded as cars took the place of horses, and welding replaced horse shoeing. Pictured are, from left to right, Joe Ryan (the owner), Sam Bray (a later owner), a Plimpton Trunk salesman, and a customer. Written on the back of the photograph is "Customer (N.Y. Bootlegger) having trunk supports made and fitted."

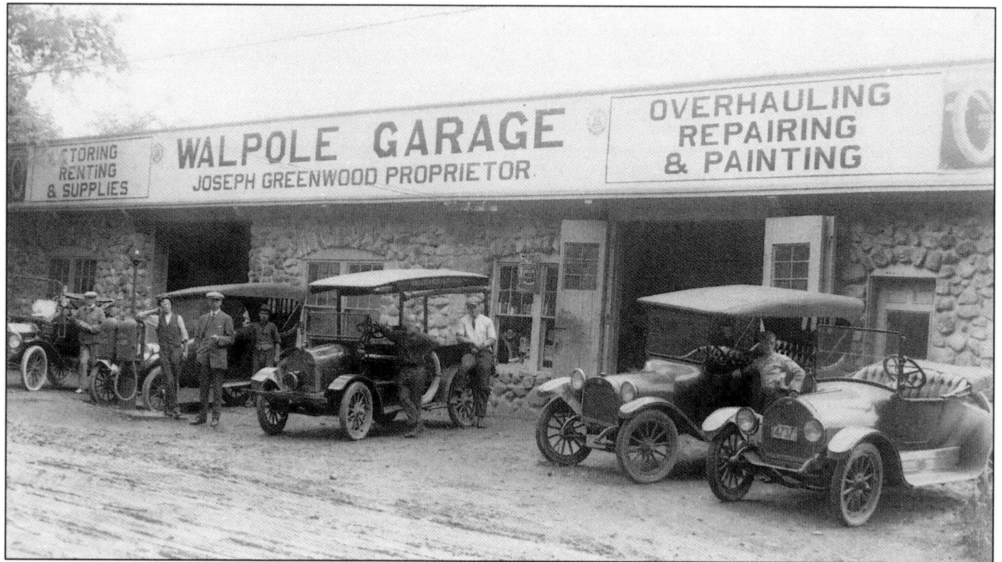

Joe Greenwood was in the right spot at the right time. Greenwood's Garage was one of the first on the state road (Route 1A) that ran between Boston and Providence. Greenwood was the local agent for Maxwell cars, and as the business grew and thrived, he was able to double the size of his building by 1916.

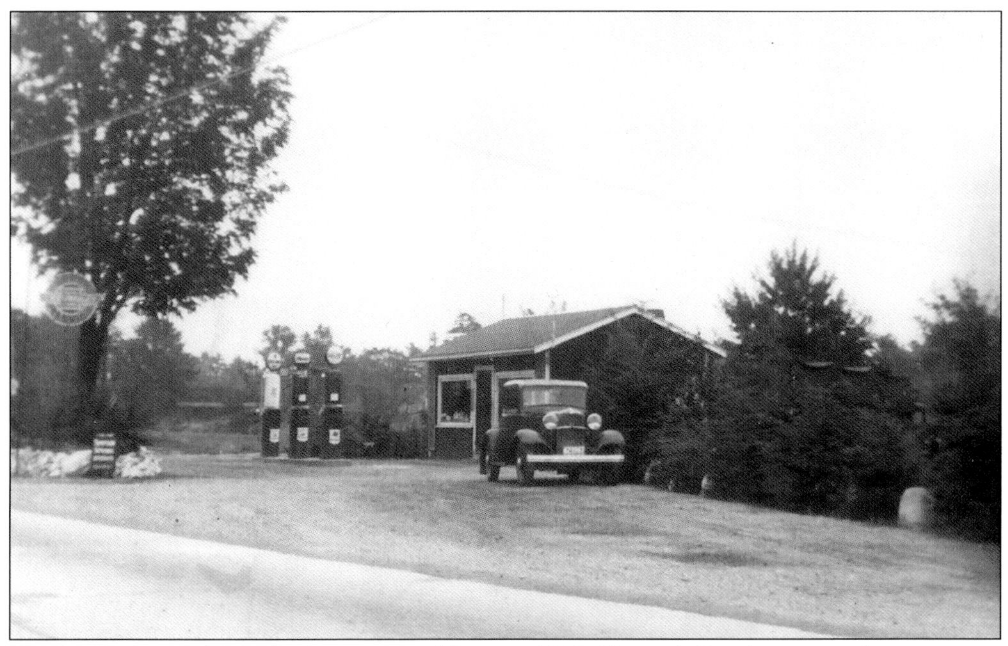

Staples Garage on Main Street is pictured here in 1932. Kenneth Staples operated a gas station and automotive repair business here for many years. Also located in this Route 1A area was Browne's Pond, a popular spot for summertime swimming and winter skating. The pond was used for practice by Walpole High School's hockey team in the 1940s. Lights enabled skaters to use the pond at night.

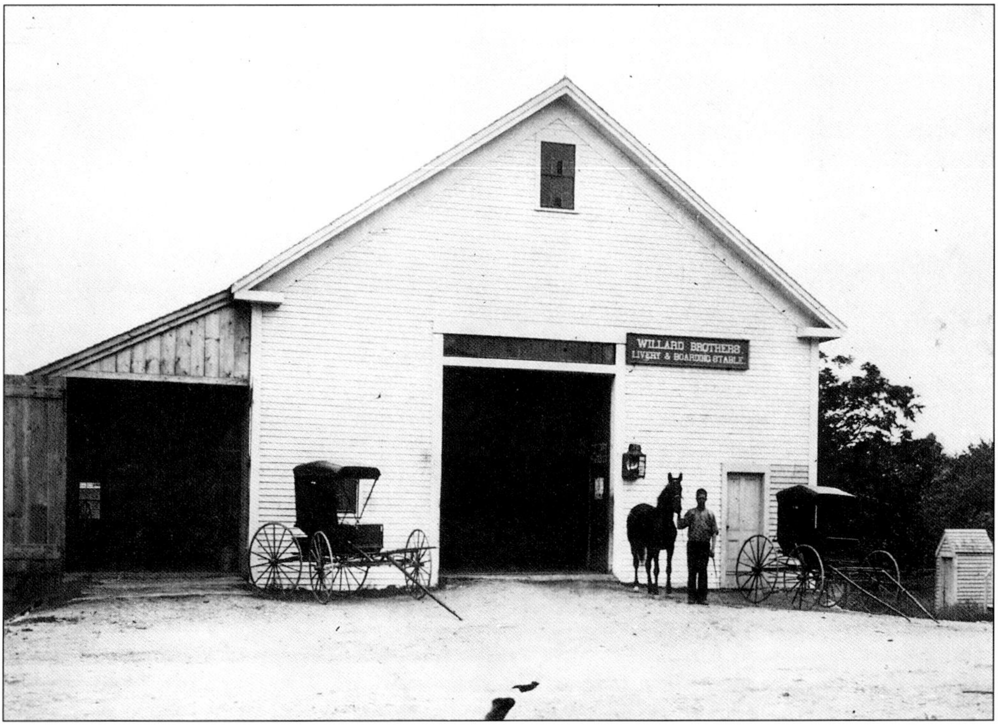

Here is one last look at a bygone era.

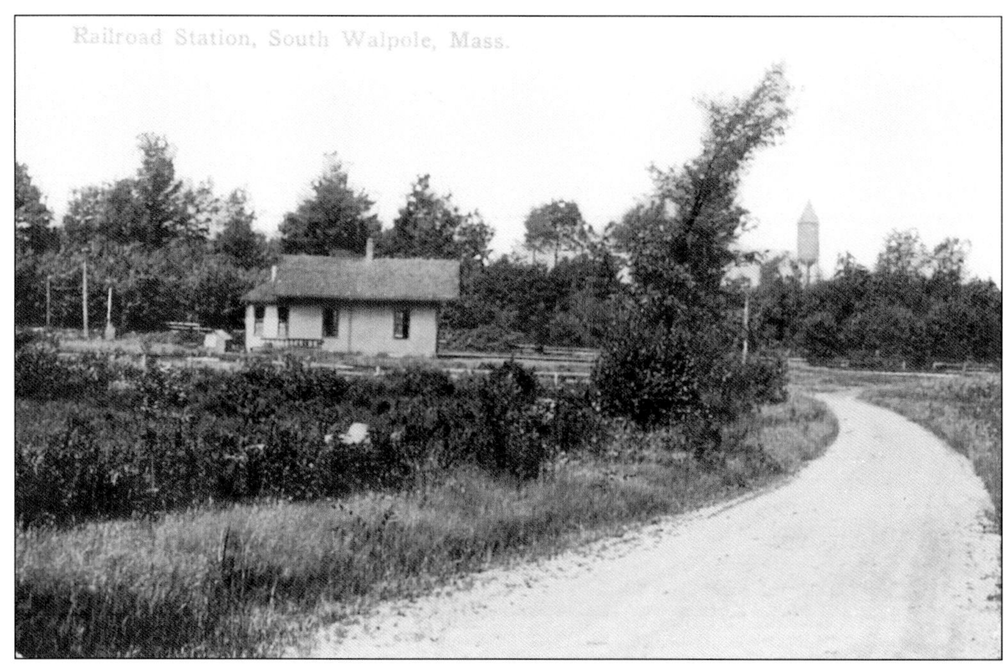

Pictured is the South Walpole train station, one of seven depots located around town. Bill Dowd, the longtime postmaster of the South Walpole Post Office, noted that the depot was converted to house the post office after the passenger service was discontinued. What looks like a missile at the right is a water standpipe.

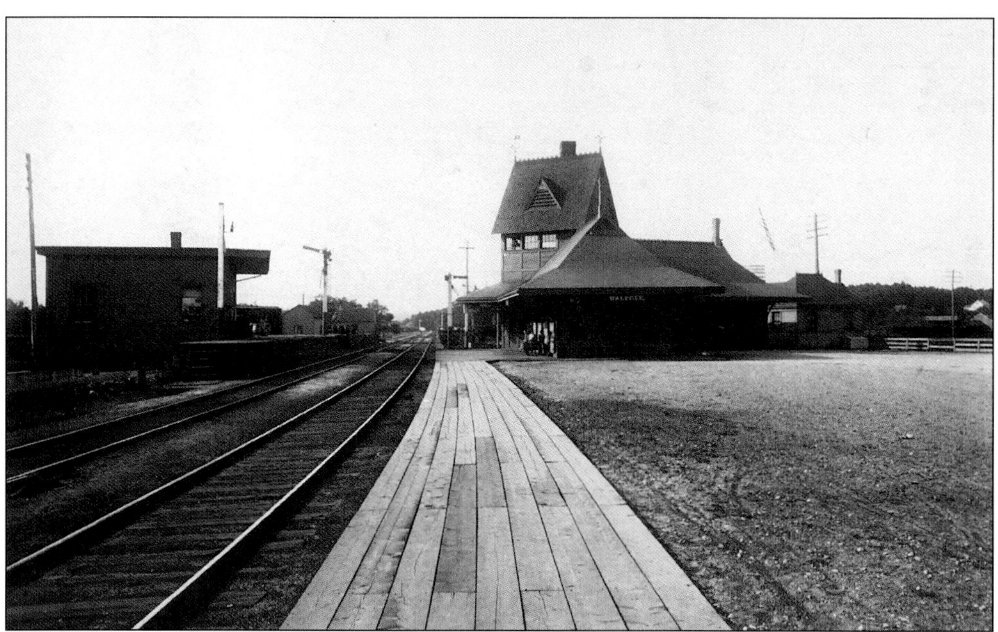

The Central train depot, on West Street, was the busiest station in town during the 1930s. F. Donovan, train dispatcher, recalls as many as 38 trains a day going east and west and 17 trains going north and south. Many extra trains would also pass through daily. The large portion of this building was the switching tower. This photograph was taken c. 1900.

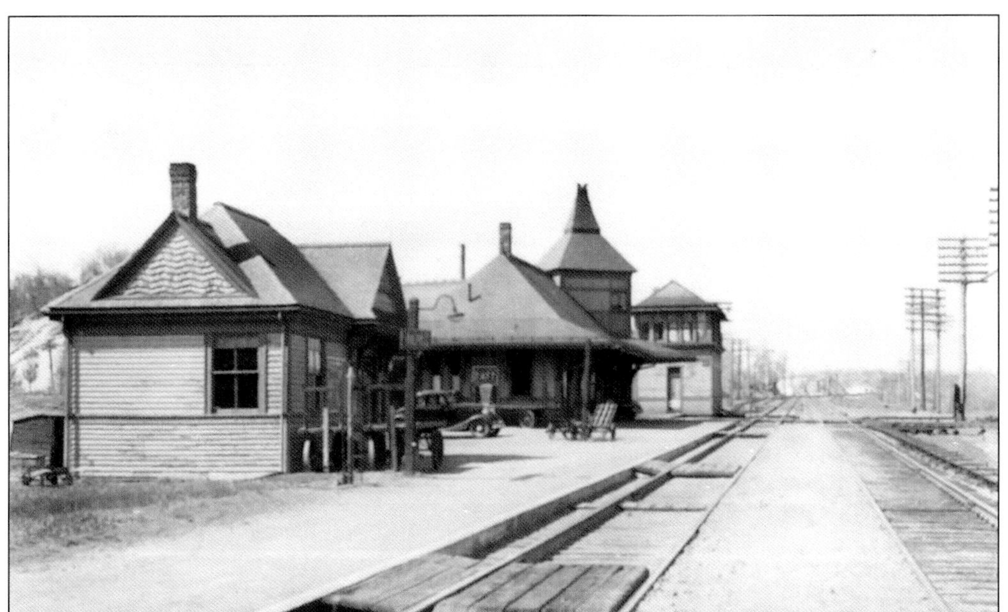

In 1932, the Central train depot was remodeled and the switching tower was removed. The architecture is a typical Old Colony Railroad style. Many duplicates of this building can be found along the Old Colony Rail Line.

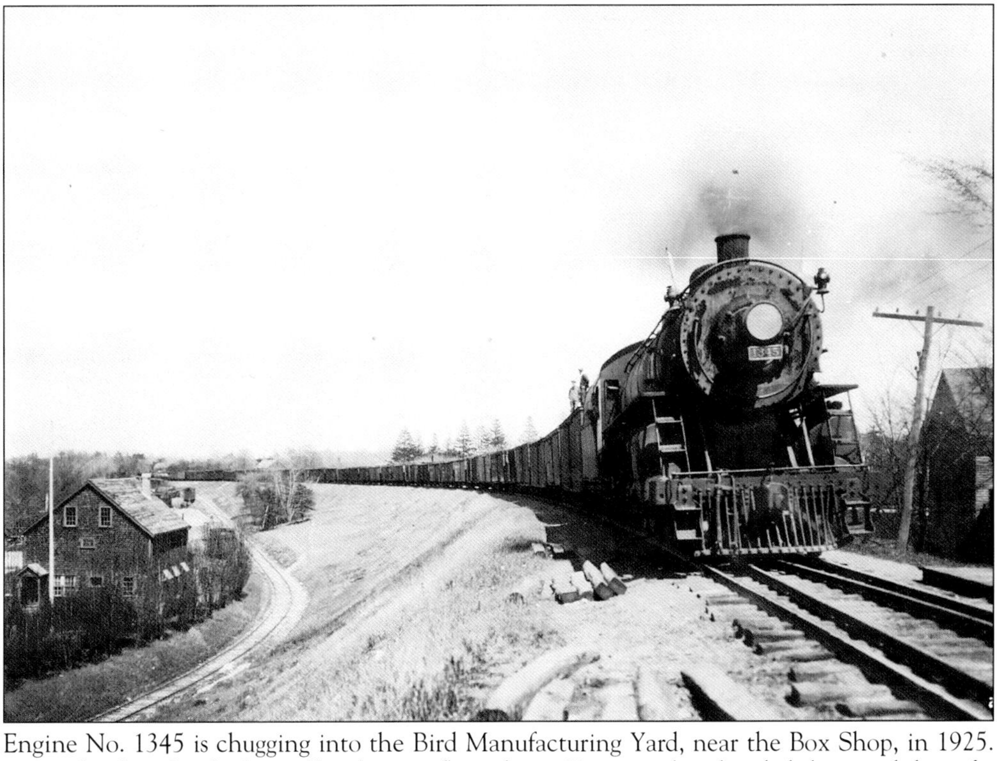

Engine No. 1345 is chugging into the Bird Manufacturing Yard, near the Box Shop, in 1925. Trains hauling freight kept all industries flourishing. Every worker dreaded the possibility of a rail strike, which could shut a mill down. Pictured in the lower left is the Hermitage, a rooming house for Bird employees and formerly the Boy Scout House.

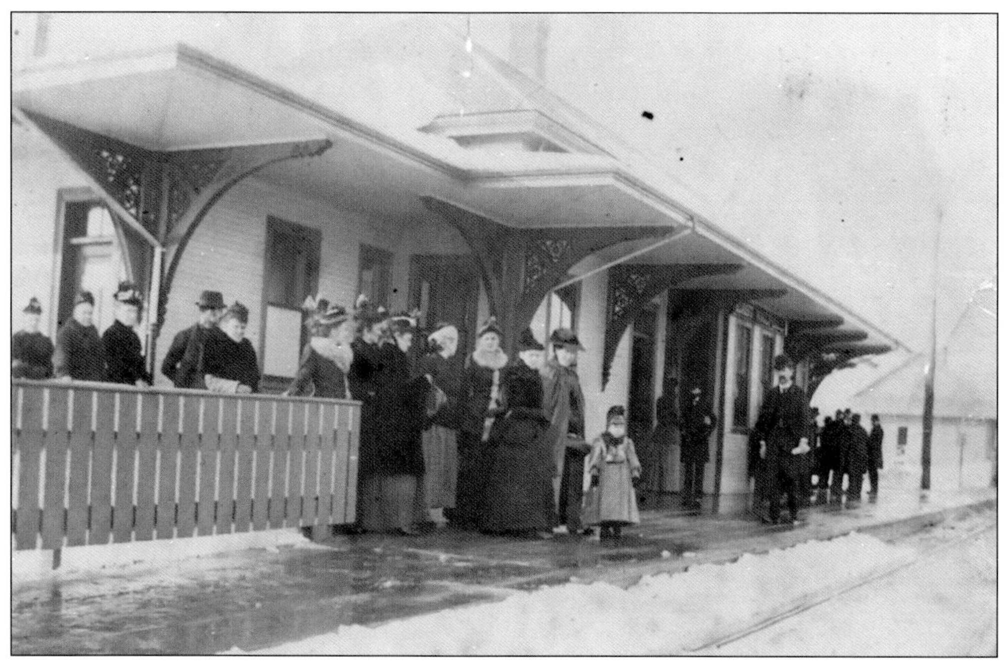

Where is everyone going on this snowy day in 1874? Waiting together at the East Walpole train station, these ladies appear to be waiting for a train to take them on an outing.

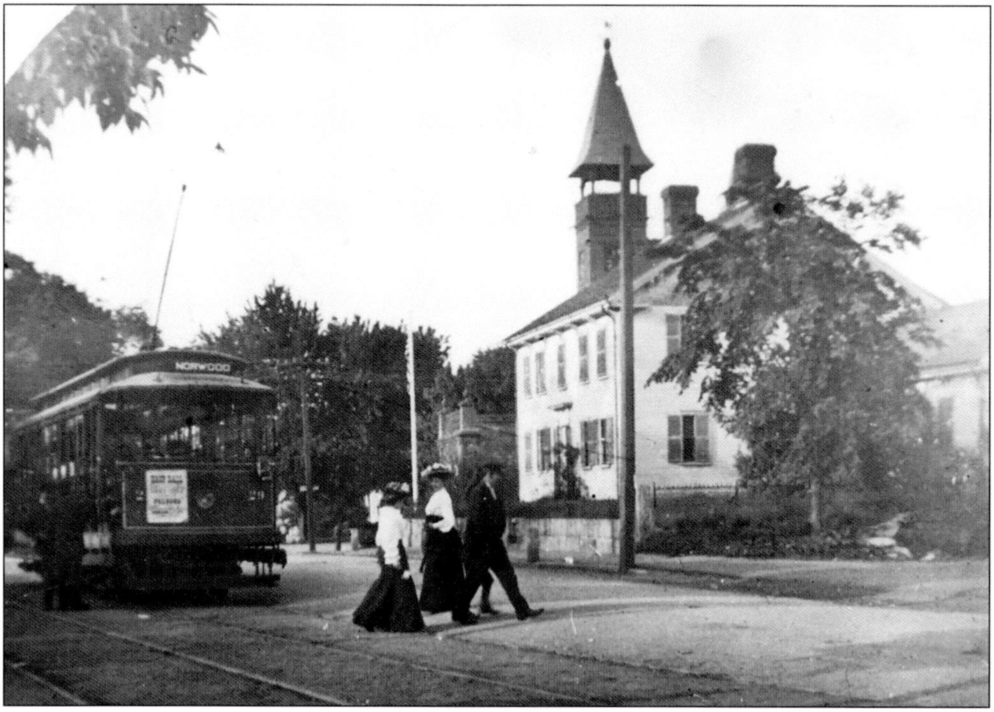

In the late 1890s, a new form of transportation came to town—the street railway system. Trolley No. 29, with open sides and bench seats, traveled the Norwood-Walpole route. It is pictured here on Main Street; also visible are the Pierce House, the telephone company (next door), and the clocktower of Town Hall (located at the corner of Stone and Main Streets).

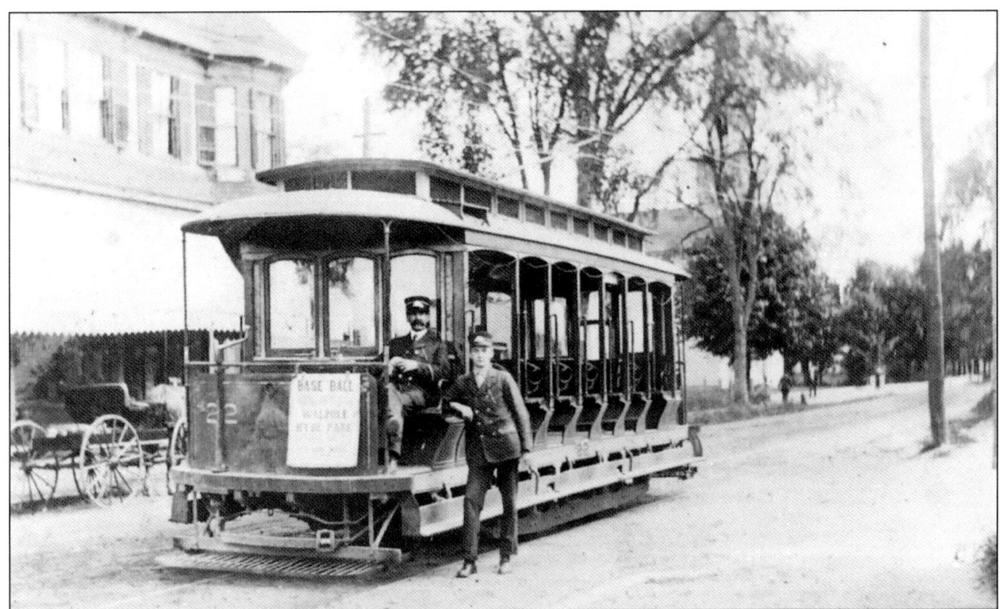

Proceeding down East Street is Trolley No. 22, an open car typically used as summer equipment. Hop on for the ride to the baseball game, for the sign states the game is Walpole versus Hyde Park. Henry Morrison (seated) was the motorman, and Thomas Leonard, who later became the police chief, was the conductor.

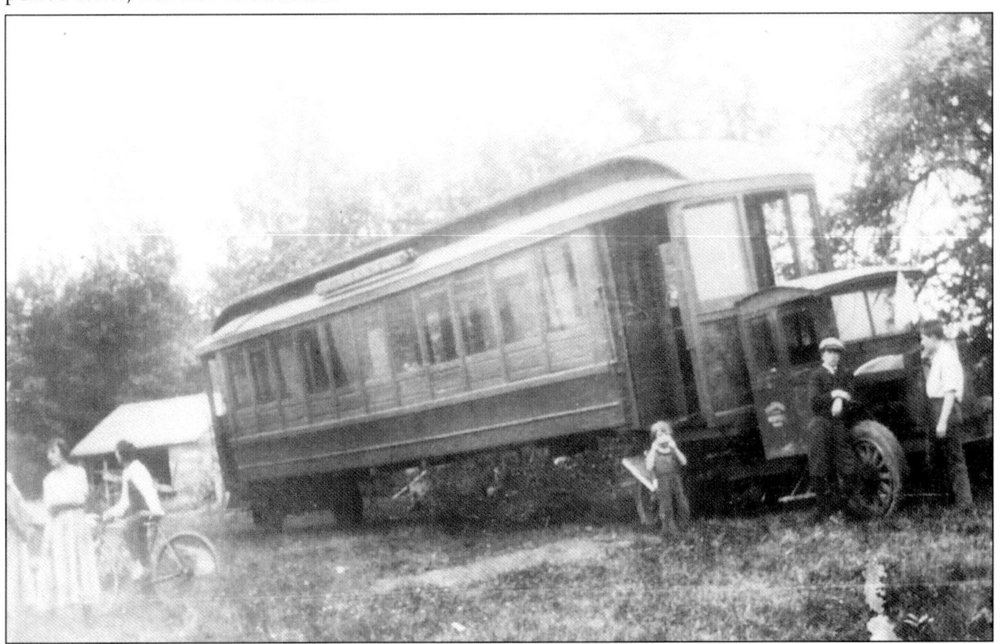

After World War I, high-operating costs and an employee strike doomed the Bay State Railway Company, and the trolley cars were sold and hauled away. Car No. 41 was purchased in 1920 and moved to 89 Summer Street, the home of Wilfred Sheehan, to be used as a workshop. On the right side of the photograph, from left to right, are E. Sheehan, W. Sheehan (with hat), and C. Guild. In 1919, the Eastern Massachusetts Street Railway Company acquired the line, and trolley service continued to East Walpole until 1932.

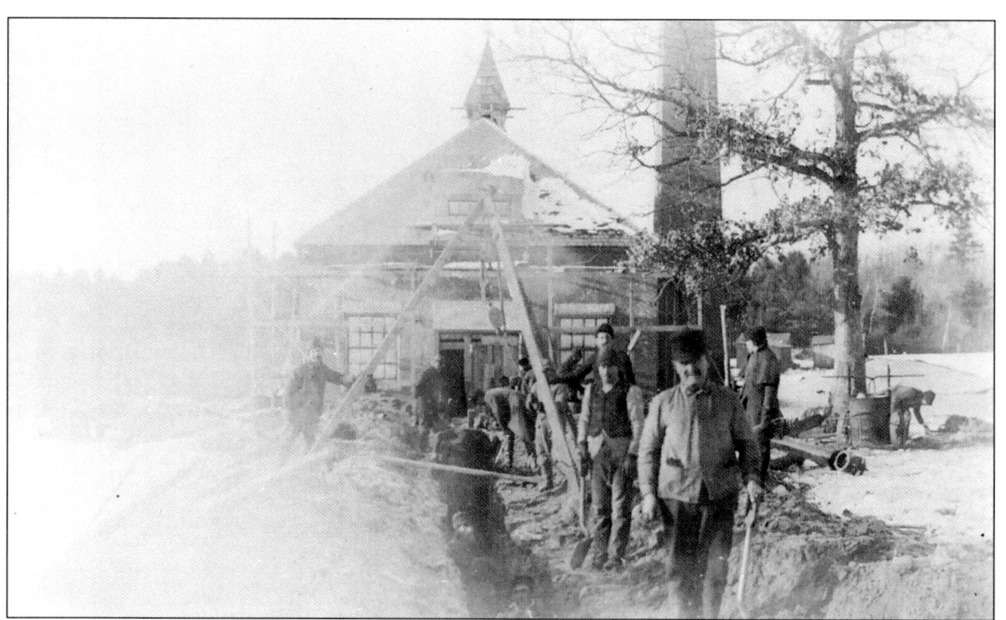

Walpole's rapid growth necessitated the building of a town water supply system. Missing from this 1894 picture is any sign of earth-moving machinery. Much credit is due the men who toiled with pick and shovel to lay the pipe lines which would greatly benefit the town.

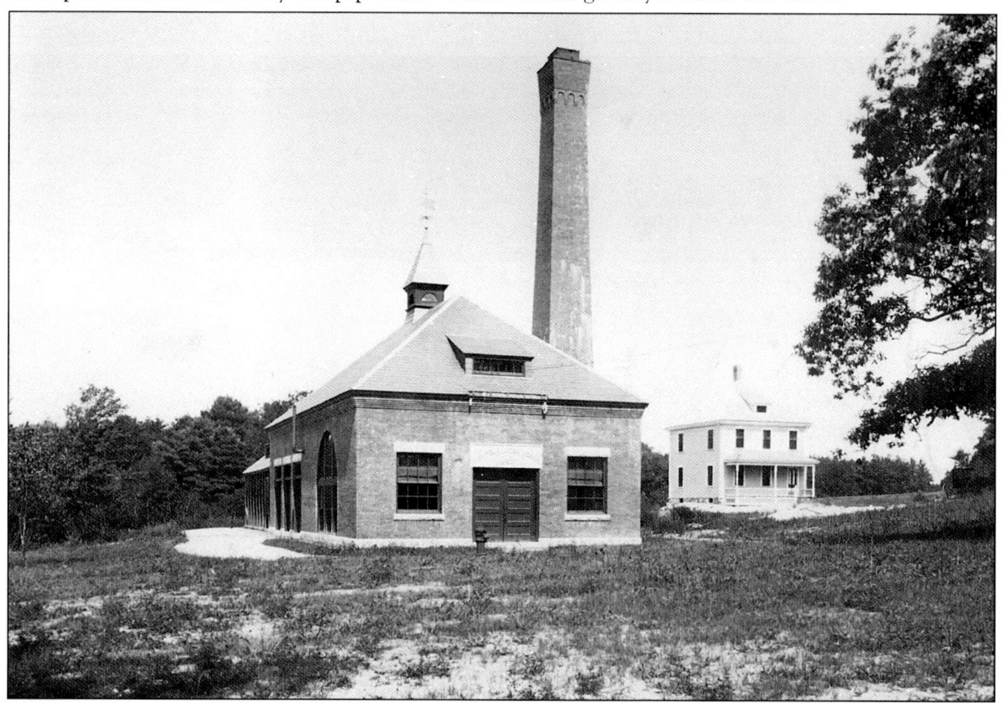

In 1895, the pumping station commenced operation, pumping from six artesian wells. There were 277 service connections, but only 77 houses had meters. The rate charge for metered houses was 22.4¢ per 100 cubic feet. Dwellings without meters were charged by the number of faucets, tubs, and water closets. The home of the Department of Public Works (DPW) director is on the right.

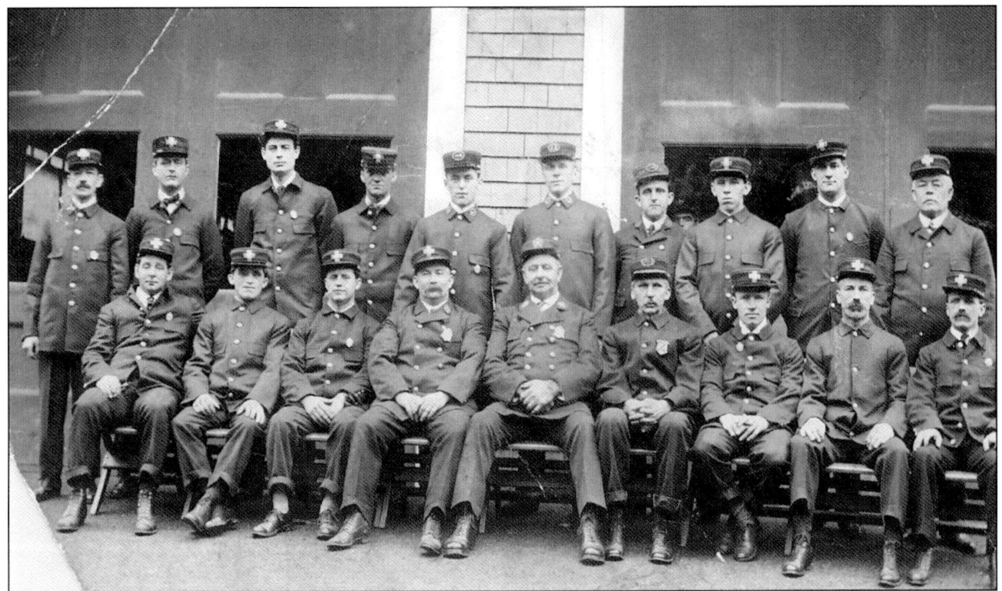

The Central Fire Department posed for a photograph in 1910. The firefighters pictured here are, from left to right, as follows: (front row) Winslow, Garby, Burns, Smith, Chief Winslow, Reardon, Walsh, Brown, and Nangle; (back row) Boyden, Mahoney, Spilane, Delaney, unknown, Hennessey, Haniford, Hennessey, unknown, and Thomas. Rank was identified on the hat—one bugle stood for the rank of lieutenant, five bugles for the rank of chief.

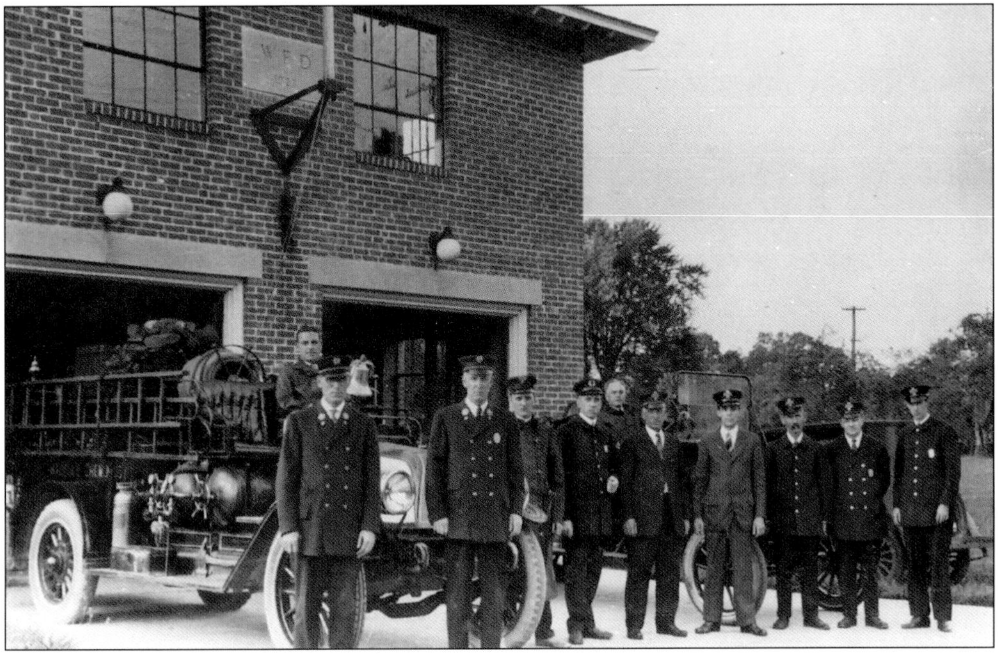

Old Clarke's Woolen Mill was chosen as the site of the South Walpole Fire Station in 1923. Ten men were assigned to this station. From left to right are as follows: Bruce Schufelt (in truck), Chief Chet Donnell, Chief Wallace Tiffany, Cliff Mills, Captain John Sheehan, John Easton (in truck), Edwin Bacon, Harold Townes, Eli Boyden, Albert Forsyth, and Charles Locke. The town's first motorized firetruck was purchased in 1917.

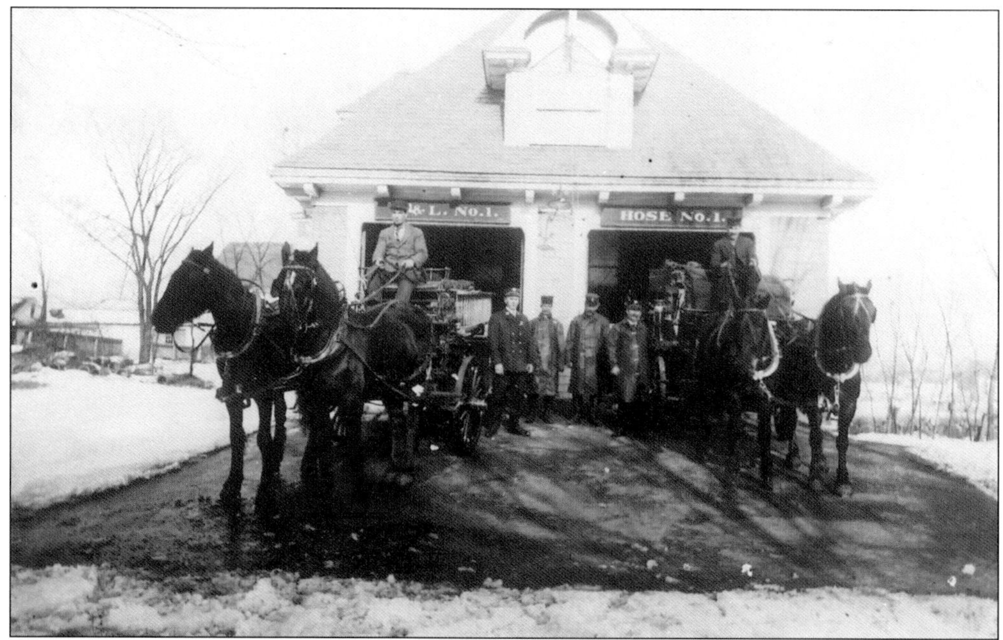

Horse-drawn fire wagons stand ready for action in 1910 outside the Central Fire Station on Stone Street. Rather than raze the station, when it was no longer needed, it was moved down Stone Street to become the Knights of Columbus Hall.

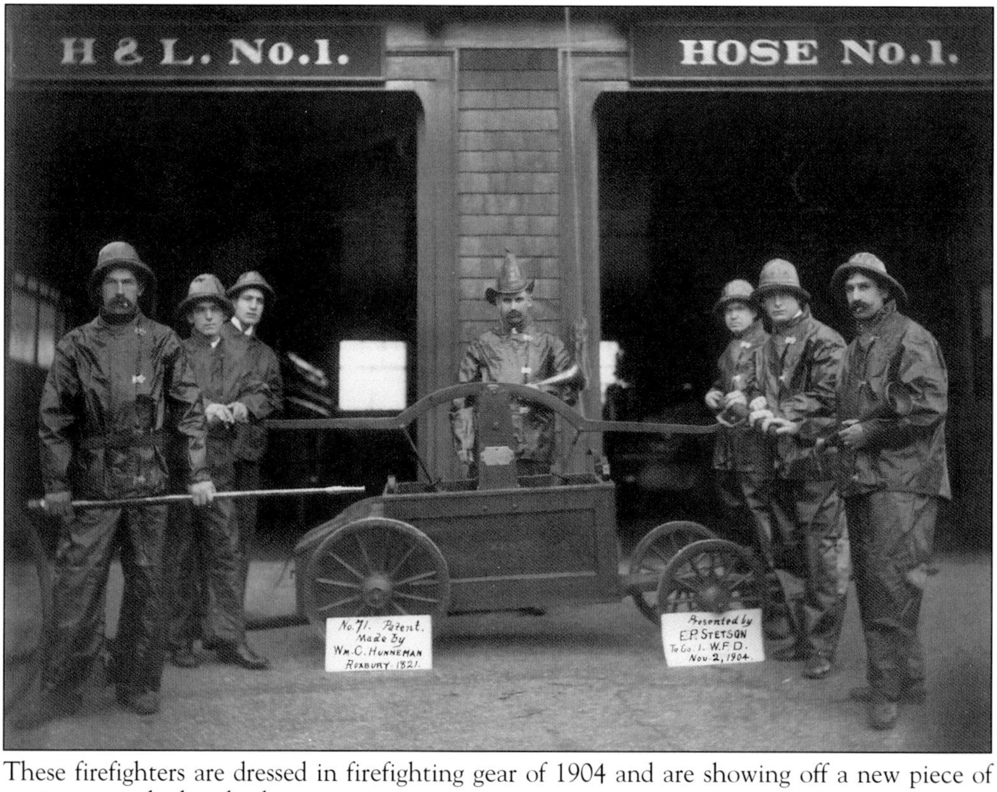

These firefighters are dressed in firefighting gear of 1904 and are showing off a new piece of equipment—the hand-tub pump.

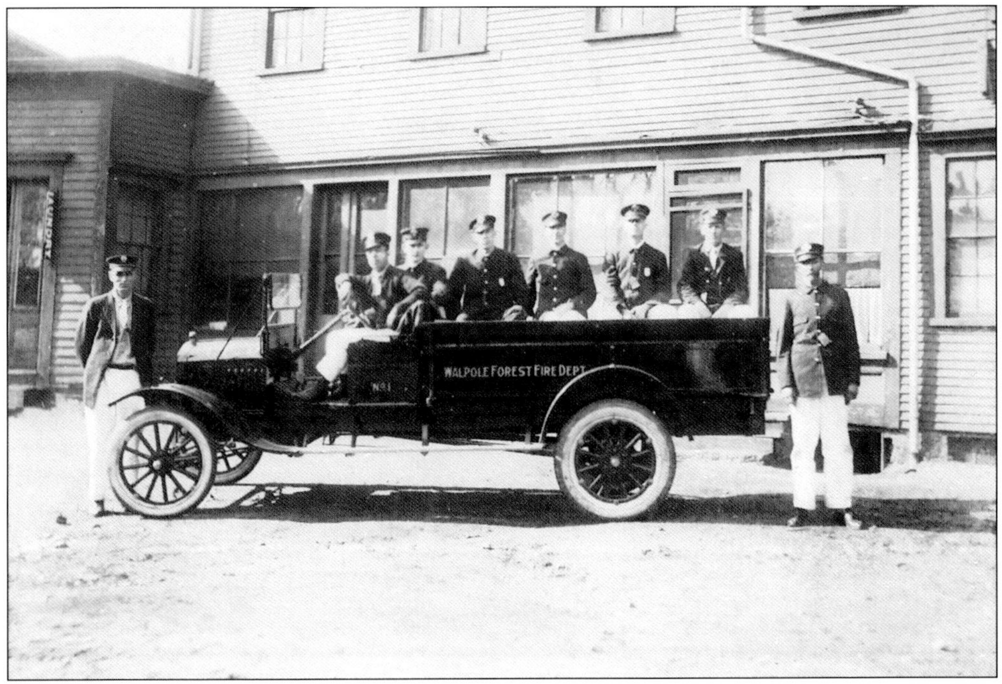

Pictured is not the forest fire department, but the muster team. During the 1920s, muster teams would participate in fire competitions with neighboring towns. Pictured in this photograph are, from left to right, Donnell, Albee, Bassey, two unknowns, Gould, unknown, and Ingram.

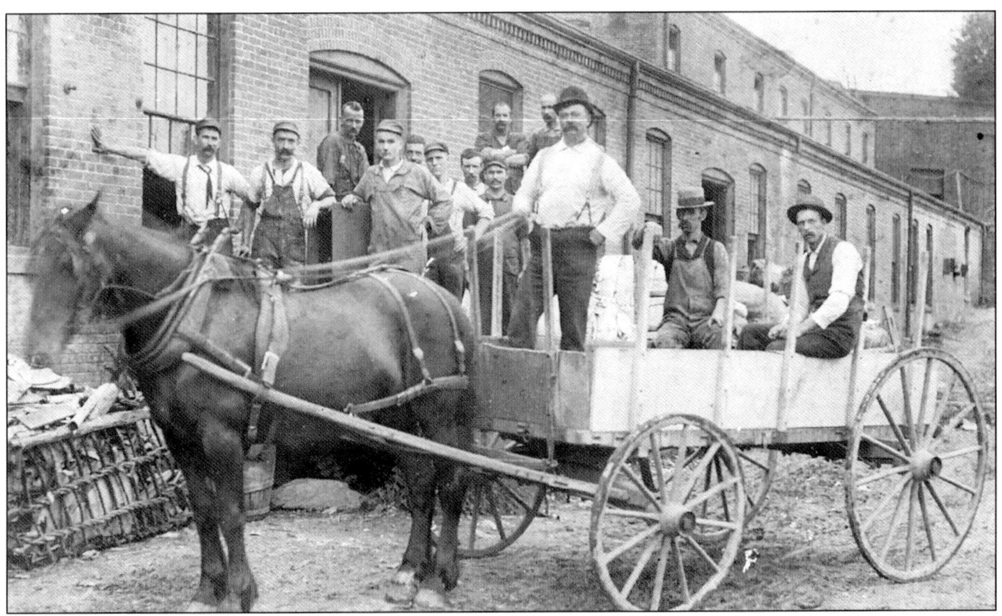

Pictured at the reigns is Bill Crowley with "Kate" outside the original Bird Company office in 1908. A take-charge type of man, Bill was one of three constables who worked with Police Chief Reardon in 1909.

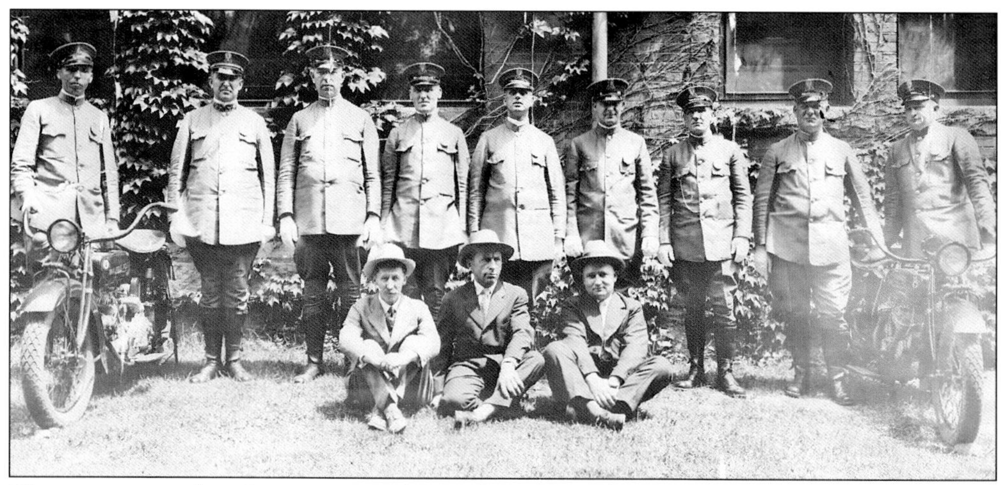

The nine-man police department and the selectmen gathered for a picture in 1927. Walpole was one of the first towns to purchase motorcycles for police use. The selectmen (seated) are, from left to right, Henry Caldwell, John Bock, and Arthur Maguire. The police are, from left to right, Timothy Cullinane, Chief Levi Thompson, Patrick Egan, Wallace Duncan, George Gould, Harold Higgins, Steve Conroy, Michael Fitzgibbons, and Daniel Hennessey.

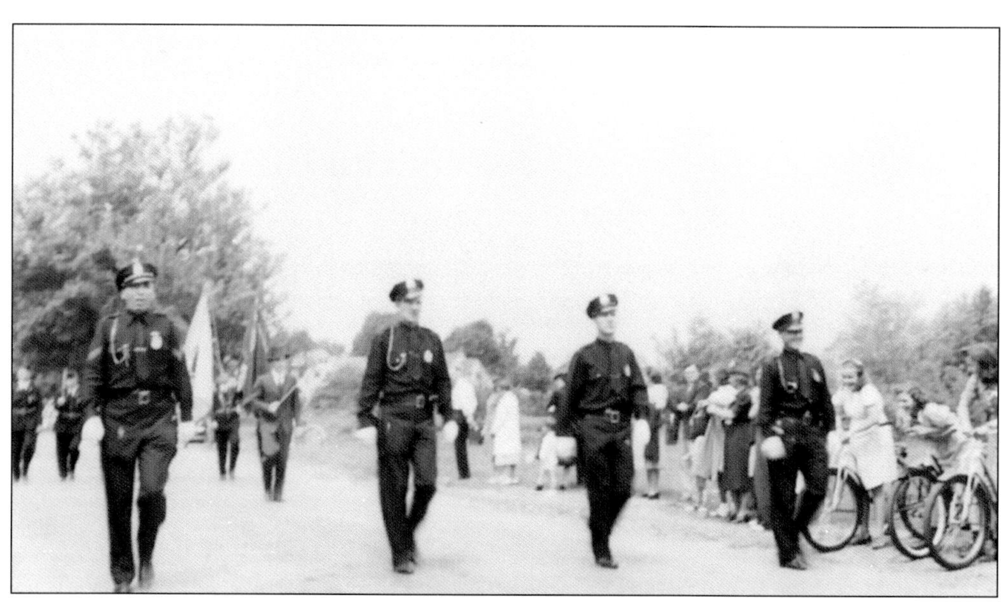

Ten years later, when the police force had grown to 24, Timothy Cullinane was promoted to police chief. Leading the field day parade is Chief Cullinane (far left) with Leo Delaney, John Buckley, and Steve Conroy (from left to right).

Five

Leisure Time

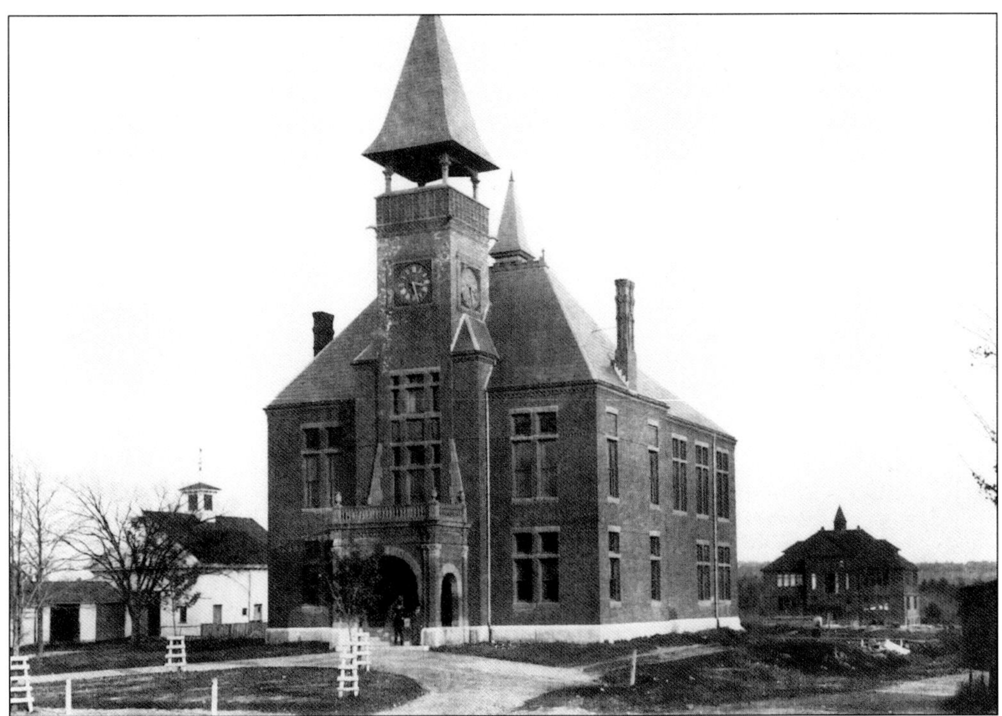

Before Town Hall was built, the meeting place for town affairs was the vestry of the First Unitarian Church. In 1881, Isaac Lewis wrote that the vestry was "ill ventilated, and at a crowded Town Meeting reeked with moisture and foul air, and was avoided in spite of a town meeting cake in the form of long sheets of nutmeg buns." The Town Hall was built for $21,800 and was dedicated on September 25, 1881 (the town's 157th year). At right is the old Stone School, built in 1885. The public library was housed in Town Hall until May 1903. The second-floor hall was rented to the public for meetings and entertainments (it was also the first movie theater in town). In 1883, hall rentals amounted to $254. Later this hall served as a courtroom. Today, the entire building is occupied by the police department.

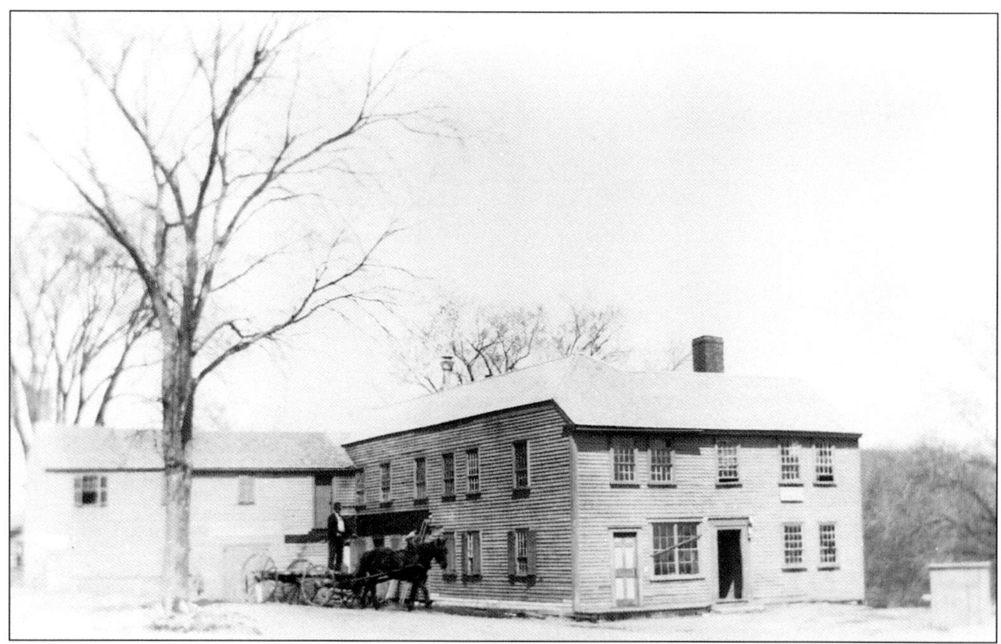

This photo shows the c. 1700 Morse Tavern on Washington Street, East Walpole, as it looked about 1892. Lafayette is said to have stopped here in 1824, and later Julia Ward Howe gave one of her early speeches in the large hall on the second floor. Walpole's first post office was located here in the early 1800s, and it was also here, in 1876, that Mary Bird started a public library. In 1903, the tavern, then owned by the Bird Company, was taken down and the "triangle" building was erected.

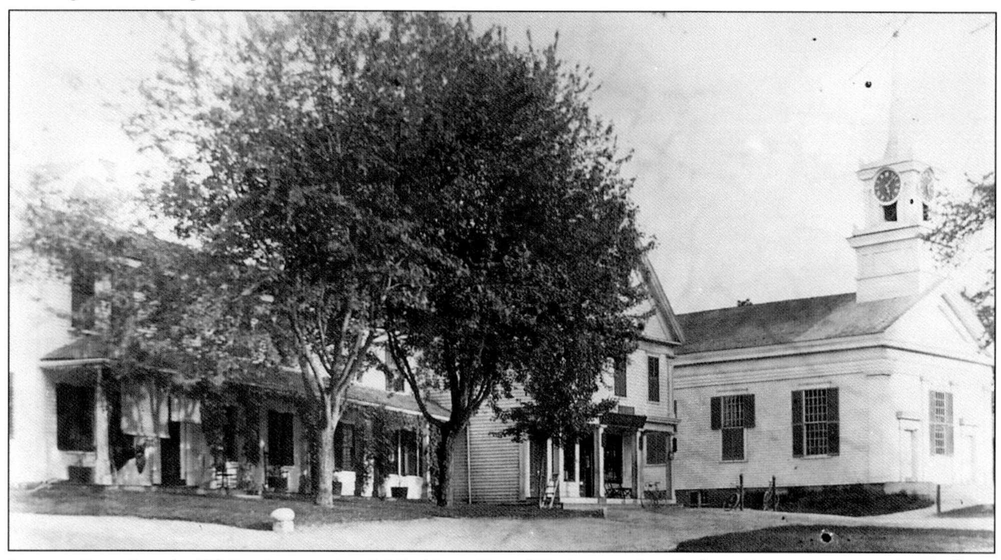

Located in South Walpole on the "Old Post Road," this is the Polley Tavern in 1897. Fuller's Tavern was almost directly across the road. Travelers going to Providence and New York would leave Boston very early in the day and stop for breakfast at Polley's. Those traveling north to Boston would stop at Fuller's for supper. Hamilton's store, located between the tavern and the United Methodist church, housed the South Walpole Post Office for many years. The Polley Tavern was taken down in the early 1960s.

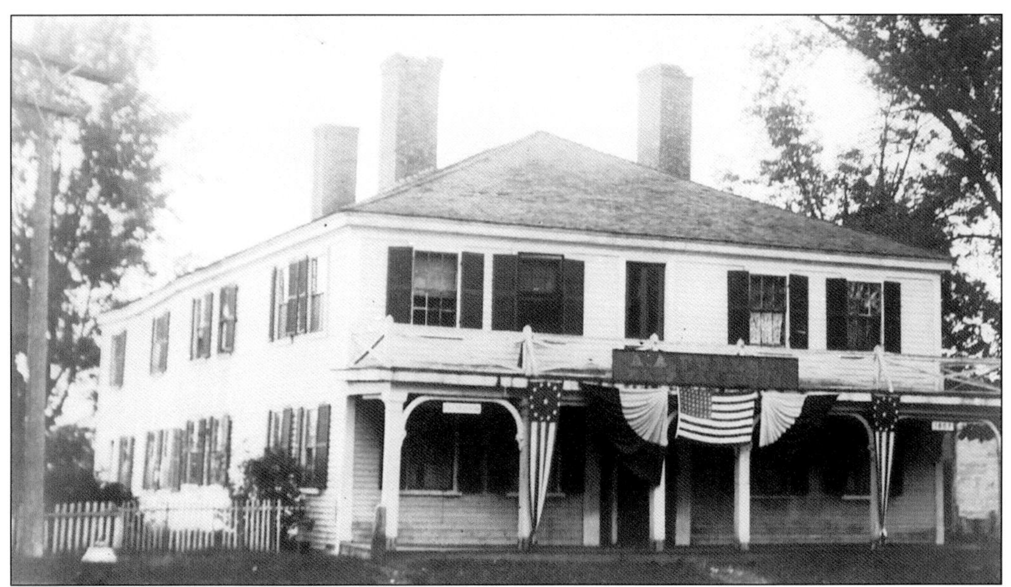

"Fuller's Tavern, the old Half Way House, one of New England's most famous hostelries was built in 1807 on the old Norfolk and Bristol Turnpike to accommodate stage coach travel between Boston and Providence." This quote is taken from an advertisement that appeared in 1927 when the old tavern, purchased and restored by Mrs Philip Allen and Mr. George Plimpton, was reopened. Early records show that Stephen Fuller purchased the Half Way House in 1809. The Fuller family operated the tavern for close to one hundred years. Today the house is a private residence.

FULLER'S 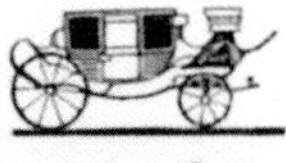 TAVERN

BUILT 1807

SOUTH WALPOLE, MASSACHUSETTS

A QUAINT OLD TAVERN, RECENTLY RENOVATED, IN A QUIET NEW ENGLAND VILLAGE
TWENTY MILES FROM BOSTON

LUNCHEON · AFTERNOON TEA · DINNER

ATTRACTIVE ROOMS FOR OVER-NIGHT GUESTS. OPEN FIRES AND STEAM HEAT.

The restful atmosphere of olden time

BALL ROOM FOR PRIVATE DANCES OR CARD PARTIES

SADDLE HORSES AND STAGE COACH DRIVES

MR. AND MRS. GEORGE E. DAVIS, Managers

TURN FROM BOSTON-PROVIDENCE
STATE ROAD AT WALPOLE

TELEPHONE
WALPOLE 613-W

Fuller's Tavern had all the comforts one could hope for according to this 1927 advertisement. Cozy open fires, steam heat, and afternoon tea were some of the amenities. Although not noted, privileges of the Walpole Golf Club were also extended to the guests.

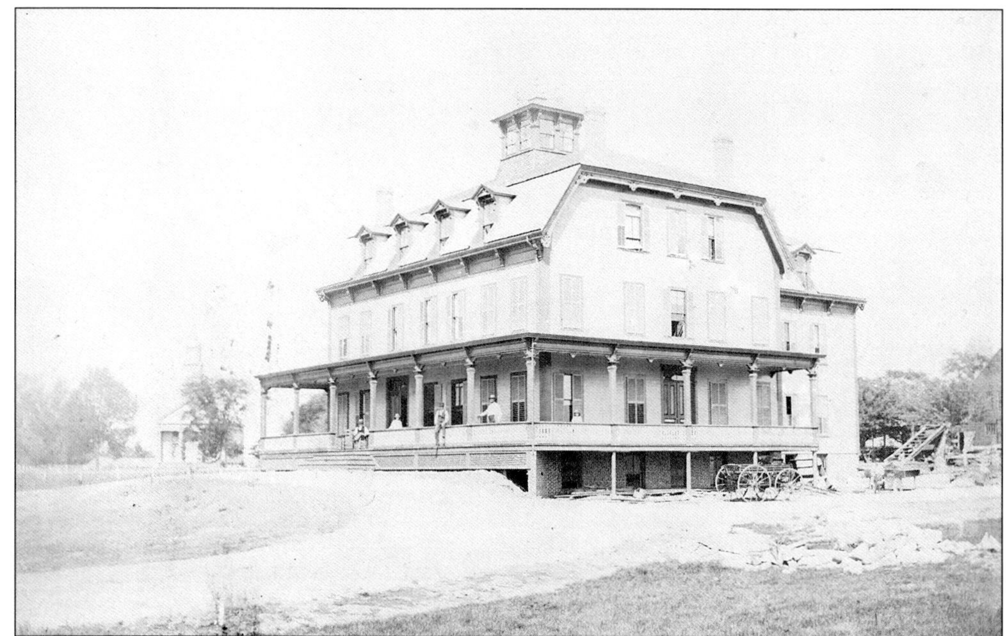

The Walpole Hotel is reputed to have been the first hotel in town, although for many years there had been numerous inns and taverns. Built in the early 1870s on Main Street (facing what is now Pete's Dream), the hotel could accommodate 50 guests. It was taken down in 1893 after being damaged by fire. The First Parish Church (the United Church today) is visible in the background.

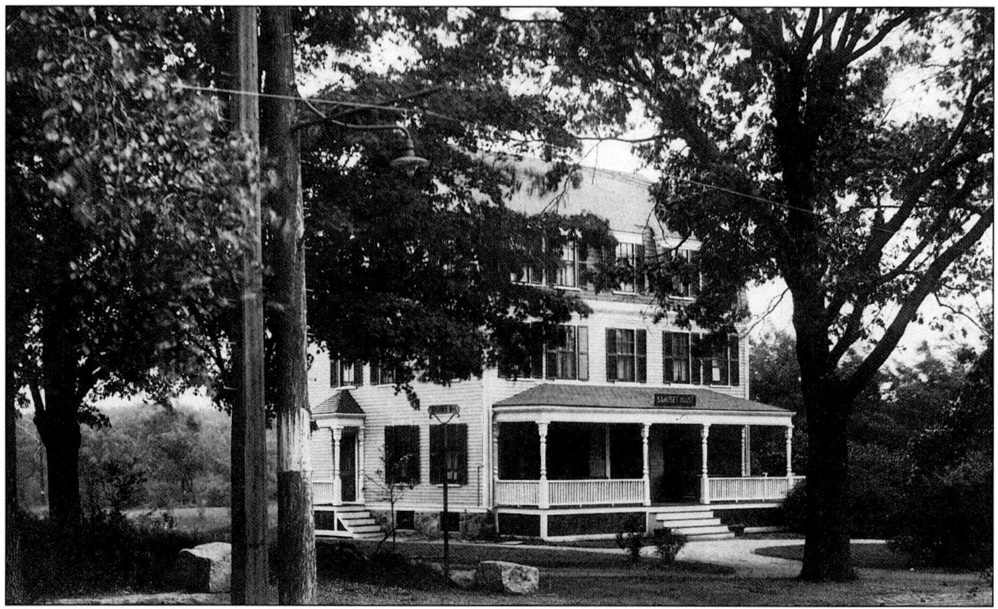

Where there was a mill, taverns and boardinghouses were nearby. In 1914, the Samoset House, located on the corner of Rhoades Avenue and Washington Street, was a gem of its time. A *Walpole Times* advertisement read, "Good Board. Pleasant Rooms. Cyclists accommodated with rest and refreshments. Terms reasonable. John Andrews, Proprietor." The East Walpole Branch Library was located in a corner of the Samoset House basement for a short time.

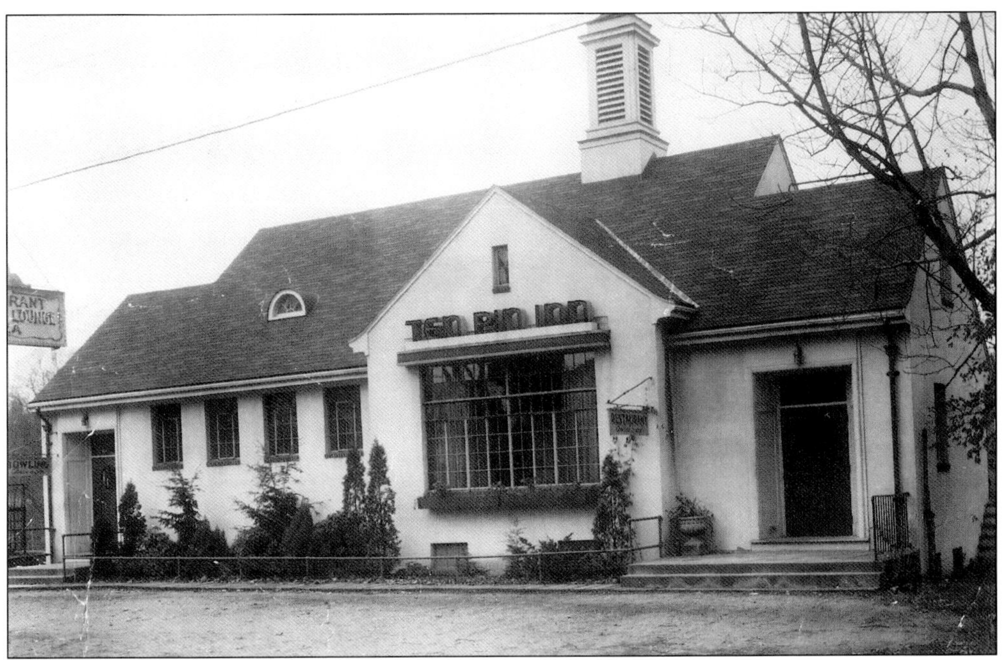

Sam Petracca's Ten Pin Inn on Main Street offered a variety of activities for diners and their families. At the picnic area in back, you could push the kids on swings or take a boat ride. Inside, ten bowling alleys were located on the lower level. Today the swings and boats are gone and the restaurant is now Pete's Dream.

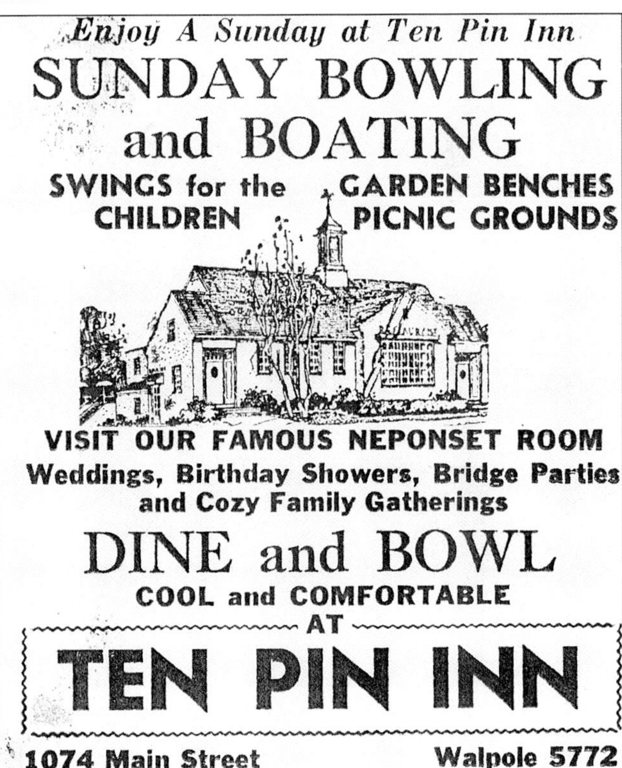

This advertisement for the Ten Pin Inn appeared in 1941 in the *Walpole Times*.

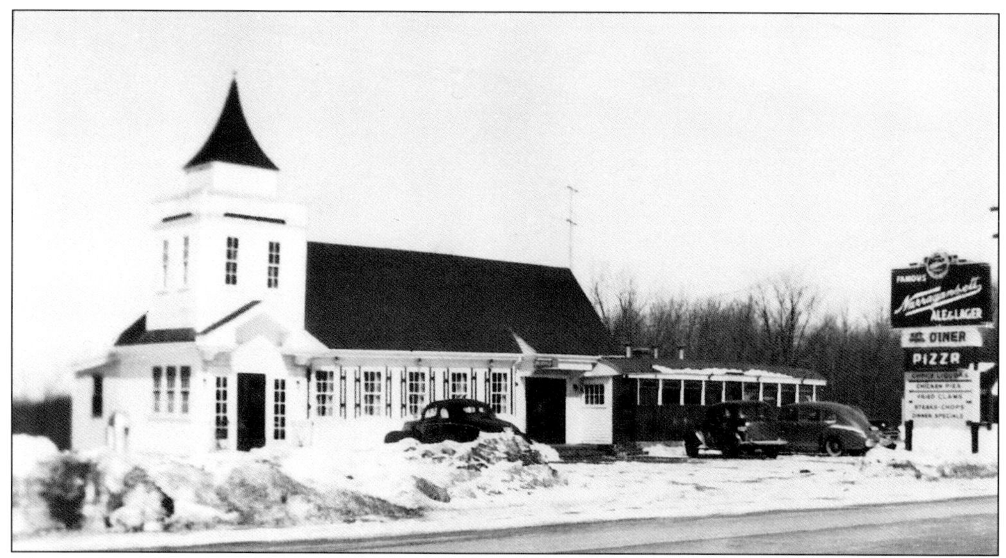

The Red Wing Diner, on Route 1 at the Walpole-Foxborough line, opened in 1932. In this 1952 photograph, the dining car, manufactured by the Worcester Lunch Car Company, can be seen at right. Later renovations removed the steeple-like tower and enclosed the dining car, making it visible only on the inside. The Campanario family has owned and operated the Red Wing for almost 50 years.

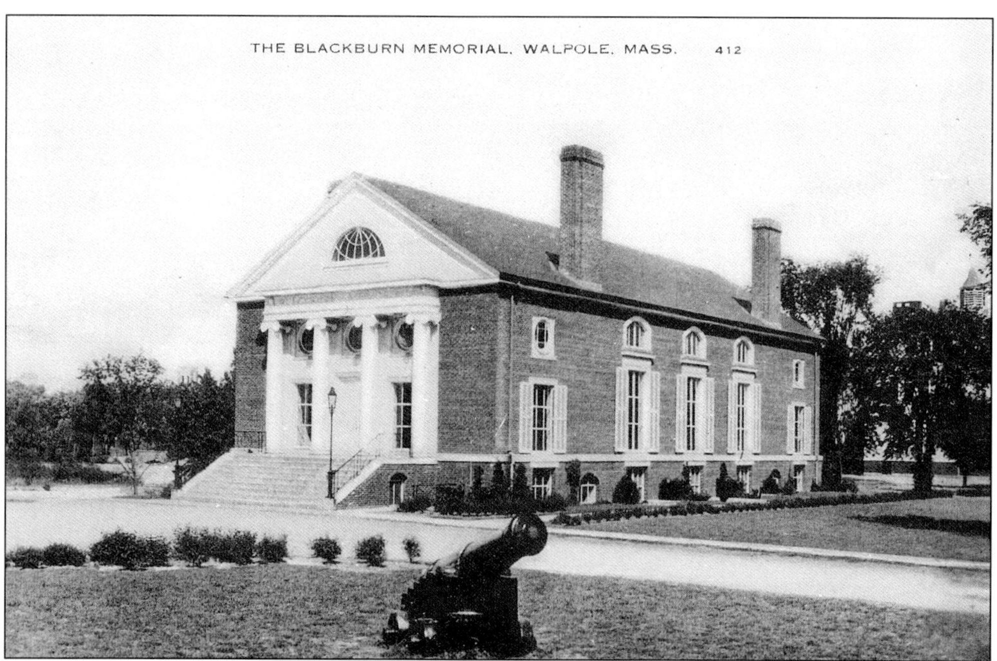

Blackburn Memorial Hall was built in 1932, funded by the generous gift of $50,000 from Harriet Blackburn Nevins. It was named in memory of her parents. The F. J. Tetrault Company was responsible for the construction of this building and the Odd Fellows building.

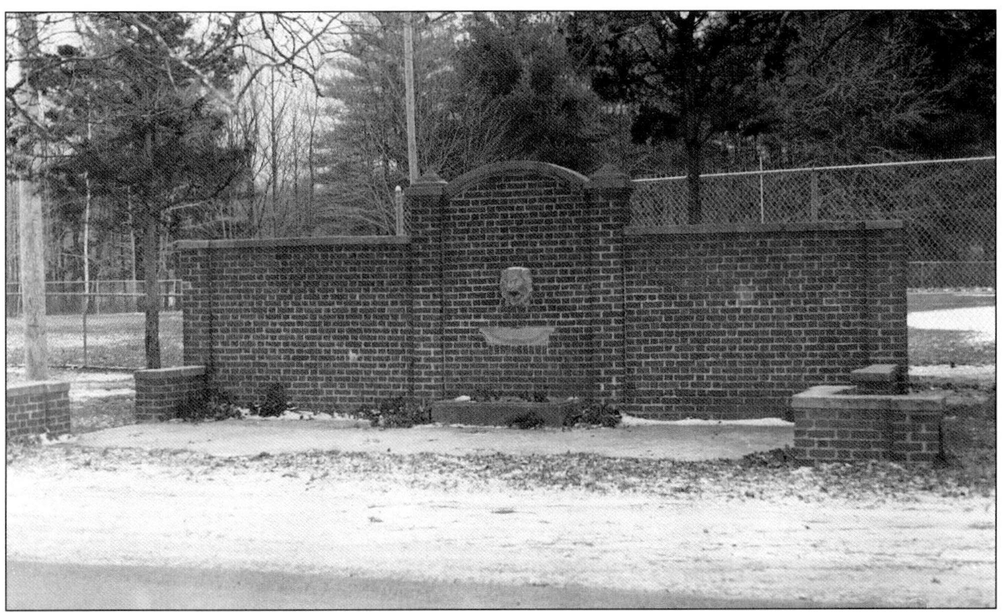

Mrs. Nevins also gifted an additional $2,500 for a water fountain. Designated for "dogs and horses," it stands on School Street adjacent to the Memorial Pool entrance.

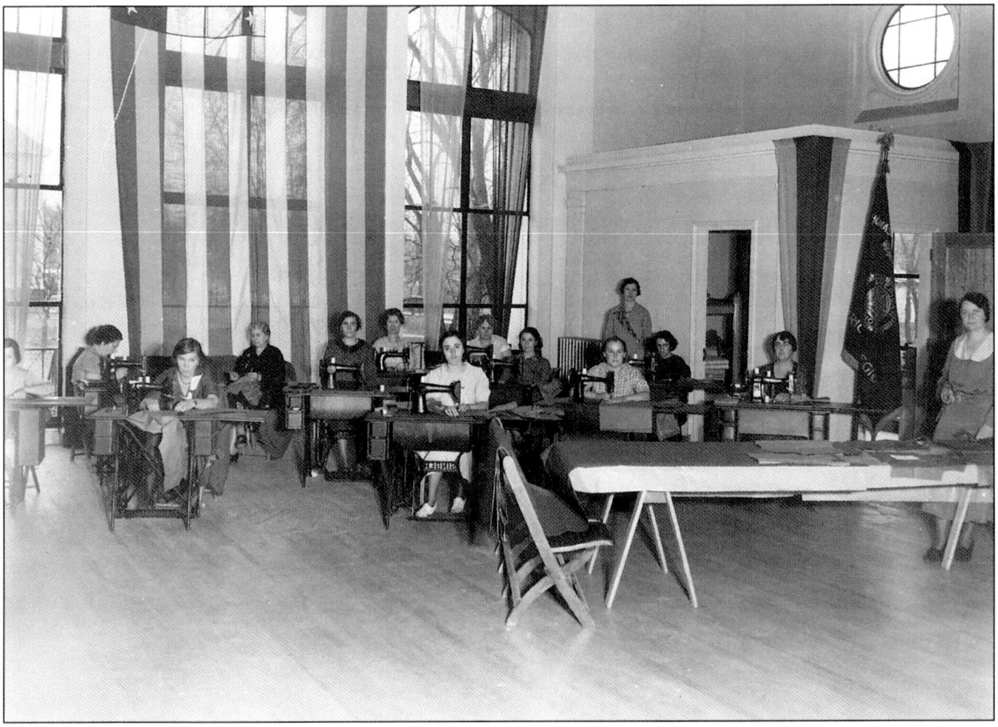

Walpole's largest function hall, Blackburn Memorial, has served as a social center for many of the town's organizations and social clubs. In 1934, these ladies were photographed sewing cloths for an unidentified community project.

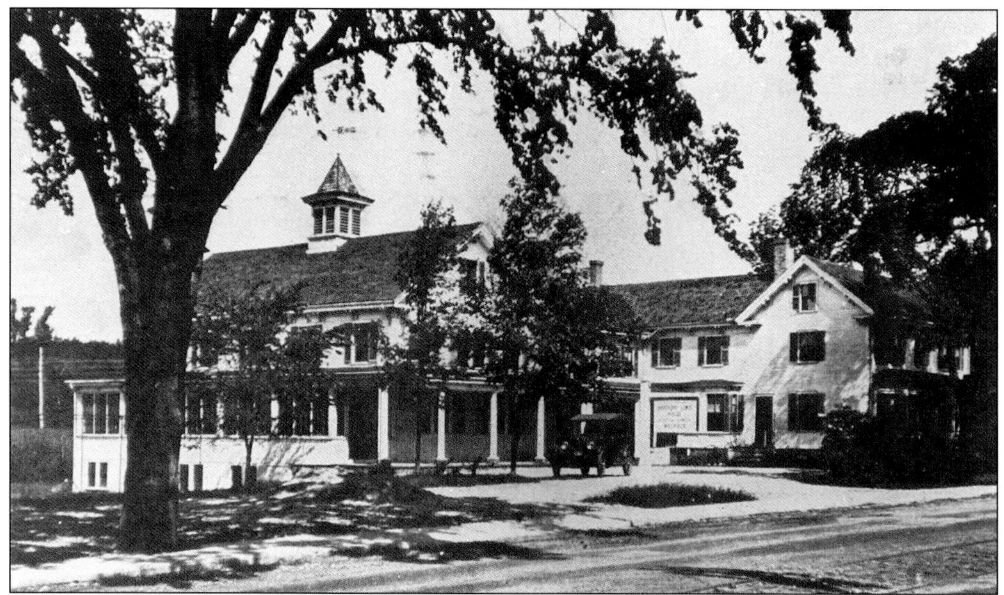

Another popular social center was the Bradford Lewis Community House, originally the home of the Bradford Lewis family. A 1918 World War I Victory Celebration Bonfire destroyed the barn. The structure was rebuilt not as a barn, but as a function hall. The Lewis property had large gardens and walkways to complement the new facility. Many wedding receptions were held here, and the United Church used this hall as its social center.

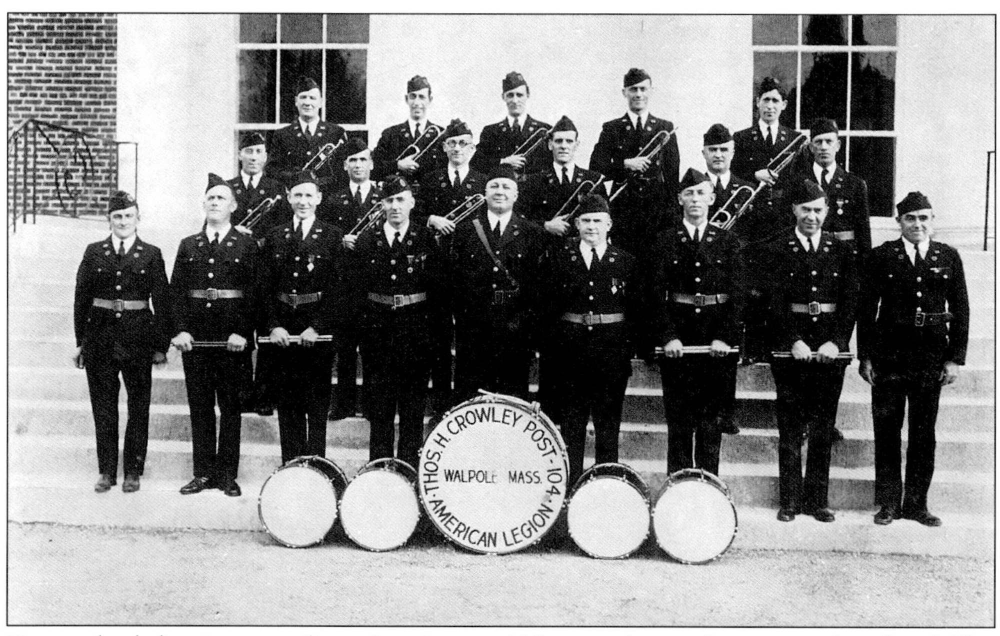

No parade, dedication, or military function would be complete without a marching band. The Thomas H. Crowley American Legion Post 104 band performed for the dedication of Blackburn Memorial Hall in 1932.

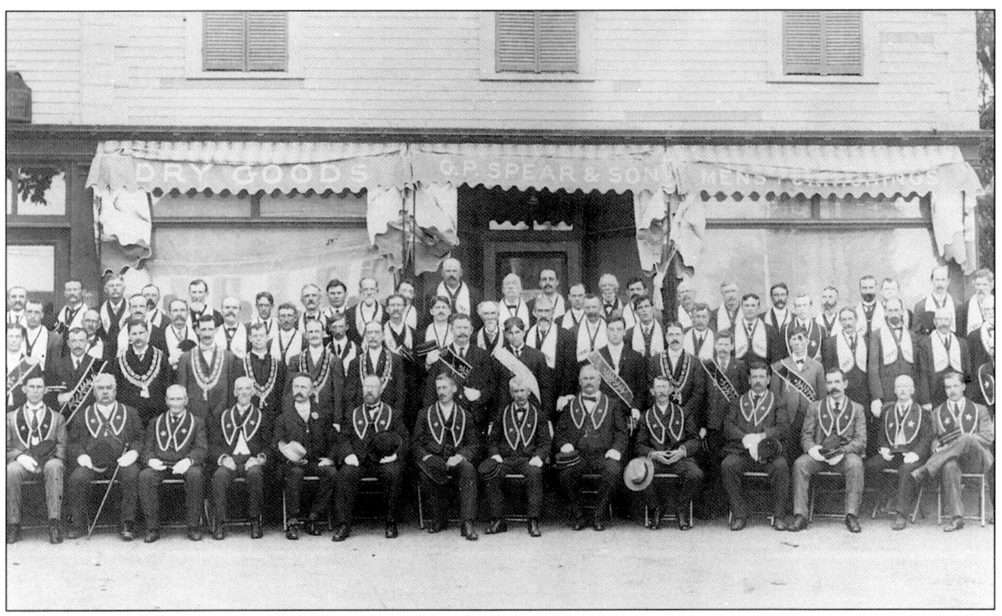

The Independent Order of Odd Fellows was founded in 1881, an organization known for its charitable work on community projects. Members assembled for this picture at the installation of a "Noble Grand" (the center man in the light sash) in 1905. A fire destroyed most records of that time, leaving names and events unrecorded.

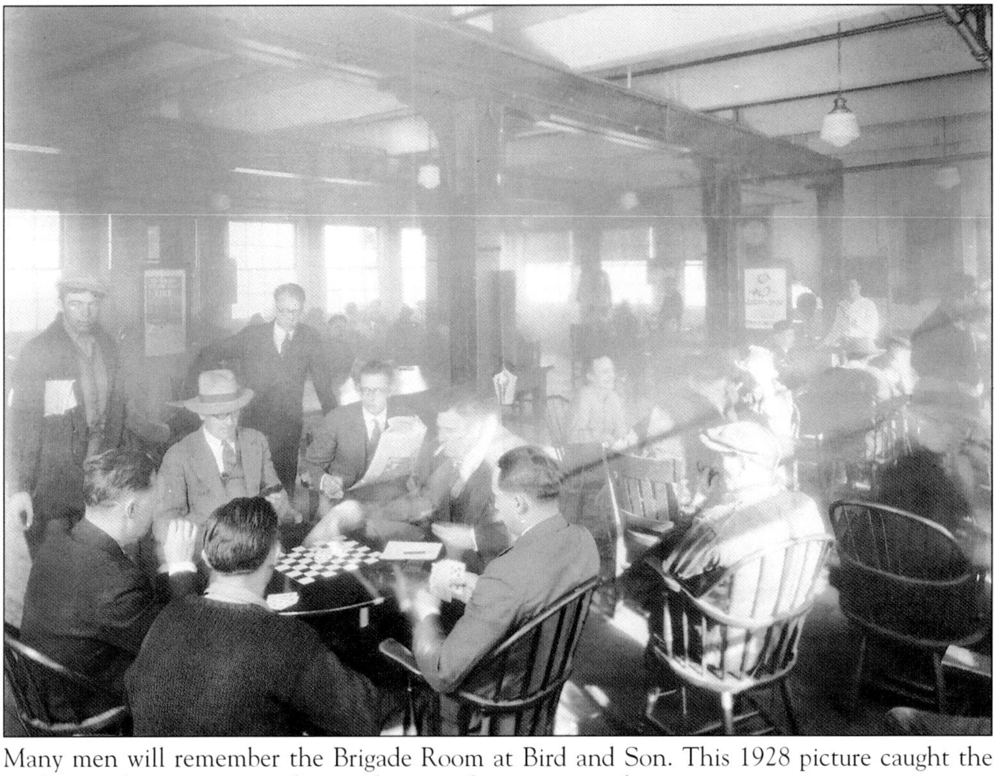

Many men will remember the Brigade Room at Bird and Son. This 1928 picture caught the workers and managers mingling at their usual noontime gathering.

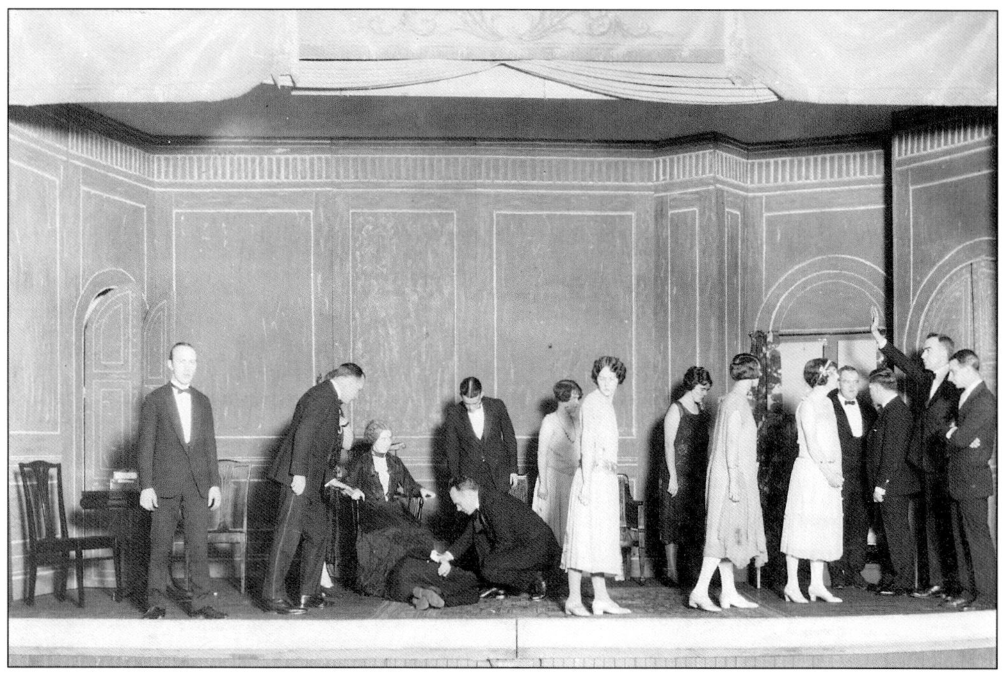

One of Walpole's many social clubs is the Footlighters theater group. In the early years, the second floor of "old" Town Hall was a courtroom by day; by night, it was a theater for performances by this aspiring theater group. This 1925 production is the *Thirteenth Chair*.

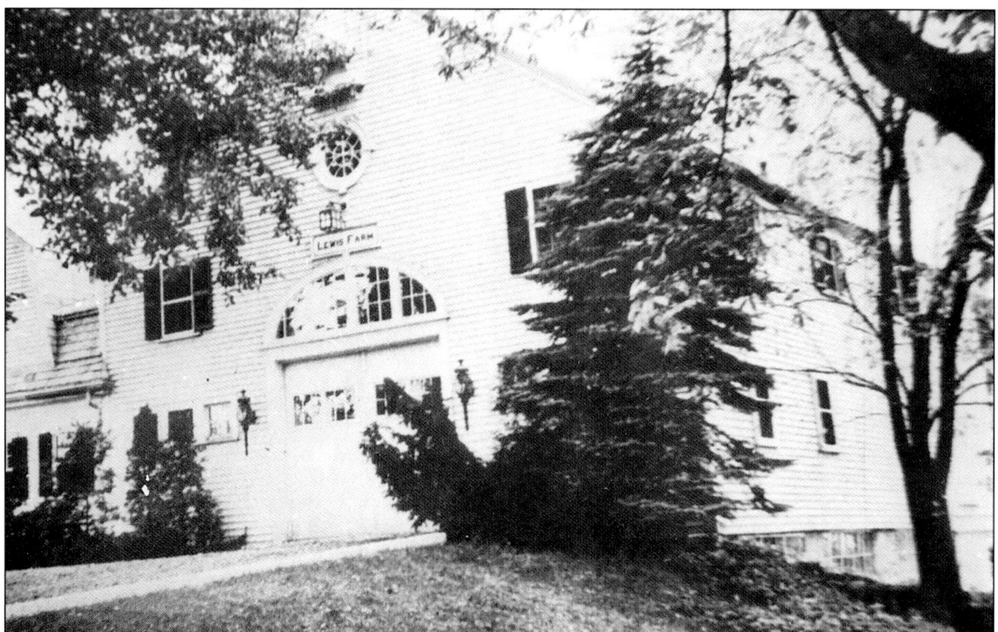

The remodeling of Town Hall's second-floor courtroom into offices brought the curtain down on theater productions, so the thespians took the show on the road. They traveled from one stage to another around town until 1939, when the barn at Lewis Farm began being used as a playhouse. In 1955, in an agreement with Charles Bird, a garage on Scout Road was converted into a theater, providing a permanent home for the Footlighters.

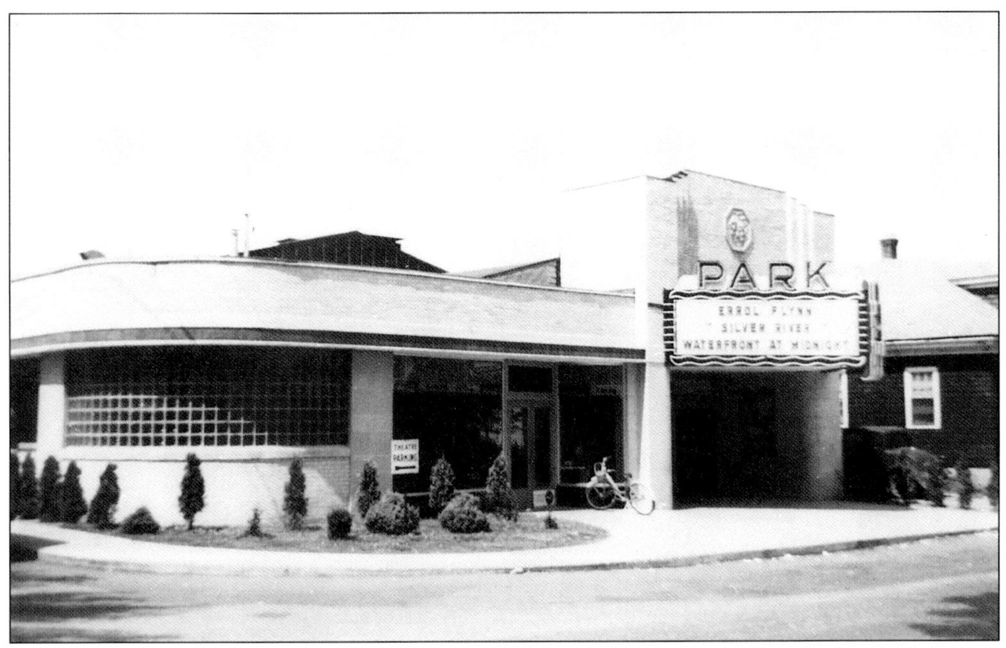

It was a short walk across Bird Park from the Footlighters Playhouse to the Park Movie Theater. A favorite neighborhood gathering spot was the snack bar pictured to the left in this photograph.

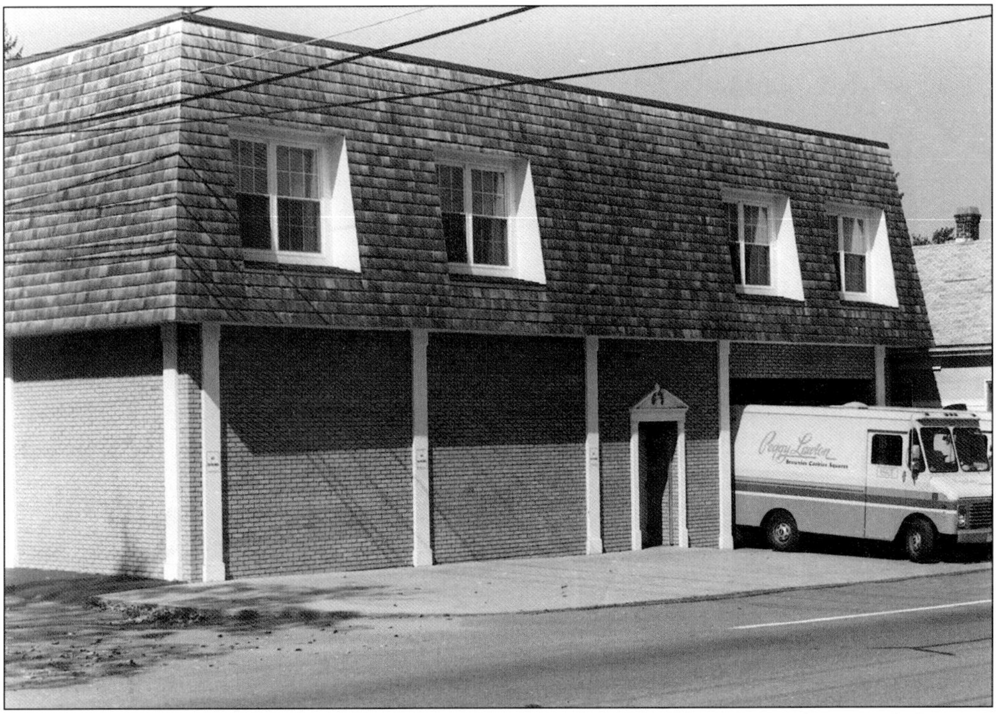

The movie house was eventually sold to the Lawton family and converted into a bakery. It is now the home of the famous Peggy Lawton Chocolate Chip Cookies and Brownies. This photograph was taken in the mid-1960s.

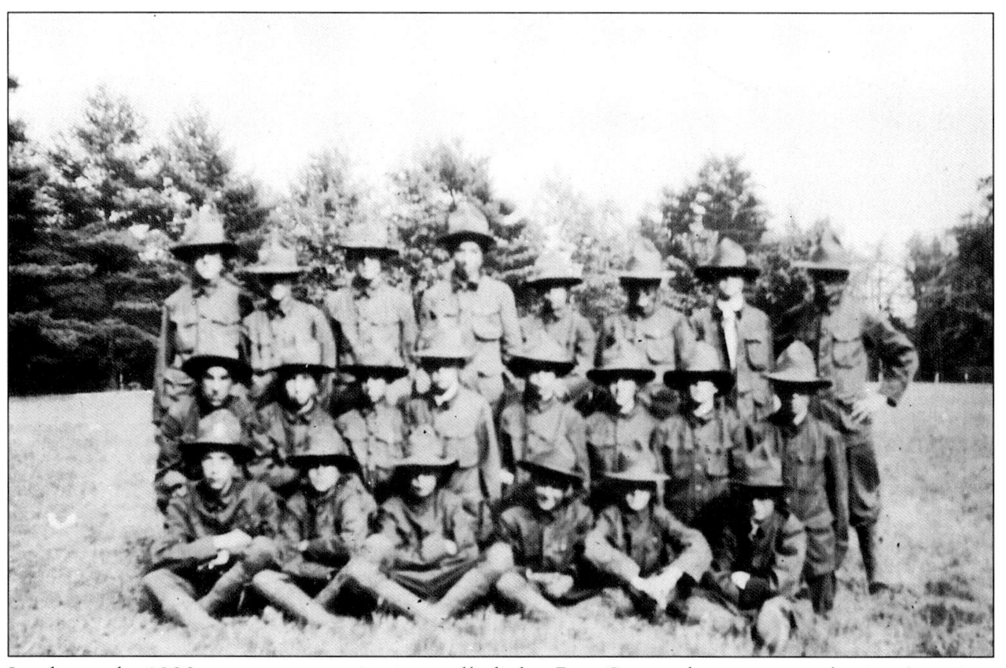

In the early 1900s, a new organization called the Boy Scouts became popular in America. Walpole's original Boy Scout troop is pictured here 1914. Meetings were held on the Bird Mill property.

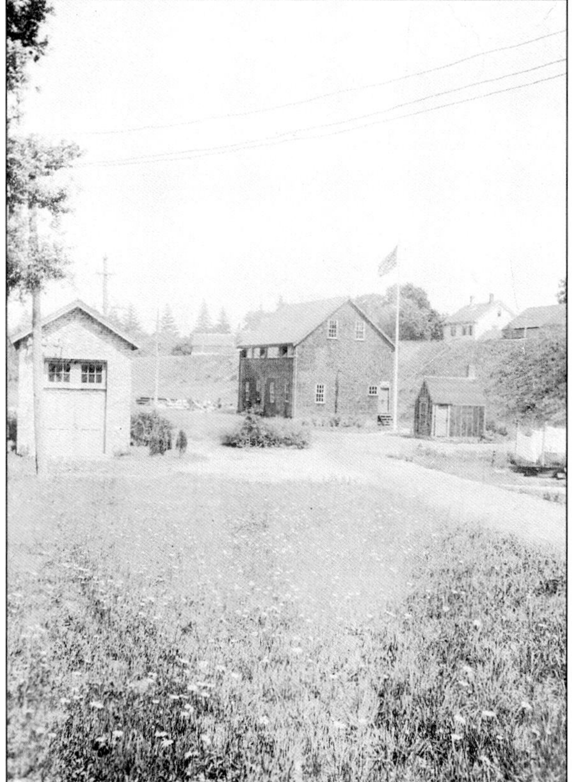

Charles Bird generously donated and furnished the two-story building shown behind the flag pole for Troop #1. The Boy Scout House had a fully equipped gym with a locker room on the top floor. The ground floor housed a library and meeting room. Mr. Bird also provided a building on Scout Lane for the Girl Scouts, which is still in use today.

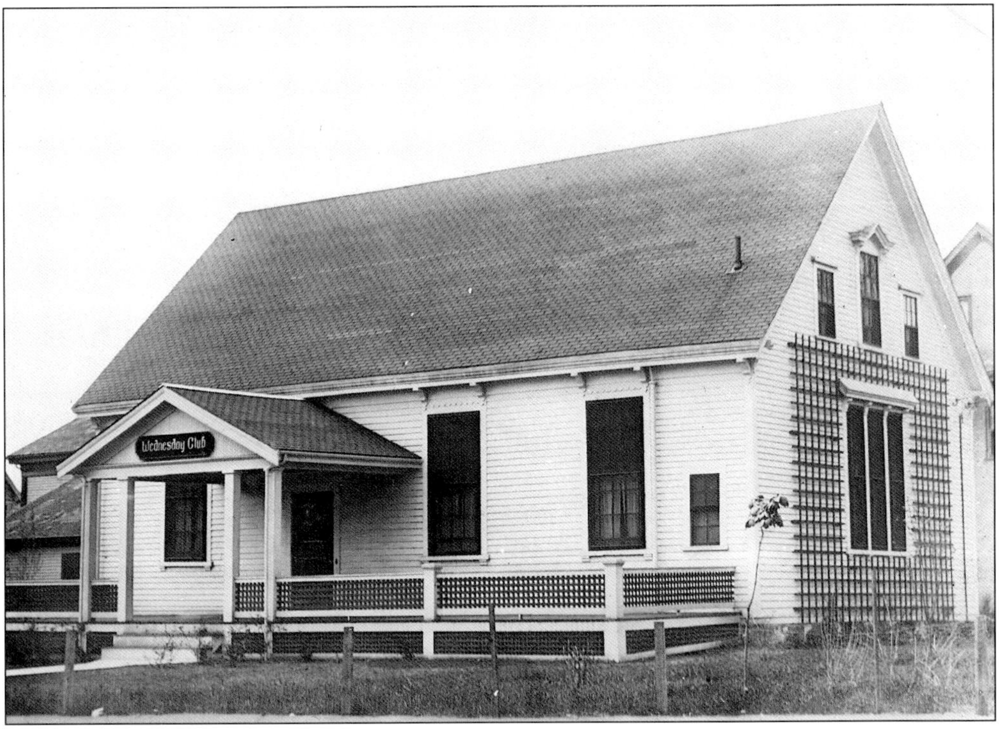

Anna Bird (Mrs. Charles) organized a woman's social awareness group known as the Wednesday Club. Meetings were held at her home, "Endean Farm," until the purchase of the old Union Congregational Church on Walcott Avenue in 1916. Many prominent people were invited to speak at the club meetings. The Wednesday Club was fortunate to have had Helen Keller as a guest.

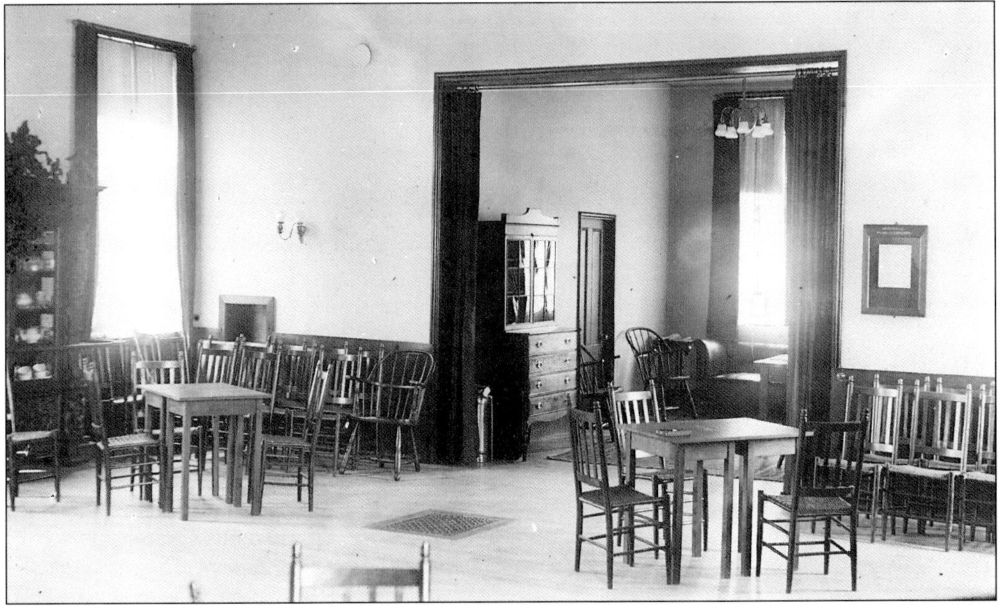

This is the interior of the Wednesday Club meeting room on Walcott Avenue. The building, in later years, became the East Walpole Library.

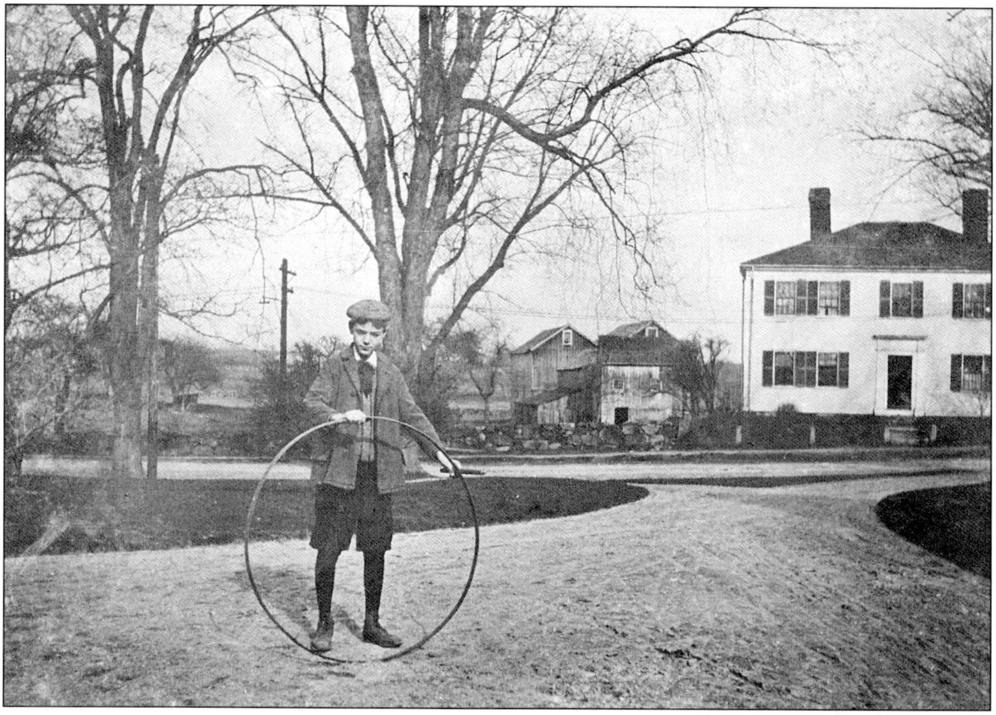

The adults had social groups, committees, and clubs to fill their leisure hours. The children amused themselves in various ways. In 1908, Philip Mann practiced hoop rolling on Willow Street in South Walpole. The Mann family homestead (to the right) is now the home of Captain and Mrs. Roy Belcher.

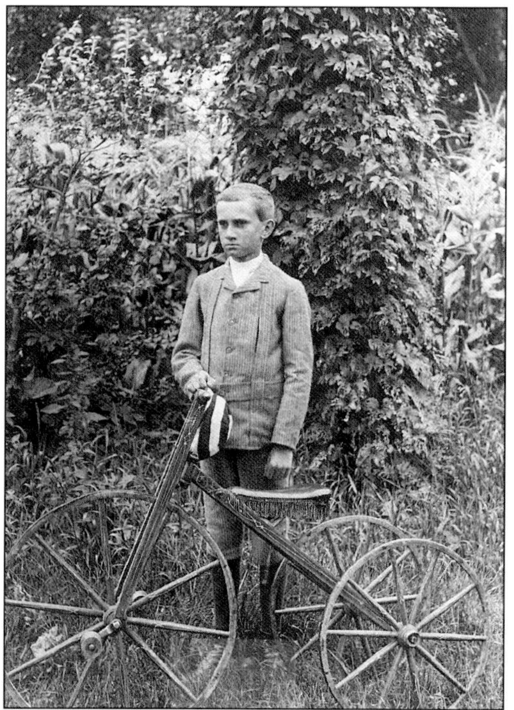

Residents had to think twice before biking on the sidewalks in 1891, as it could be costly. The town meeting voted on September 24, 1891, that "no person shall ride a bicycle upon any sidewalk in the town. The penalty is not less than $5.00 not more than $20.00."

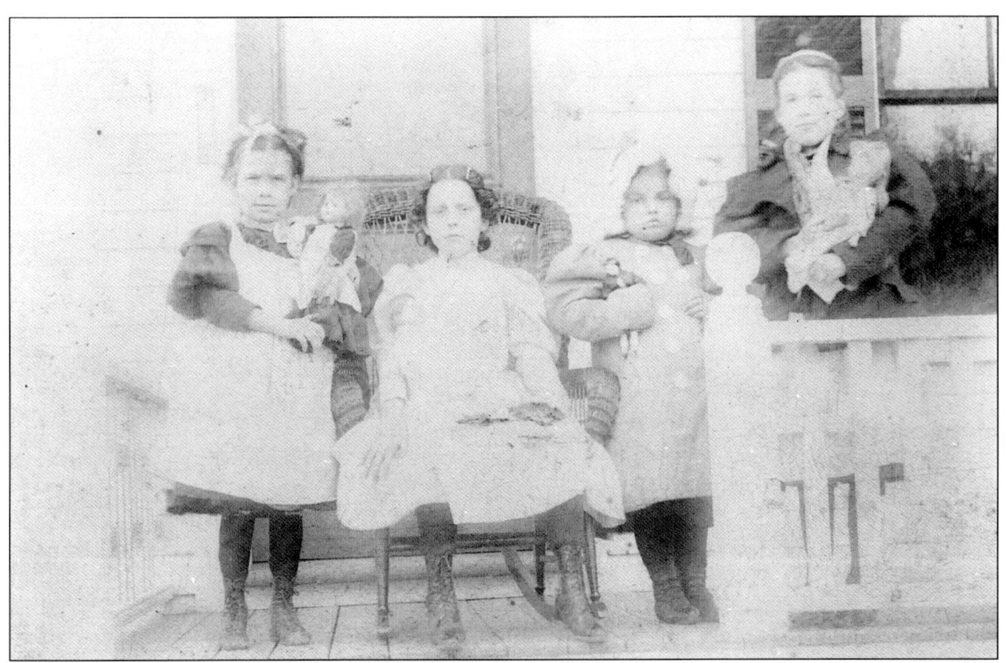

This front porch on Burns Avenue was a favorite place for Catherine Gould, Lila Misuer, Jennie Burns, and Annie Gould (from left to right) to play with their dolls.

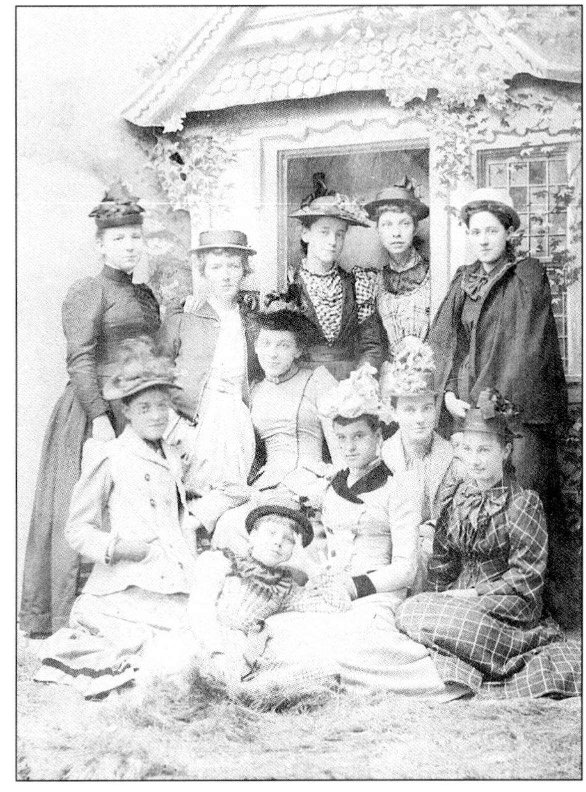

These ladies spent an afternoon posing for a group picture at the E.E. Reed Studio in Franklin. From left to right, they are (front row) Carrie Spear; (middle row) Sarah Moore, Mary Morse, Rebecca Hartshorn, Jessie Willet, and Ida Gardner; (top row) Grace Spear, Rebecca Stetson, Betty Stone, Mirabelle Spear, and Jennie Wetherbee.

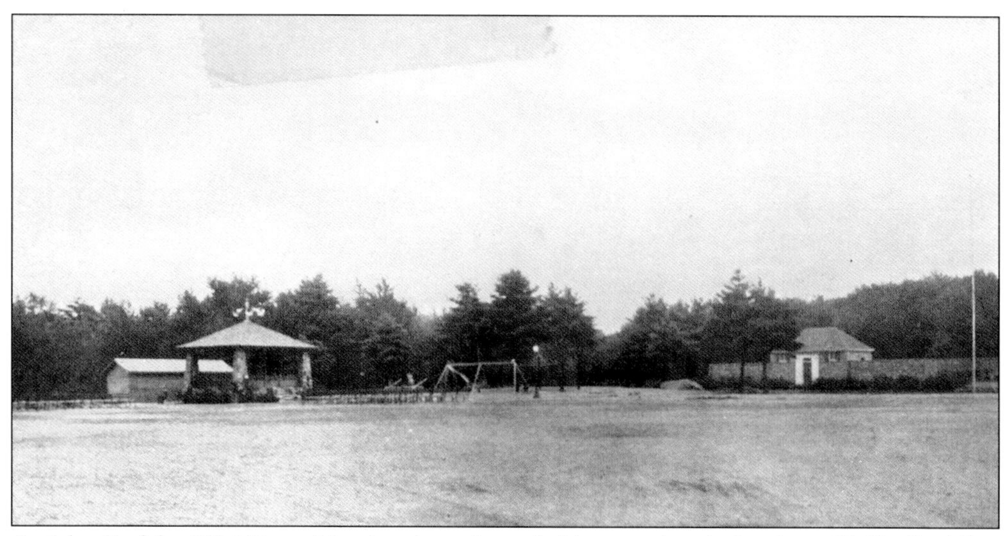

Article #5 of the 1926 Town Meeting Agenda reads,"Accepted with thanks to Phillip R. Allen to build a swimming pool and bath house in Memorial Park." Article #6 reads, "$2,914.95 will be transferred from the surplus War Bonus Fund to build a bandstand in an area of park land." Memorial Park was gradually added to each year following the plan of John Nolen, a landscape architect from Cambridge. This photograph shows the pool and bandstand before the tennis courts and the skating rink were completed.

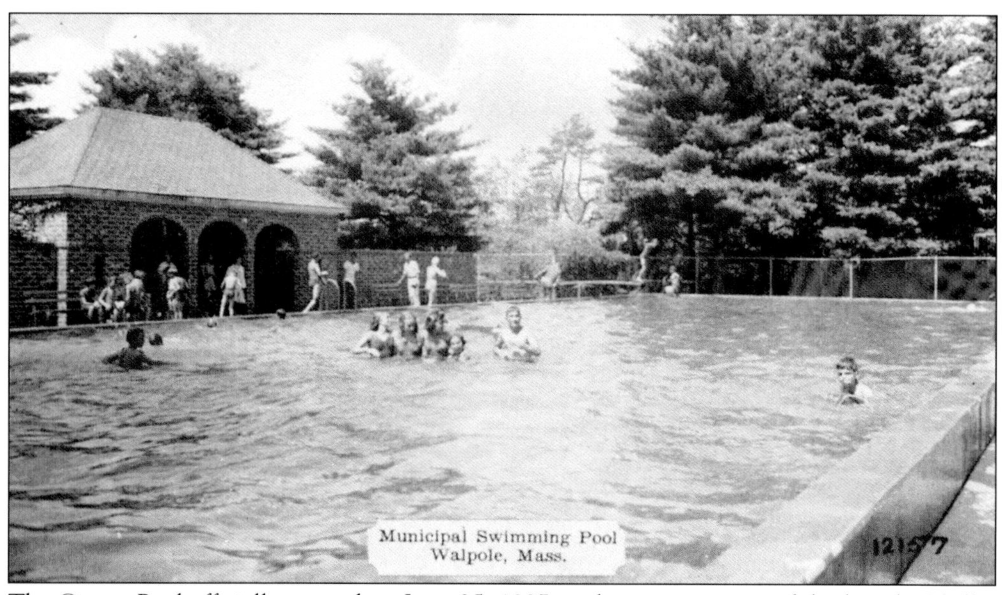

The Center Pool officially opened on June 25, 1927, with a presentation of the keys by Phillip Allen to Selectman Henry Caldwell. The following was recorded in the town report: "1,116 residents registered for use of the pool that first season. The largest number using the pool on one day was 308 people!"

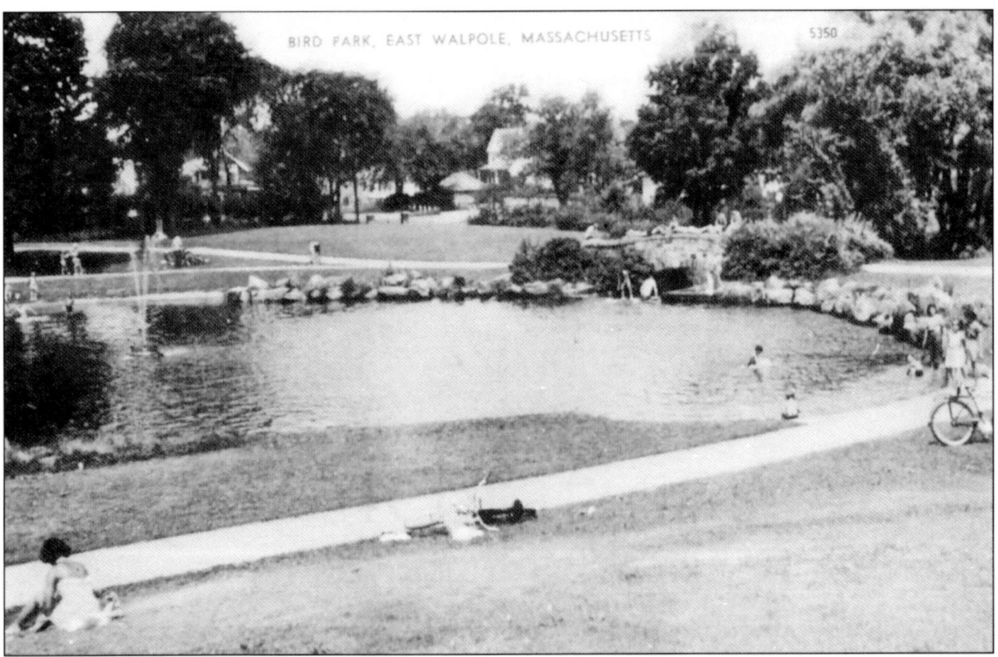

A much different swimming pool was located in the 70-acre Bird Park—not a square cement pool, but a lovely natural-looking pool designed to complement the surrounding area.

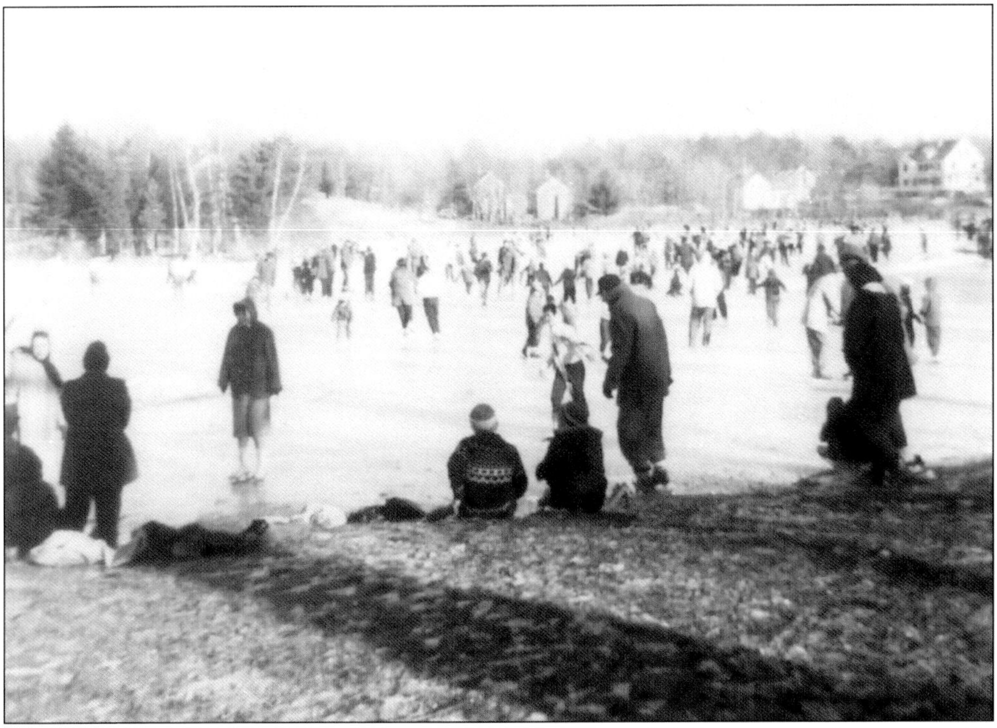

Summer has passed. The cold days of winter provided the needed element to make an enjoyable afternoon of skating on Memorial Pond. Seven acres of meadow land were purchased and dredged to create a new pond for additional recreational use in the Memorial Park area.

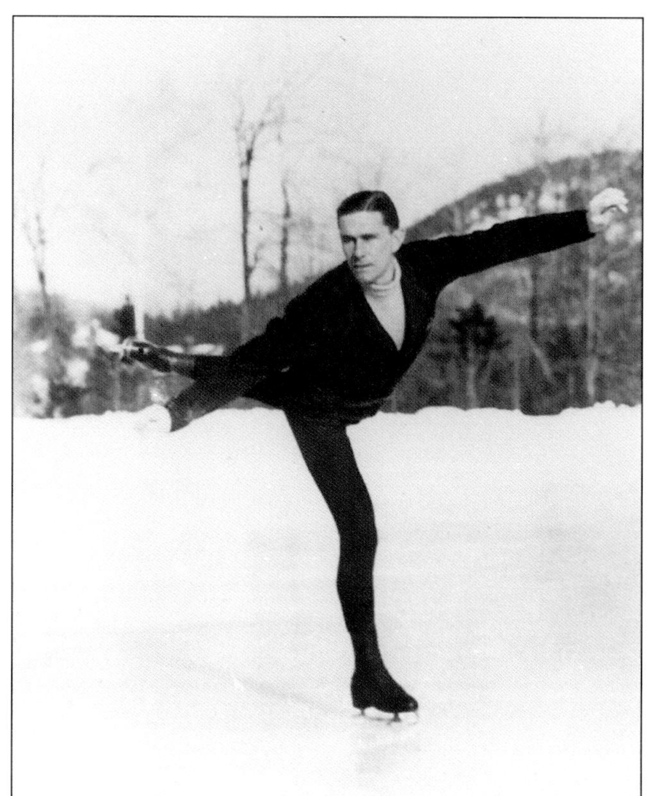

Turner's Pond on Elm Street (Route 27) was the property of Roger Turner and fittingly so. Mr. Turner's career in figure skating began on a local pond. After winning local competitions, he glided along to win the National Men's Figure Skating Championship, a record seven times. His greatest achievement was being a member of the 1928 and 1932 Olympic Figure Skating Teams.

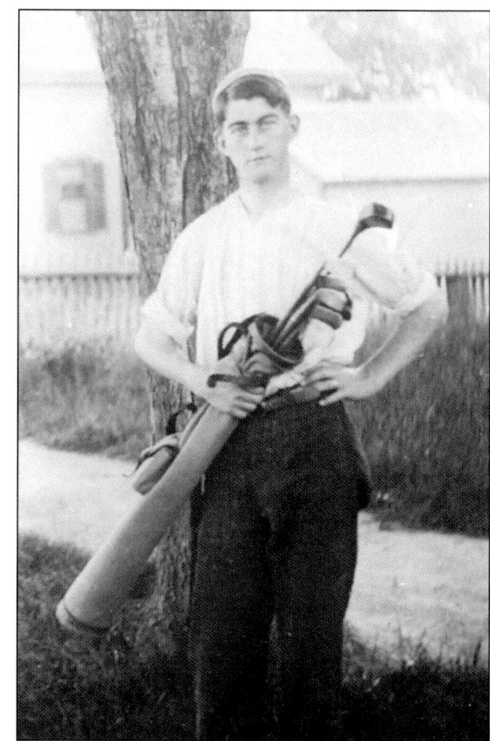

Howard Garby doesn't appear to need a caddy to carry his golf bag in 1906. Walpole's first nine-hole golf course was located adjacent to the Maple Grove Cemetery on Kendall Street.

Six

Celebrations

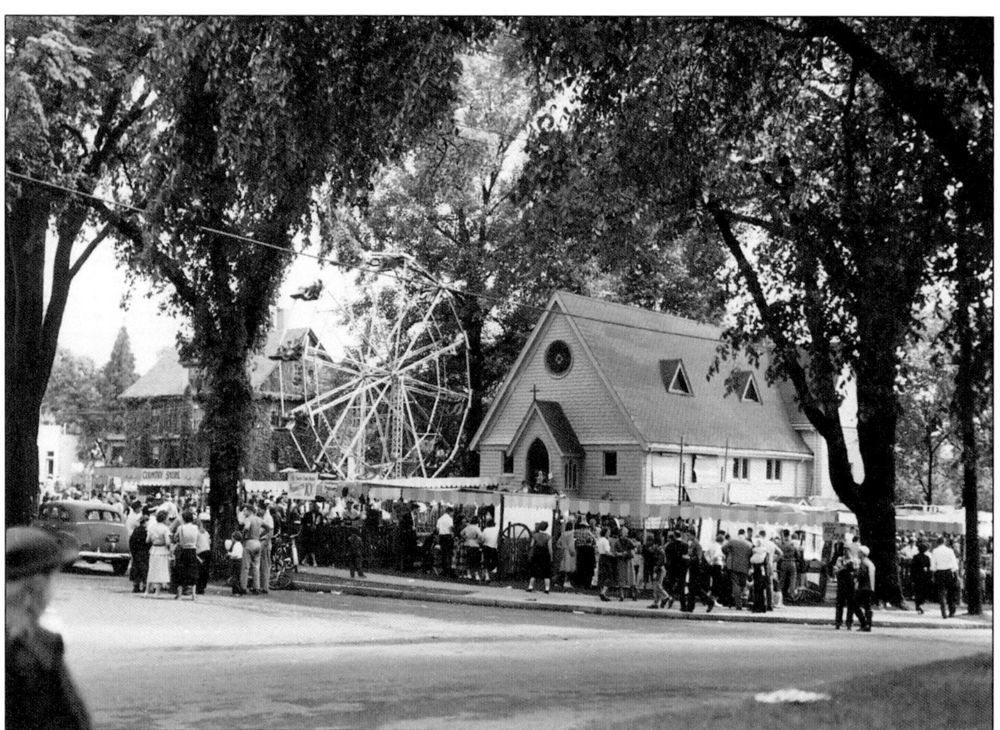

Social life in early New England centered around the church. Since 1949, the Epiphany Church has followed the old tradition on the second Saturday in June with its annual Village Fair. A parade down Main Street starts the festivities. Many remember the doll carriage parade and the live frog-jumping contest. The Ferris wheel went around, the boat ride went up and down the river behind the church, and games of chance were played. By noon, the chickens were roasted and strawberry shortcakes were served. An evening block party capped off a wonderful day at the fair. The house of Dr. Banks at left is the present parish house.

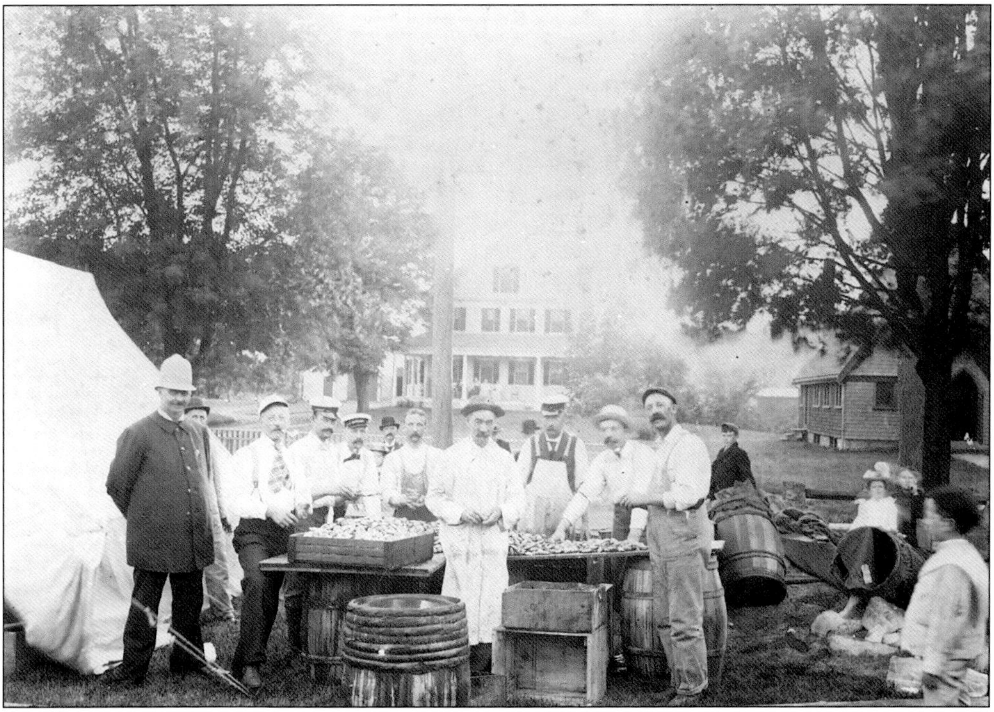

Clams were packed in ice (lower right corner) and hauled to Walpole for a clam bake sponsored by the fire department in 1898. The Epiphany Church is to the right, and Mrs. O'Brien's Boarding House is in the center.

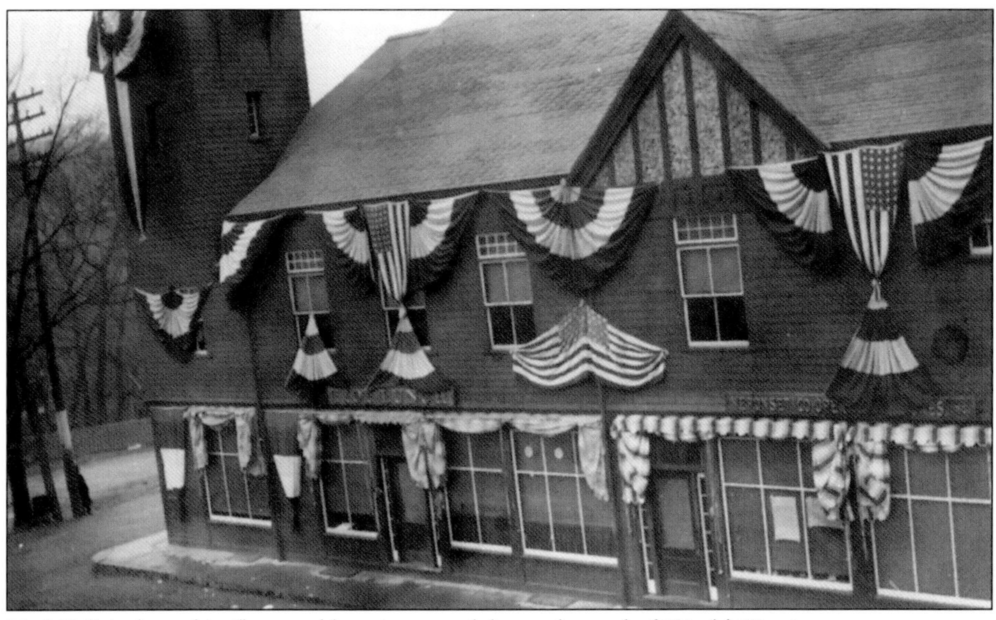

Bird Hall is draped in flags and bunting to celebrate the end of World War I.

Walpole's town forest was dedicated on May 5, 1916. In attendance were Lieutenant Governor Calvin Coolidge (to the left, in the absence of Governor David I. Walsh), George A. Plimpton (center), and Charles S. Bird. Fifty-seven acres bounded by Common, South, and Washington Streets were given to the town by George Plimpton, who had previously donated 30 acres for the building of the Plimpton Elementary School and the high school. Preceded a few weeks earlier by the town forests of Brookline and Fitchburg, Walpole's town forest became the state's third.

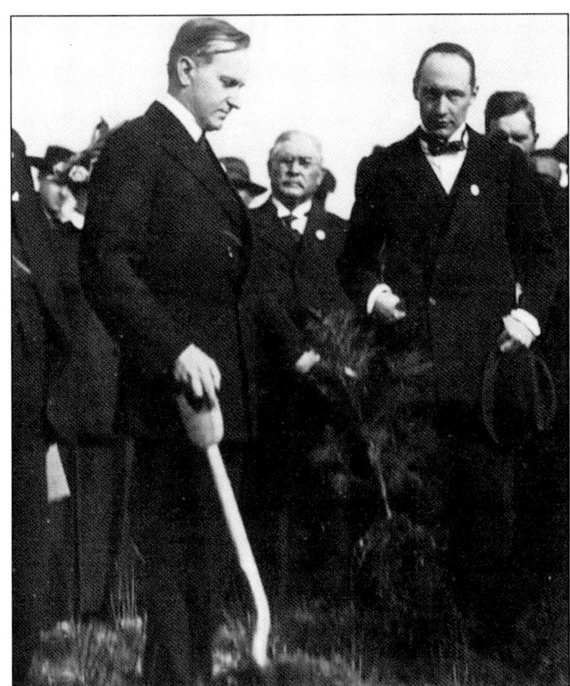

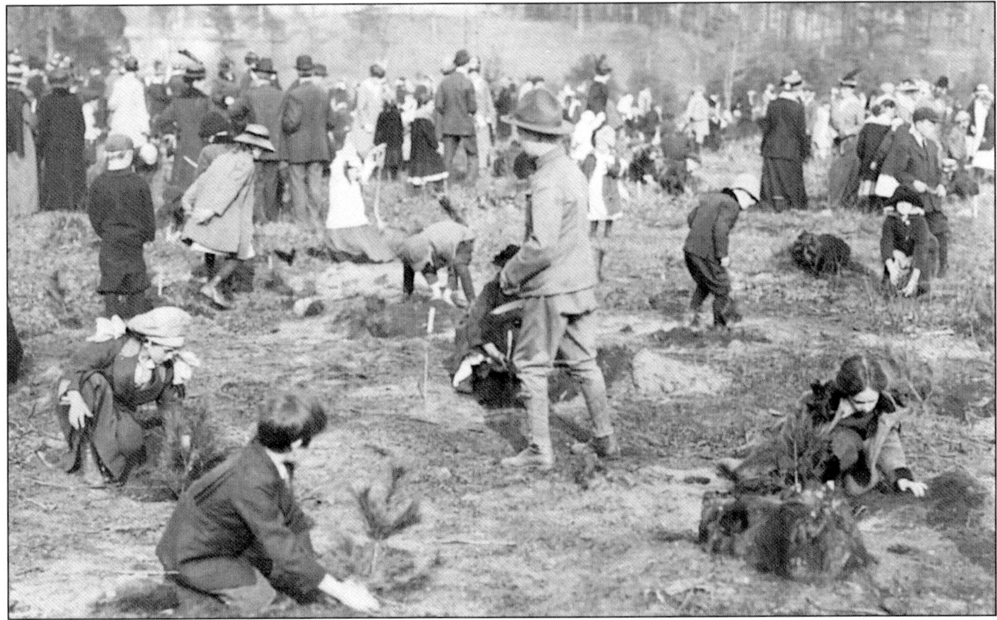

Part of the dedication ceremony was the planting of 1,000 white pine seedlings by 900 schoolchildren. By the end of May, an additional 11,000 white pine, 2,500 red pine, 600 douglas spruce, 115 scotch pine, 113 red spruce, 200 aborvitae, and 30 red cedar had been planted by the park department. A detailed map (on file at the town hall) was created at that time showing the location of each new tree and the identification of each child planter. In 1966, the Town observed the 50th anniversary of the dedication. In attendance were some of the grandchildren of the original young planters, who planted saplings in memory of family members.

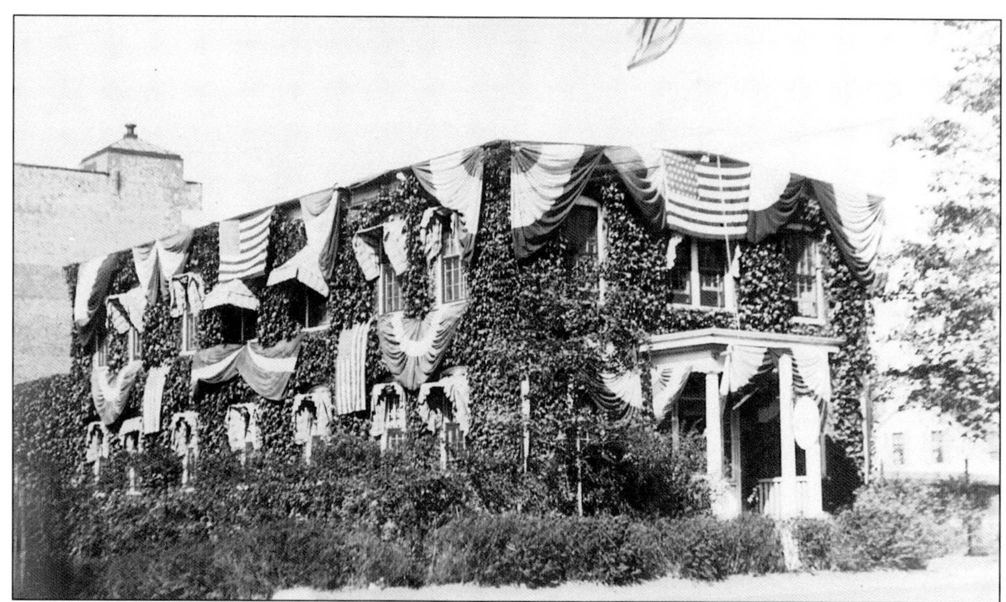

Enthusiasm for the gala celebration of Walpole's 200th birthday spread throughout the town. On West Street, away from the parade route, the blanket of ivy on the Kendall Co. office building is mantled by flags and bunting. The two-day bicentennial celebration included a banquet, parade, speeches, and the unveiling of the Memorial Bridge tablets.

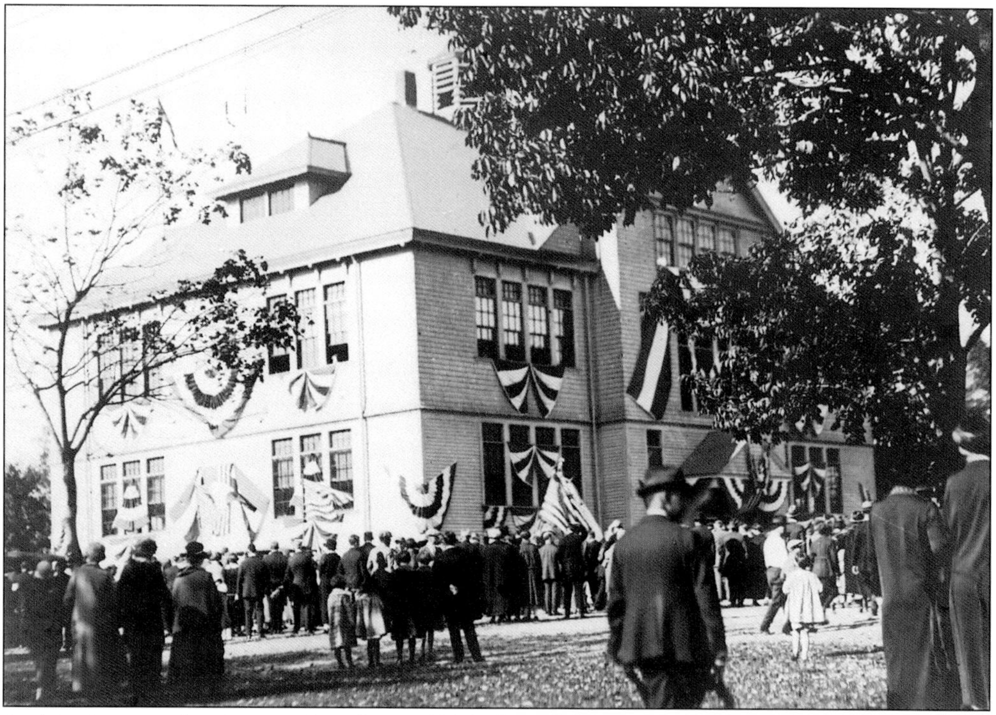

In this photograph, taken on October 4, 1924, the "old" Stone School wears her colors proudly for the celebration. The school grounds served as one of the marshaling areas for the crowd of more than 3,000 celebrants who joined the procession from the dedicatory services at the bridge on Memorial Pond to the high school.

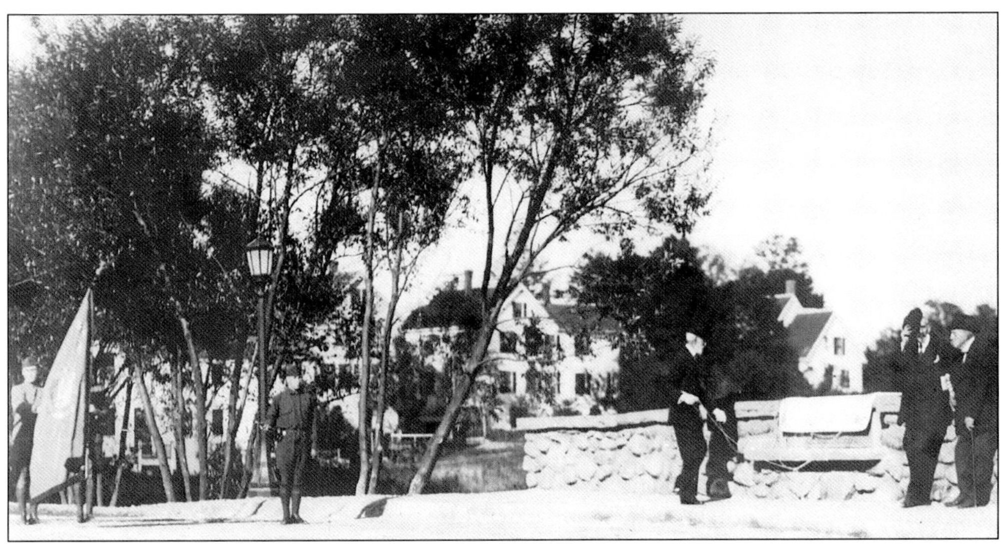

The bronze dedication tablets on the new bridge at Memorial Pond were unveiled by two of the three surviving veterans of the Civil War, Joshua Allen and Fred A Hartshorn. The tablets read as follows: "THIS MEMORIAL BRIDGE IS DEDICATED BY THE CITIZENS OF WALPOLE TO THE SOLDIERS, SAILORS AND NURSES WHO HAVE GONE OUT FROM WALPOLE TO SERVE THEIR COUNTRY IN TIME OF WAR 1724–1924" and "DEDICATED ON THE TWO HUNDREDTH ANNIVERSARY OF THE INCORPORATION OF THE TOWN OF WALPOLE THIS MEMORIAL BRIDGE MARKS THE FIRST STEP IN THE DEVELOPMENT OF THE MEMORIAL PARK 1724–1924."

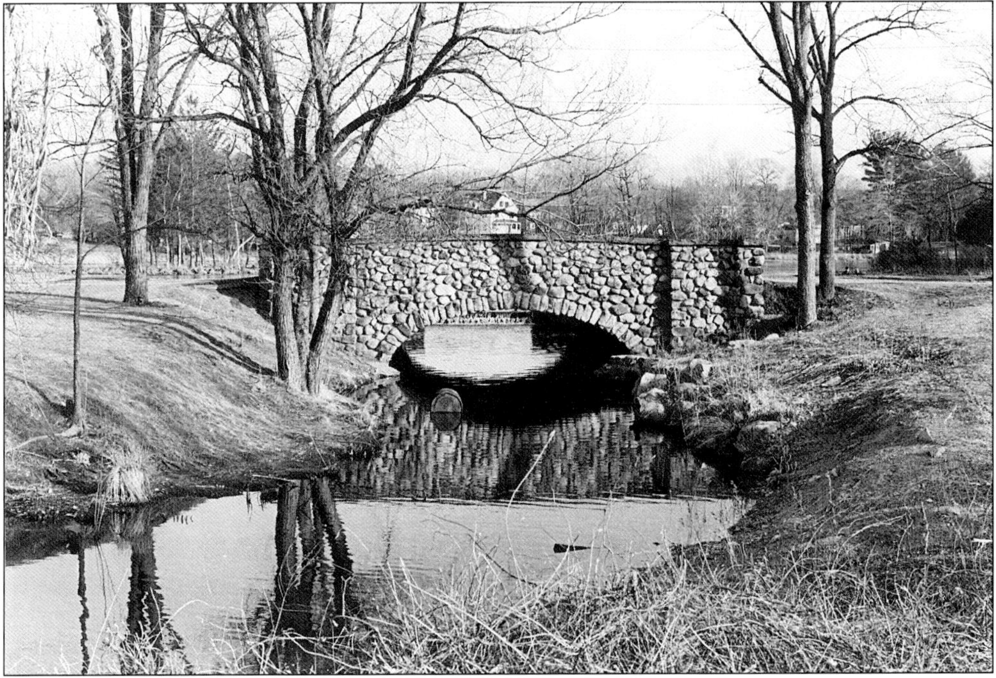

This idyllic view of Memorial Bridge is a serene reminder of the peaceful calm that was won by those veterans to whom it was dedicated. It has survived the torrential floods of 1955 and continues, as did many of its commemorated veterans, to perform above and beyond the call of duty, carrying a volume of traffic far in excess of the traffic anticipated in 1924.

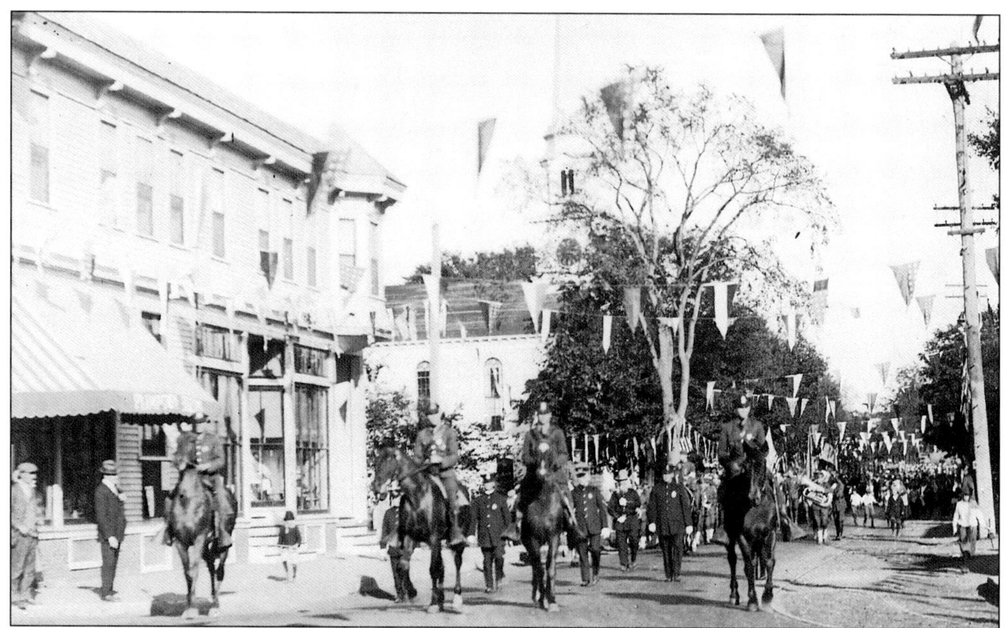

After the bridge dedication, the parade of 3,000 Walpolians, carrying small flags, marched to the high school. Here they are shown coming down East Street to the corner of Main Street! Leading the parade are Police Chief Daniel Crowley and four patrolmen (from left to right): Mike Fizgibbons, Coleman Hogan, Tim Cullinan, and Charlie Jones. Music for the parade was provided by the Weymouth Legion Band and the Norwood Brass Band. To the left is the Plimpton Block, and in the center is the Orthodox Congregational Church (now the location of Gallo's greenhouse).

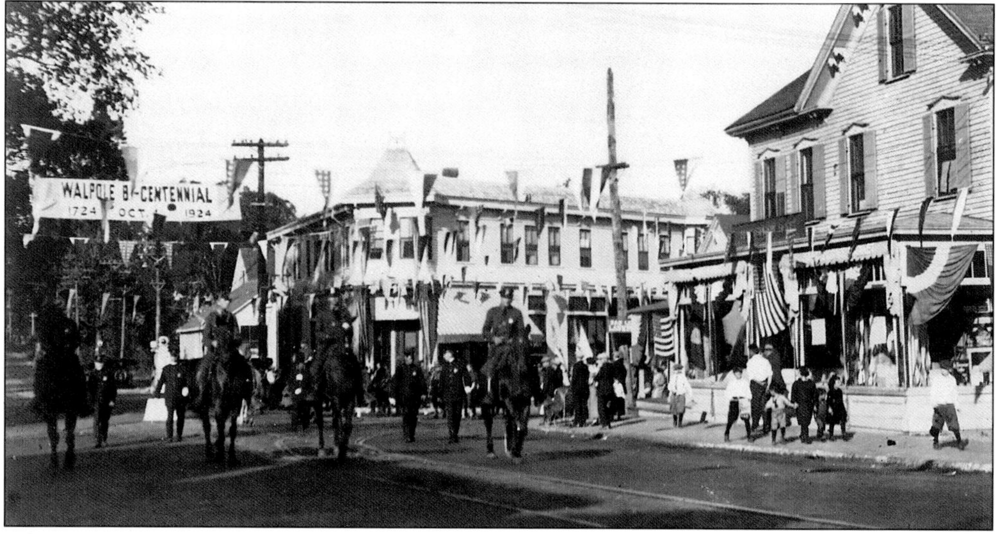

After successfully negotiating the corner, mounted police led the procession up Main Street. The store on the right is Hartshorn Brothers market. On the utility pole can be seen a simple, but informative, sign identifying the adjacent location of Sam Lee's Laundry. Walpole's well-dressed men entrusted soiled shirts in exchange for a slip of paper. The ticket, printed in oriental numerals, was later returned (provided, of course, that it had not been misplaced) with a minimum fee in exchange for immaculately clean and stiffly starched shirts.

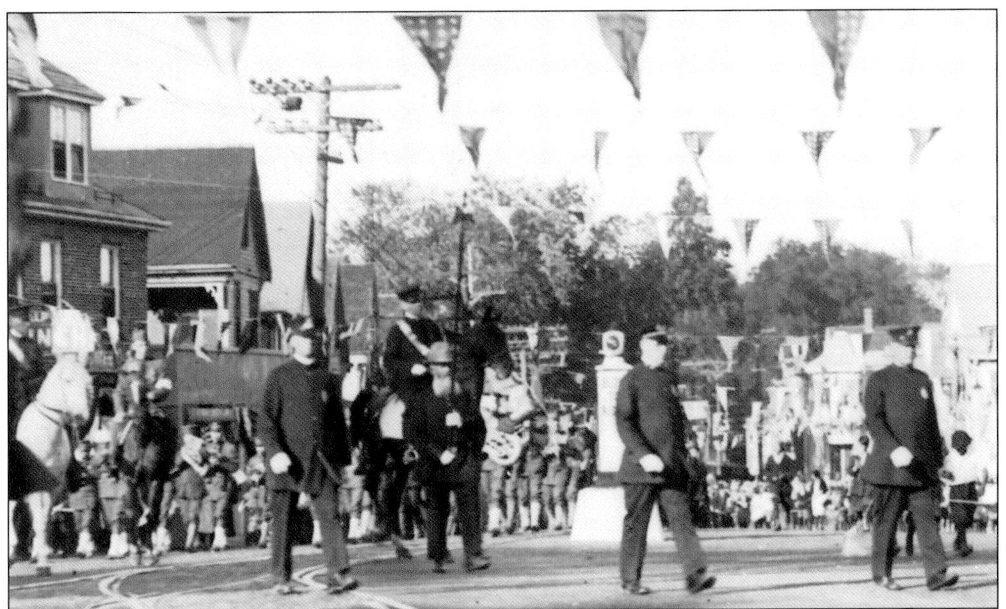

The leaders have passed Town Hall and a 1920s vintage traffic dummy (with only one light!). John Dalton is the bearded man carrying a halberd (a sixteenth-century weapon consisting of a battle ax and pike mounted on a 6-foot handle), a symbol of authority. On the street can be seen trolley tracks and a bed of cobblestones. Although the defunct trolley company had been bought by local luminaries, the service was never reinstated, and the Main Street tracks were removed at the expense of the taxpayers. Having reached the high school grounds, the marchers were treated to a bean supper. As night fell, there was a presentation of ten live dioramas illustrating the town's historic milestones.

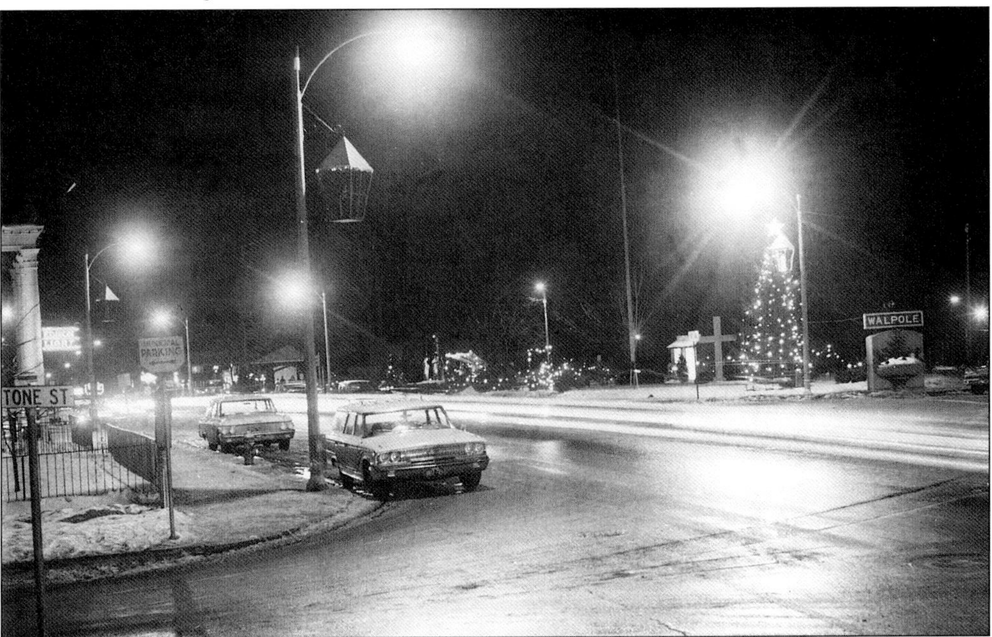

Merry Christmas, 1963. Clear skies and twinkling lights set the tone of holiday spirit. The department of public works has done a fine job of lighting the town common.

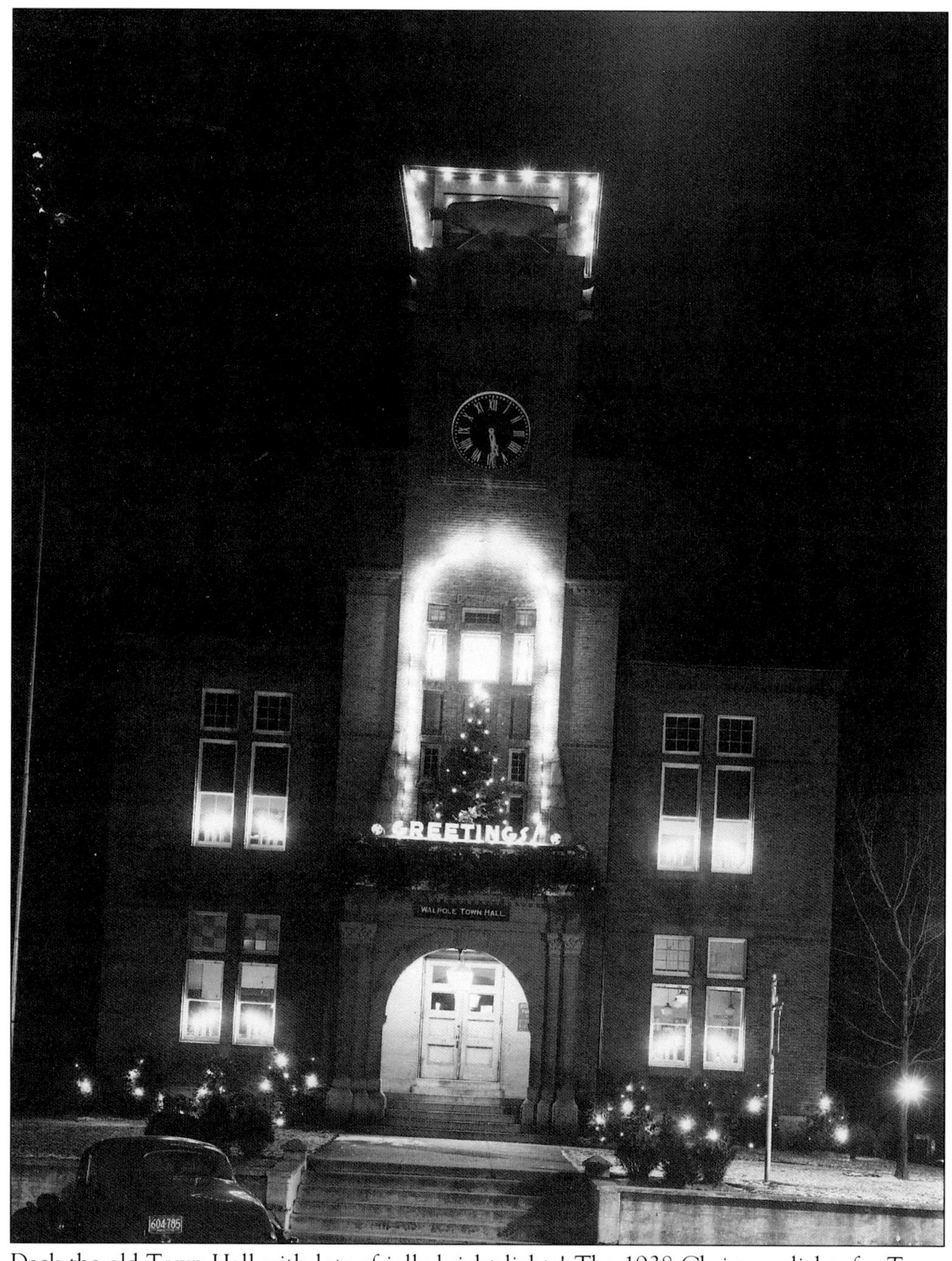

Deck the old Town Hall with lots of jolly bright lights! The 1938 Christmas lights for Town Hall were courtesy of Boston Edison.

Seven

Good Times, Bad Times

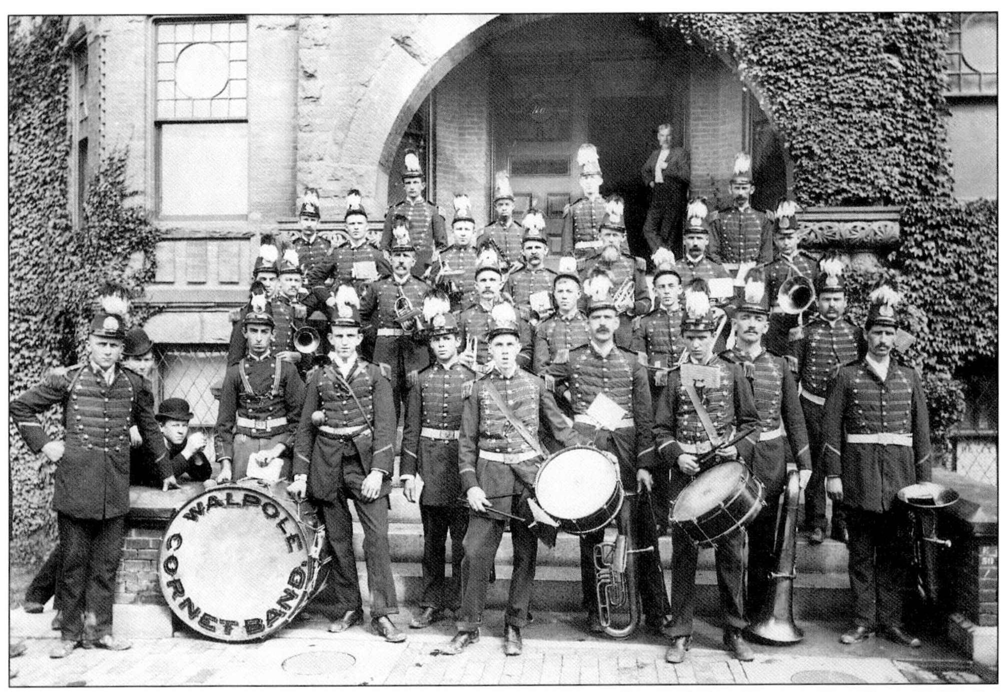

Everyone loves a parade! Twenty-six men of various ages formed the Cornet Band in 1892. In addition to participating in Walpole parades, this band was also called upon to perform concerts at area schools.

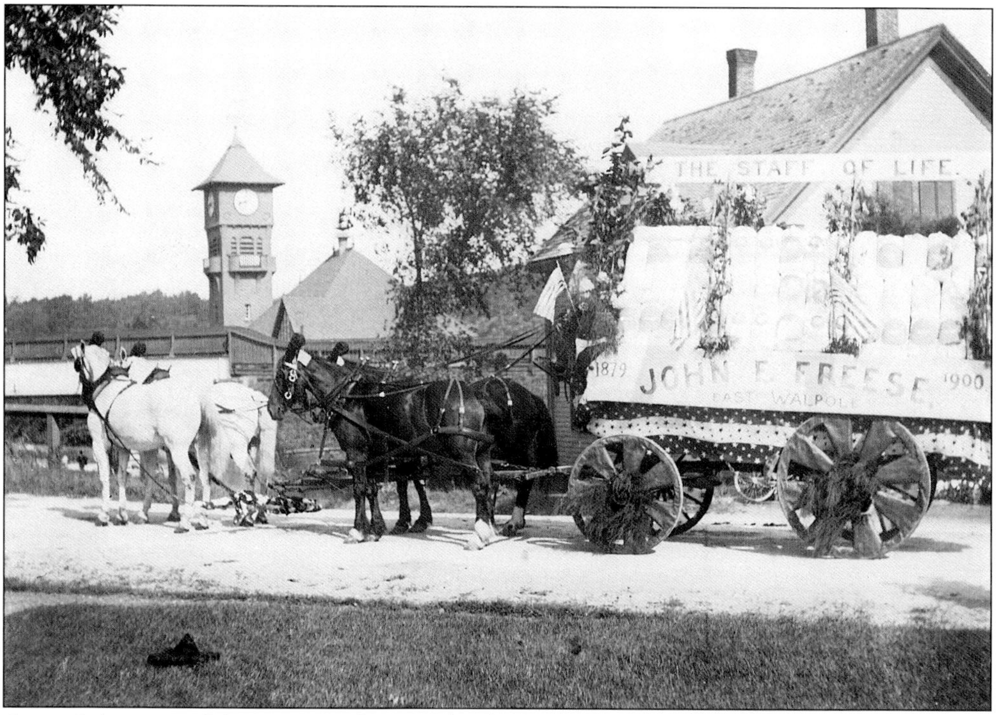

Around the turn of the century, the Fourth of July was a grand celebration in Walpole. John Freese, the owner of Freese General Store, is displaying sacks of flour on his float titled, "Staff of Life in 1900." Mr. Freese is barely visible on the wagon seat.

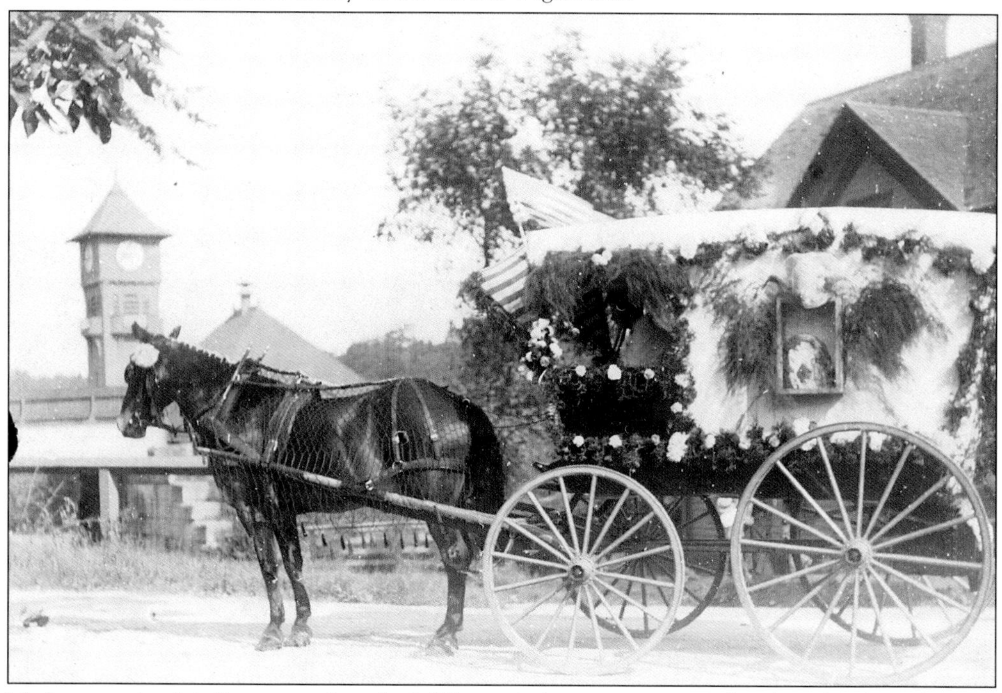

Unfortunately, this float is unidentified. What can be seen is a ram's head made of wool over a shadow box. The horse is draped with netting to keep the flies away.

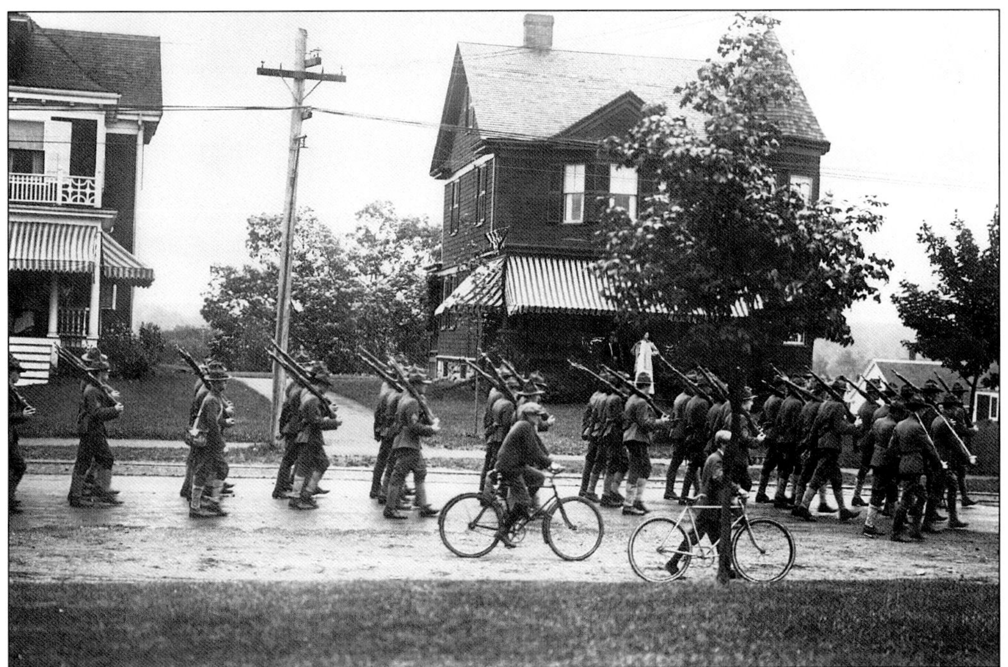

The following photographs were taken on July 4, 1915. Forty-five floats representing five divisions stepped out at 8:30 from Bird Hall and marched to the high school. Awards were presented to the best in each division. The 11th Company Coast Artillery Corps. won first place in Division One: Uniform Marching Bands division.

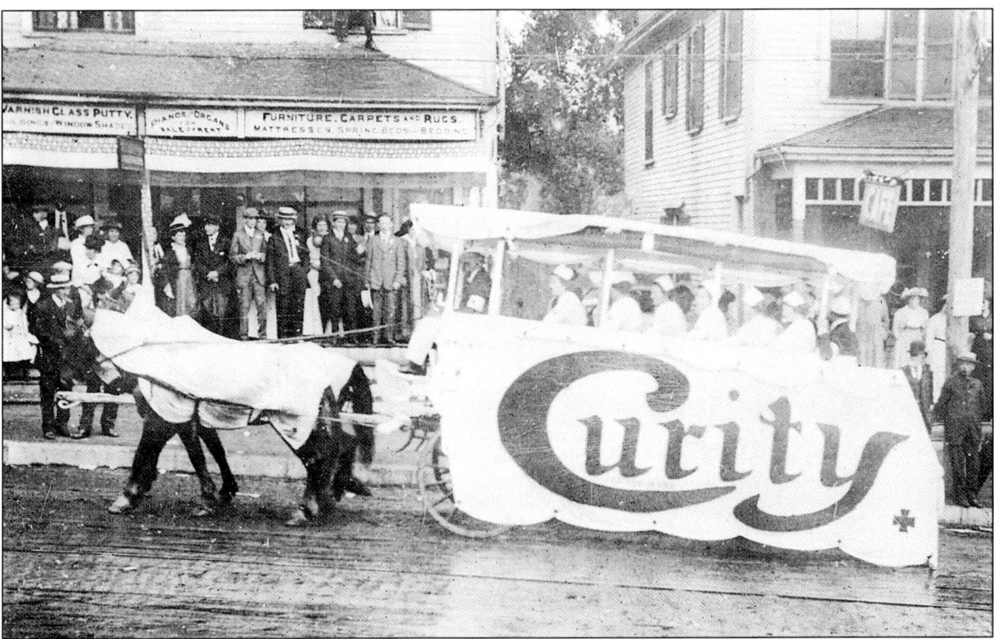

This picture shows the winner in Division 2: Trades and Manufacturing division. First place was awarded to Lewis Manufacturing Company. In second place was Fales Manufacturing.

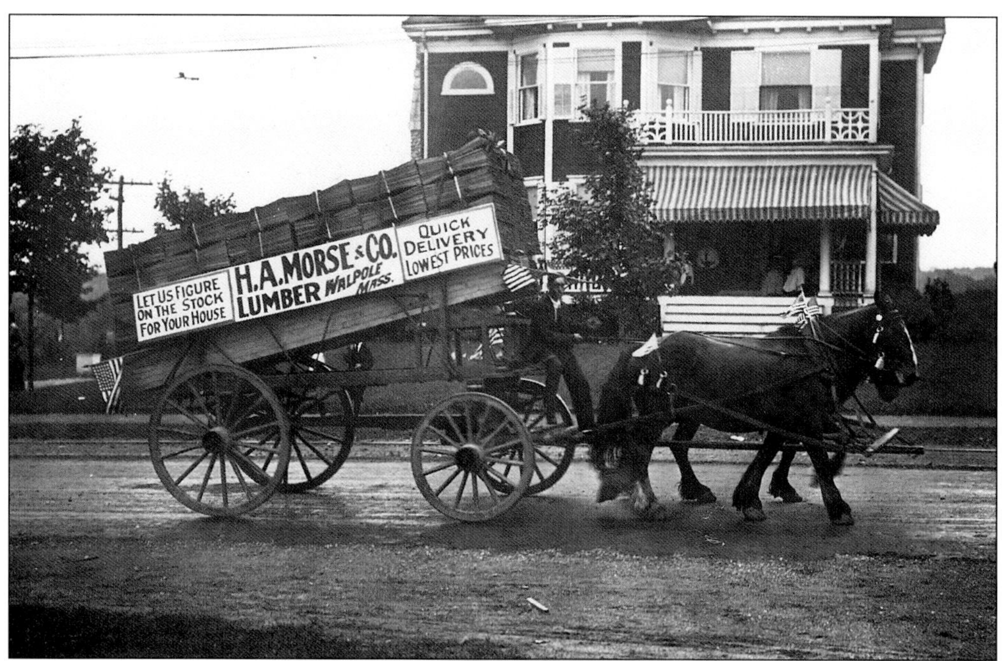

H.A. Morse had a unique way of advertising his stock and trade.

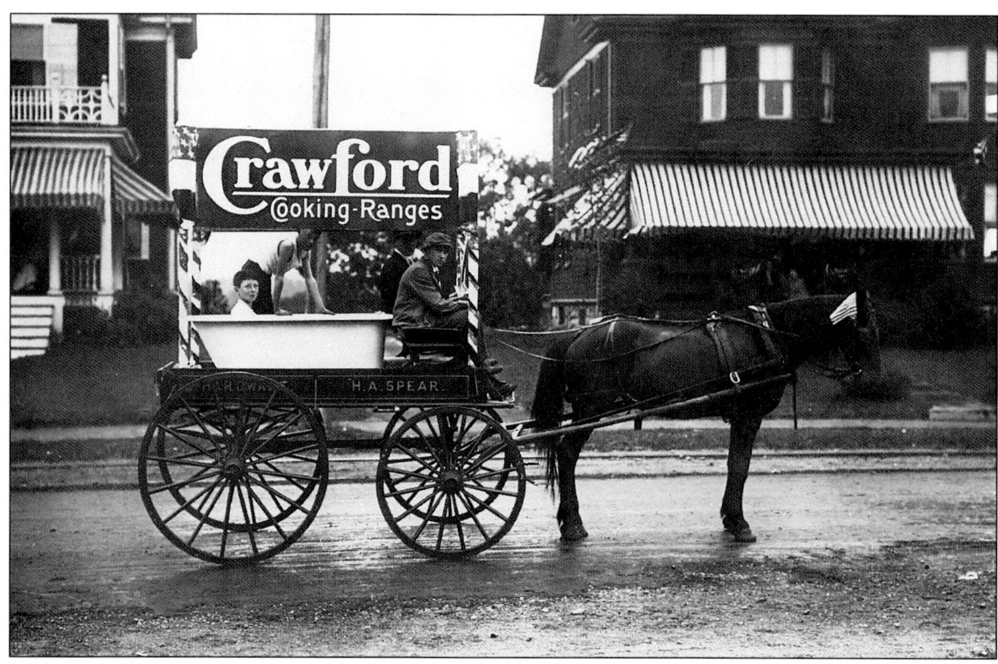

H.A. Spear's wagon sports an advertising sign for "cooking ranges and a fine line of bath tubs."

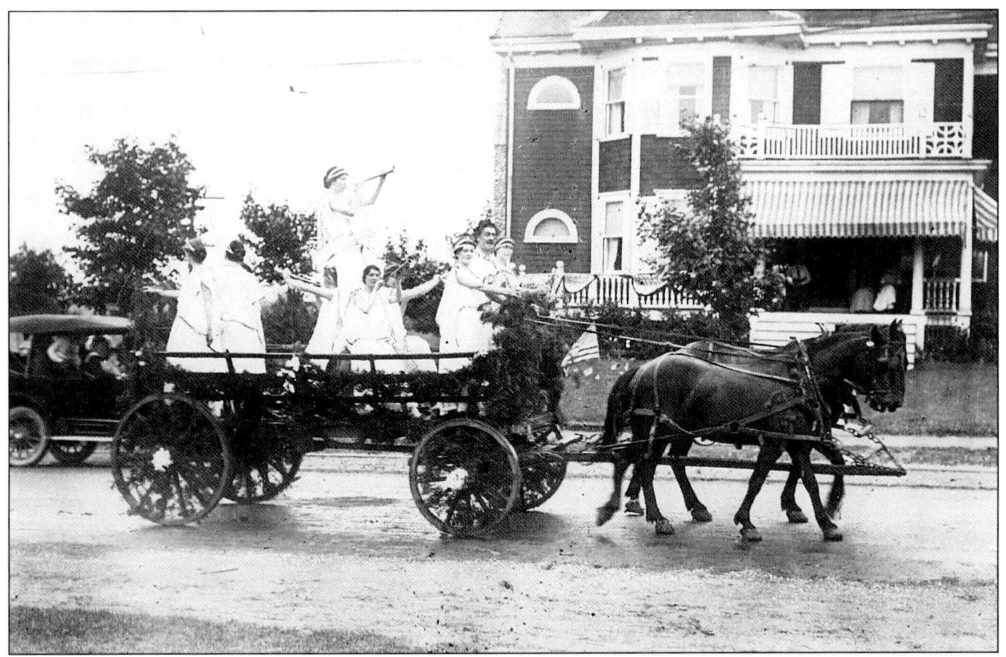
First Place in Division 3: Choral division went to the Walpole Choral Society. The driver of the float is Chester Gove.

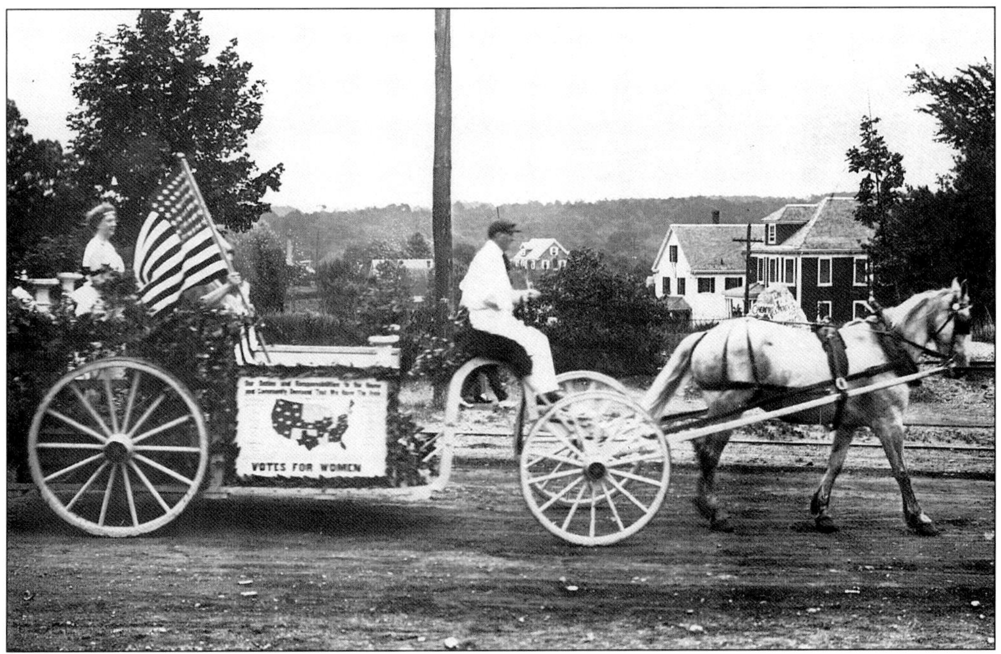

The second place winner in Division 3 was the Votes for Women Float. Mrs. Hunt posed as Victory. The sign states, "Our duties and responsibilities to the community and home demand that we have the vote." Women achieved the right to vote in 1920.

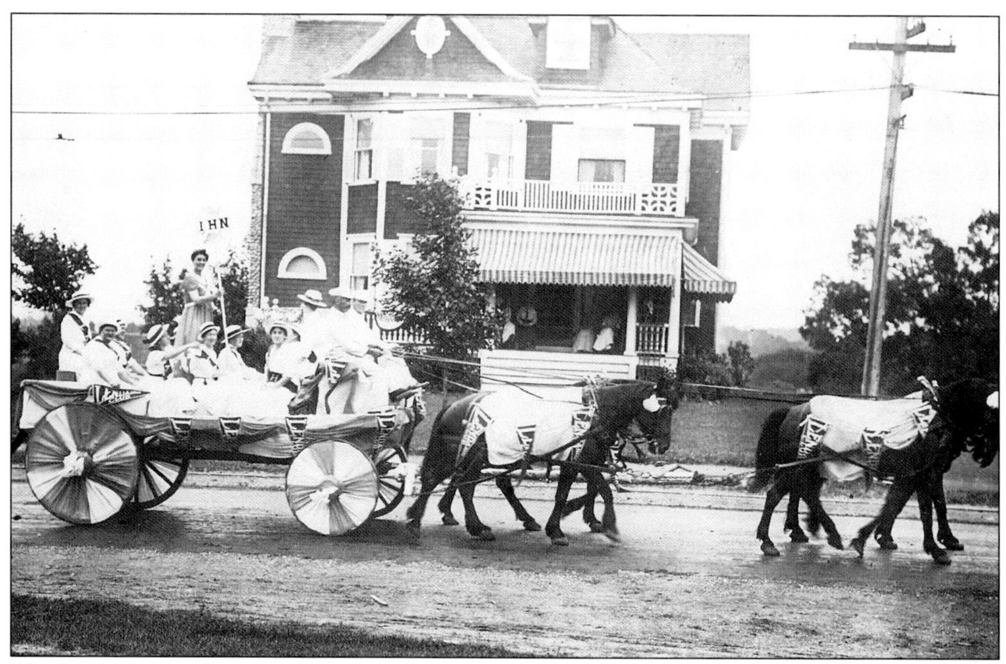
The Lend-A-Hand Club was organized for the purpose of aiding needy residents. In later years, Nellie Barlan Miner and Mrs. George served as presidents of this organization.

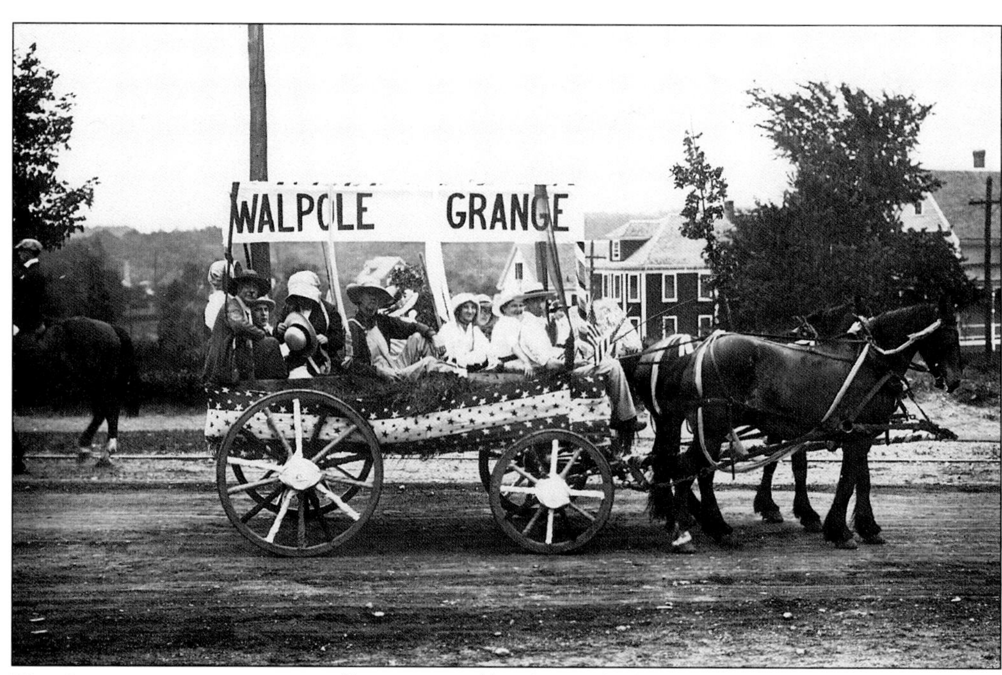

The farming community was well represented by the Walpole Grange, an old society formed to educate, lend aid, and provide social activities for the agricultural community.

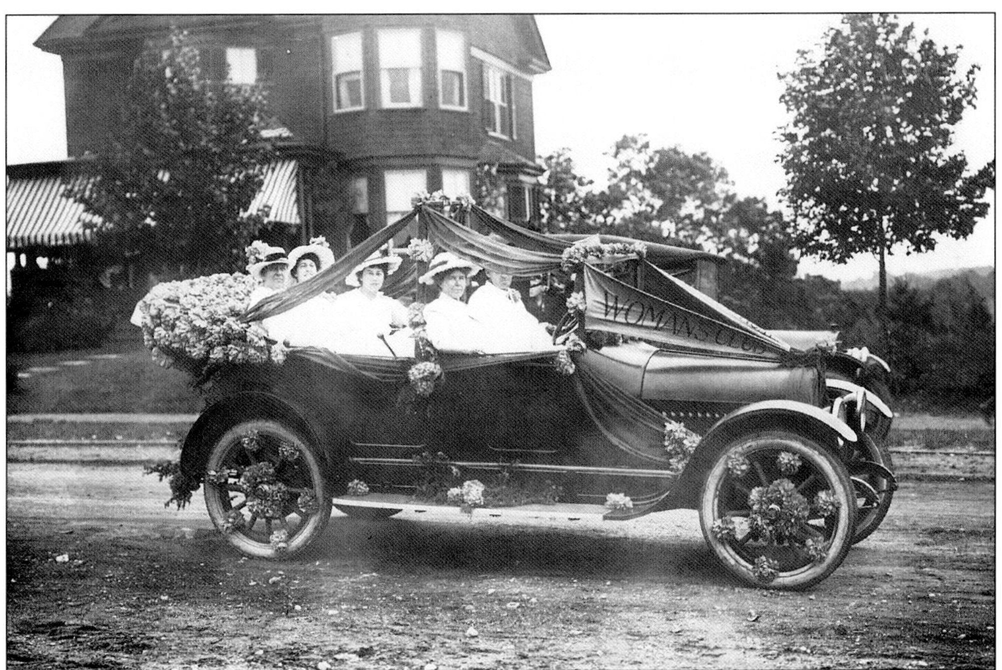

Representatives of the Walpole Woman's Club ride by the reviewing stand in style. Elizabeth Spear, president, is seated in the front while Lizzie Spear, vice president, sits behind her.

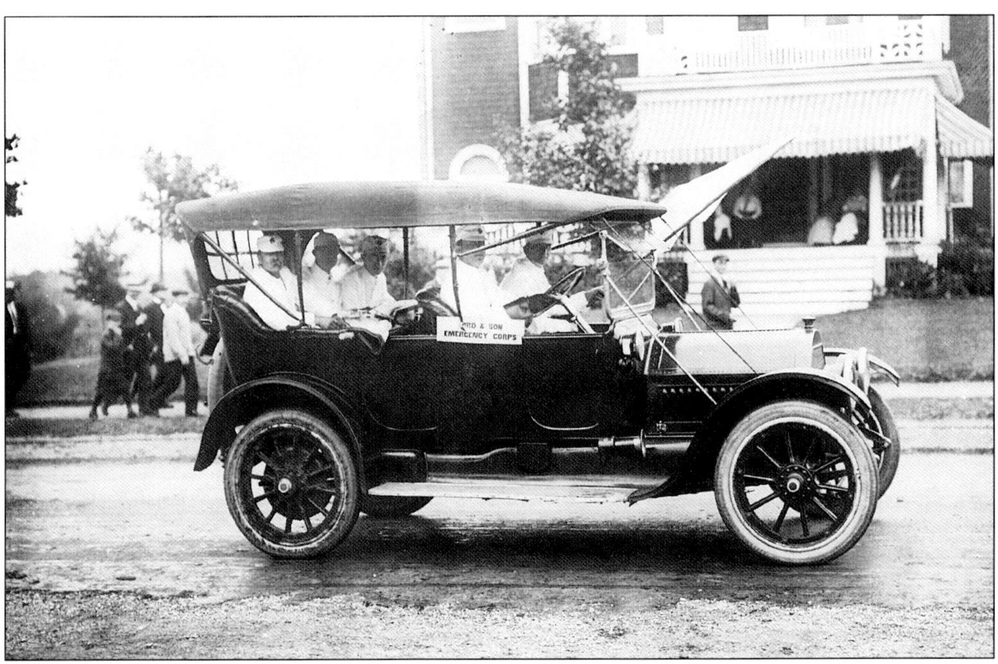

In Division 4: the Automobile division, the winner of first place was E.E. Simmons. Pictured here is the second-place winner, the Bird and Son Emergency Corps.

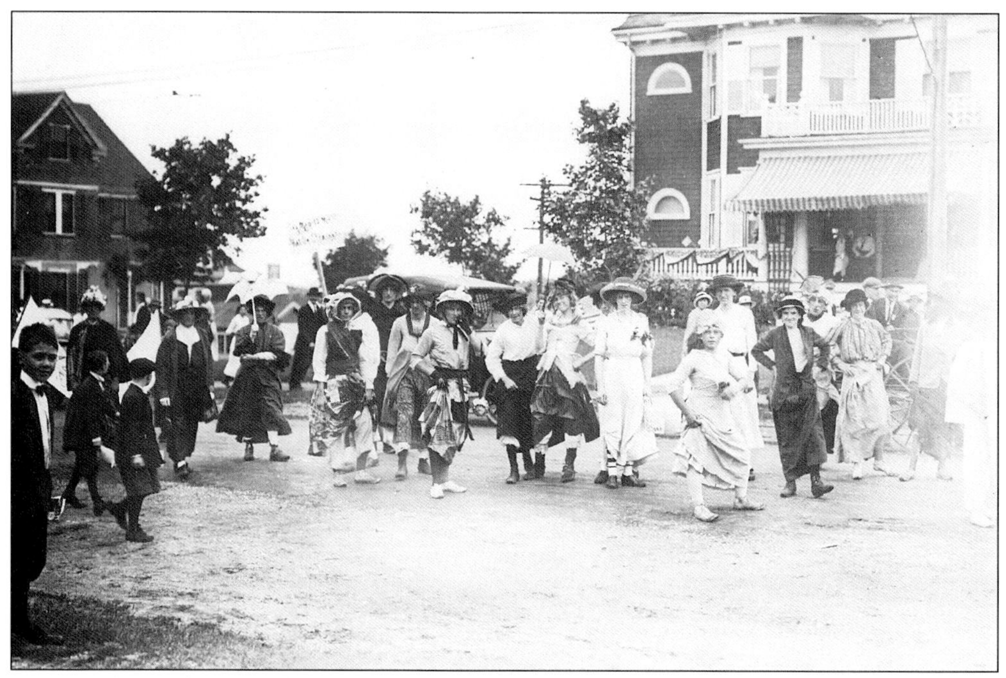

Division 5 was the Horribles division. A group of 50 marchers made up this division, which poked fun at various organizations in town. The first place winner was a parody of the Woman's Club, with second place going to a spoof of the water department.

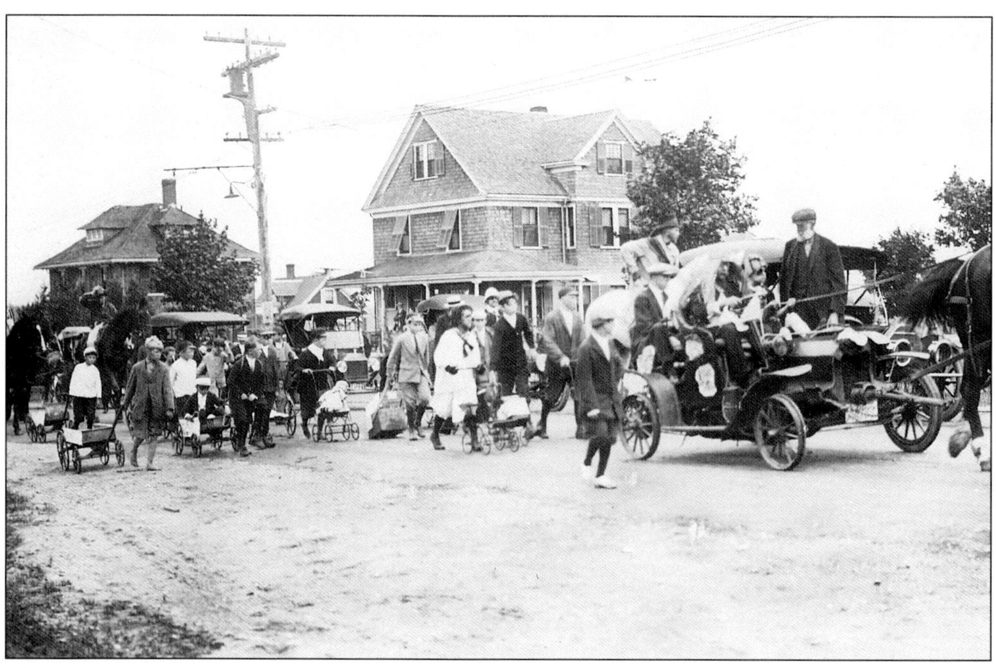

This is another Horribles division entry. No explanation was given to clarify what was being made fun of here.

There are many and various reasons to hold a parade. In 1919, Memorial Day was observed with a gala parade and ceremonies. Here the Regiment Band strides down Main Street to Rural Cemetery.

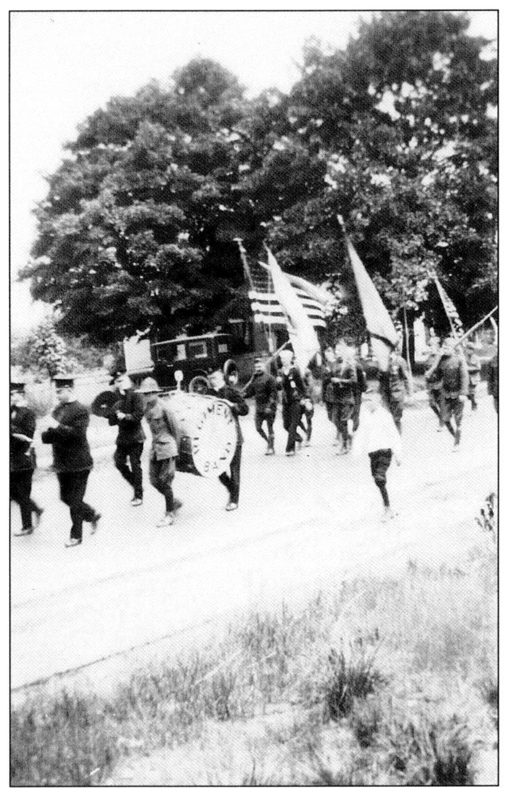

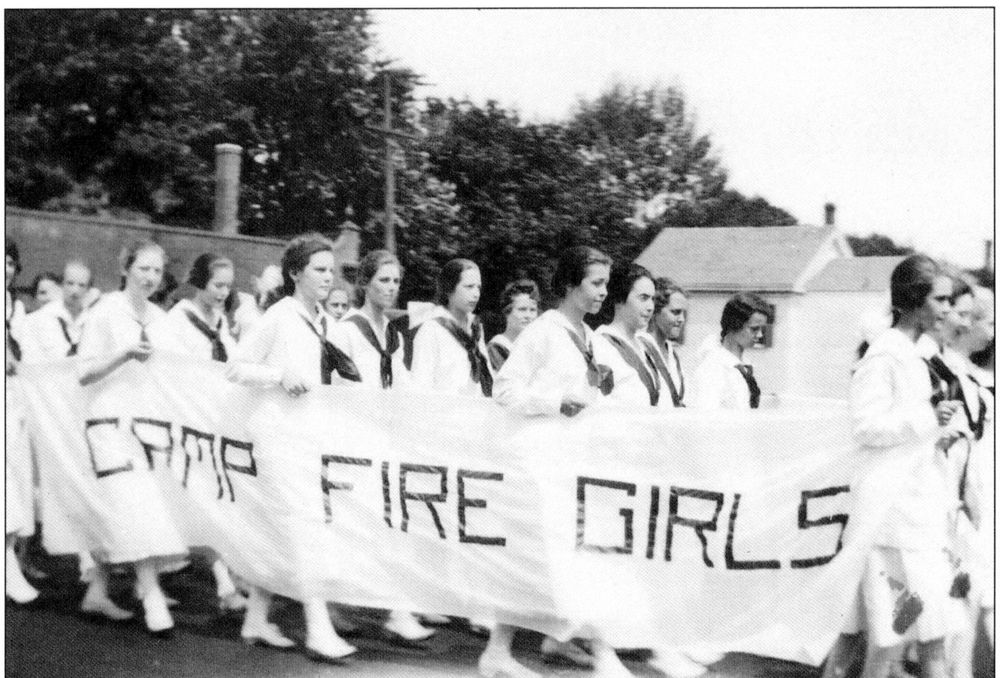

These Camp Fire Girls are representatives of the group that was organized in 1911 by Mrs. McKenzie. Her husband was the minister of the Orthodox Congregational Church.

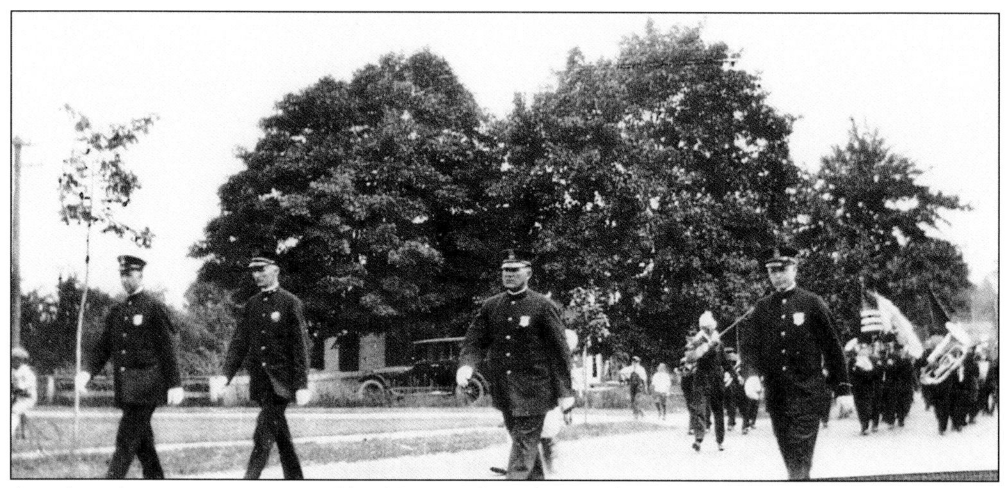

A police department escort—Chief Leonard, with patrolmen Egan, Fitzgibbons, and Hogan (from left to right)—led the 1920 Field Day Parade.

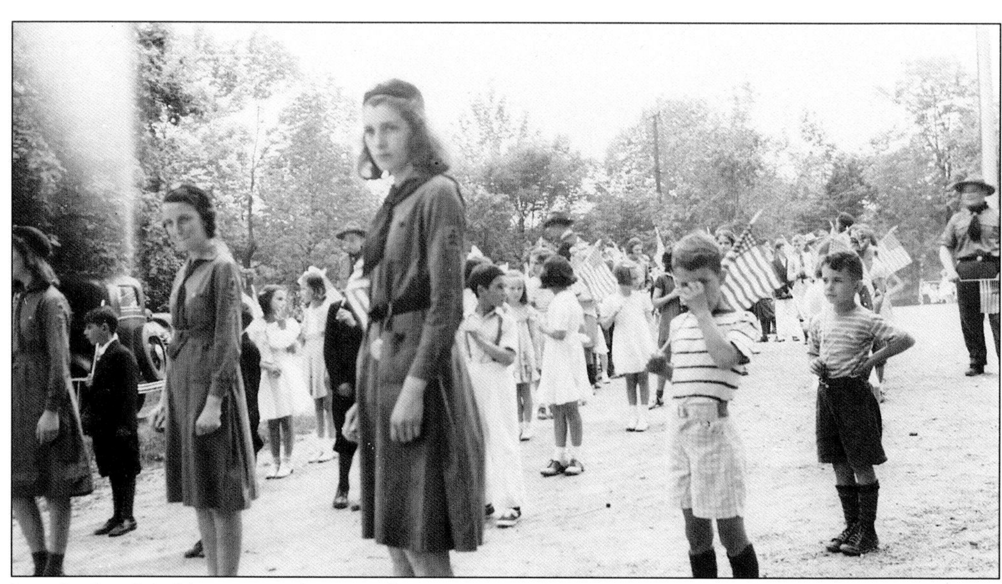

Local schoolchildren pay tribute to the American flag at a ceremony on Flag Day 1940.

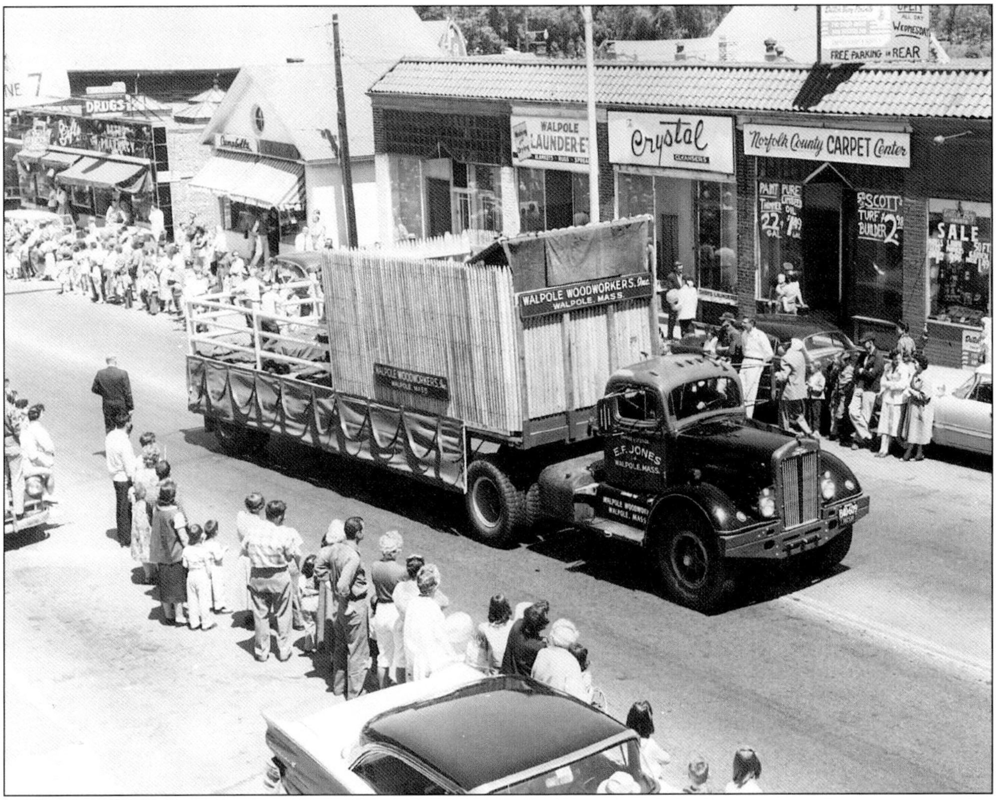

Many changes have taken place around Walpole since Mr. Freese entered his float in the July 4th Parade in 1900. The Village Fair has kept the parade tradition alive. Pictured is the Walpole Woodworkers entry in 1958.

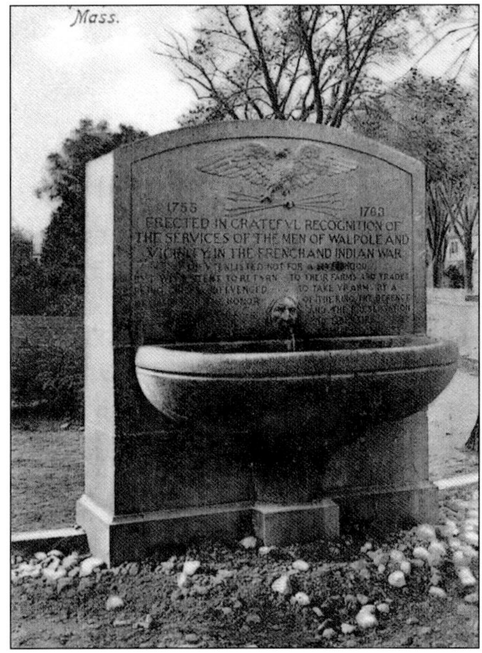

There are many memorials honoring citizens for outstanding service and dedication to the town. The French and Indian War Memorial Fountain was a gift to the town by George Plimpton in 1901. The fountain was placed over the original town well.

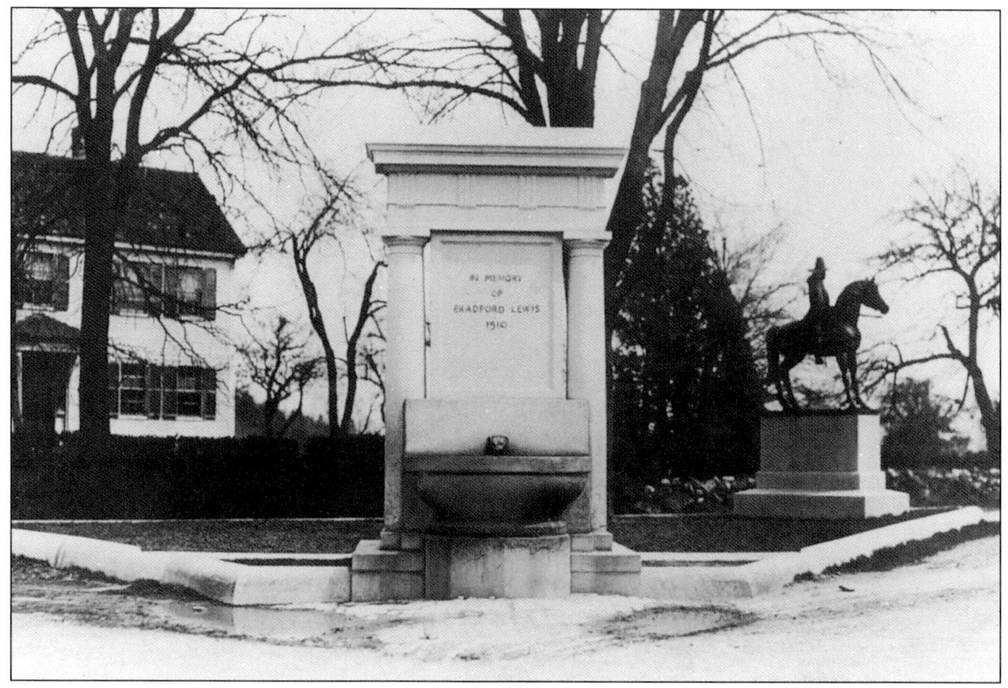

Lewis Square on East Street was a gift to the town by Issac Lewis in 1775 to be used as open space. E. Frank Lewis erected the granite fountain as a memorial to his father, Bradford Lewis, in 1910. Why and when the horse statue was moved is unknown.

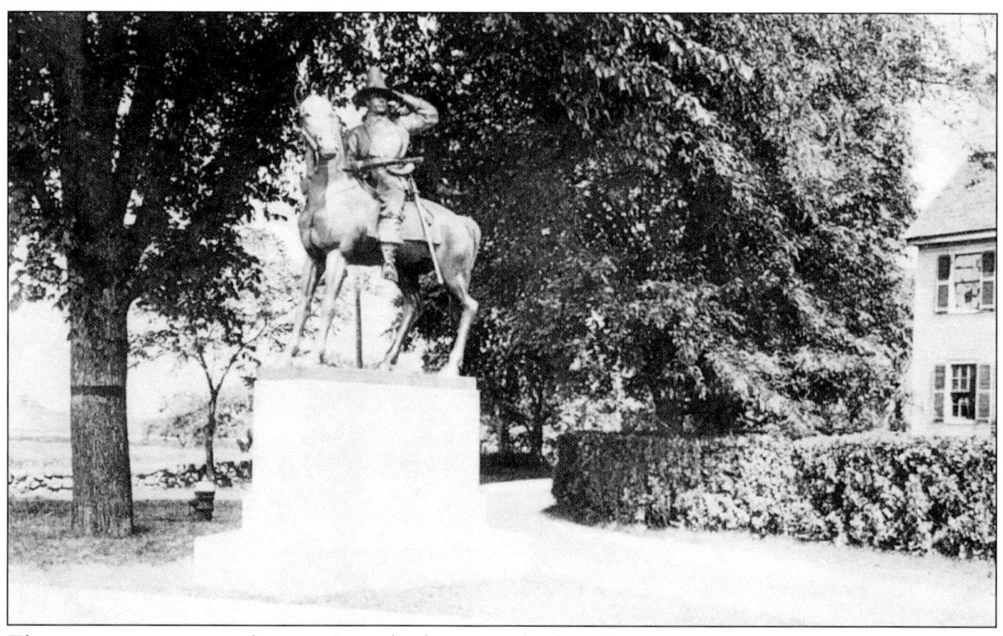

This equestrian statue honors Barachiah Lewis for his illustrious service as an officer in the French and Indian War. It was dedicated as a memorial to William and Judith Lewis by their children, Mary R. and Issac Newton Lewis, in 1911.

On July 4, 1917, Issac Newton Lewis posed for this picture at the dedication of a flag pole honoring the 26th Division of the Grand Army of the Republic (GAR). Lewis was a noted local historian who published several books on Walpole and was responsible for the construction of Lewis Castle (page 16).

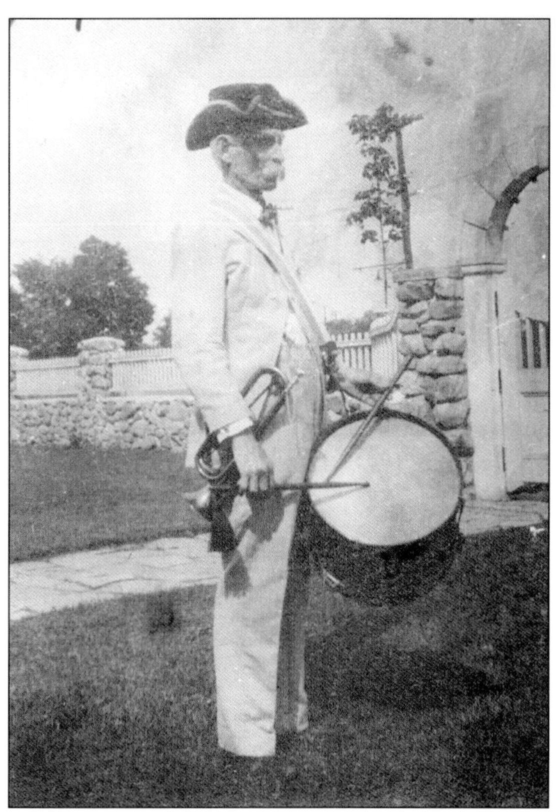

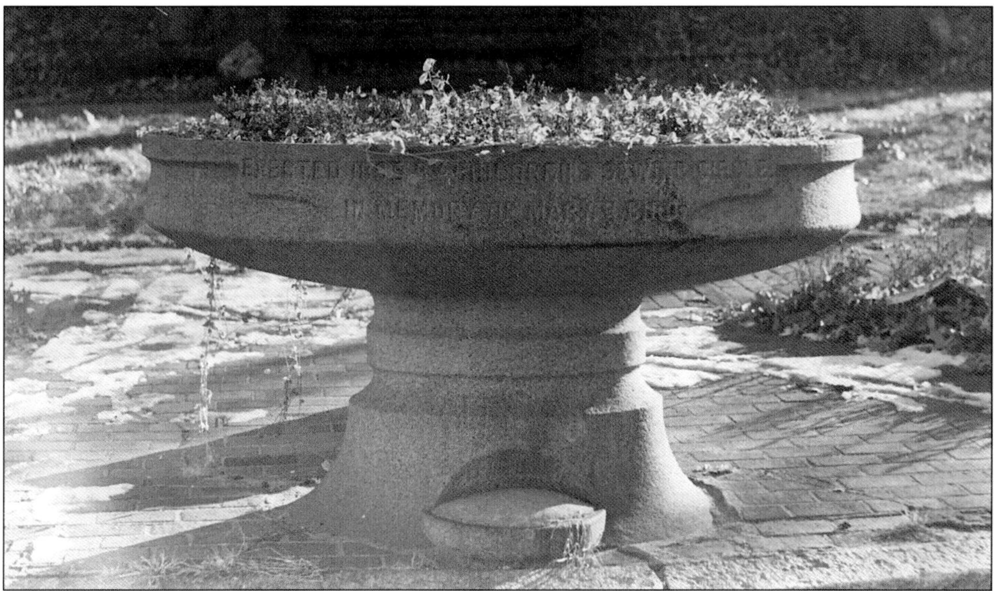

Mary Reynolds Bird was fondly remembered by the Childrens Sewing Circle, as can be seen by the dedication of a fountain in her honor. Miss Bird would be considered an activist by today's standards. She spoke out against slavery, was president of the Improvement Society, promoted children's programs, and formed a citizens group to start a public library.

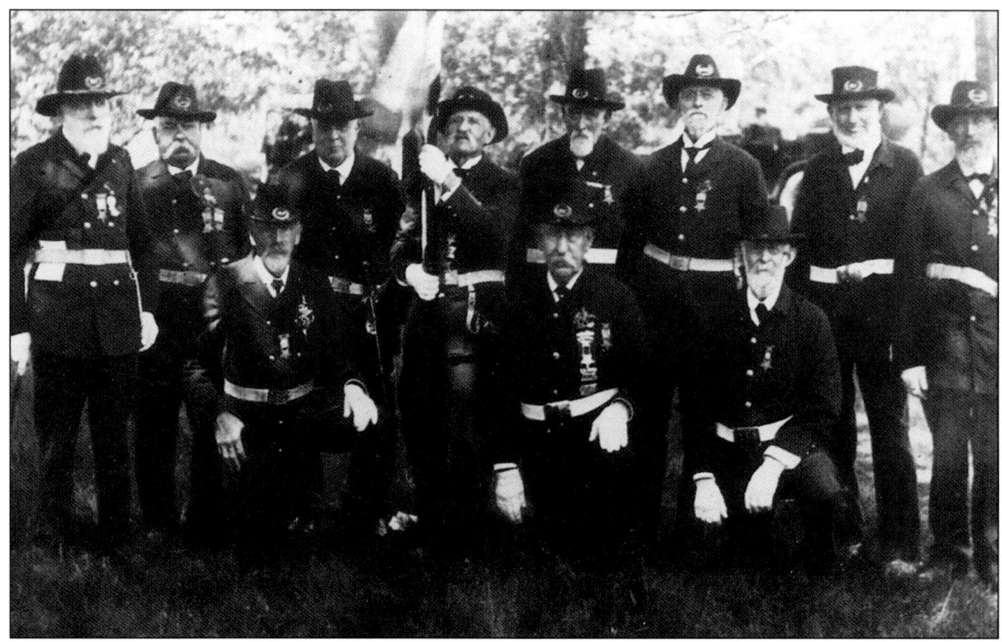

The July Fourth celebration of 1896 brought the Grand Army of the Republic veterans together. Henry Achorn of East Walpole (bottom row, second from left) served in the 26th Regiment. A memorial sign at the corner of Pleasant and Union Streets was dedicated in his honor.

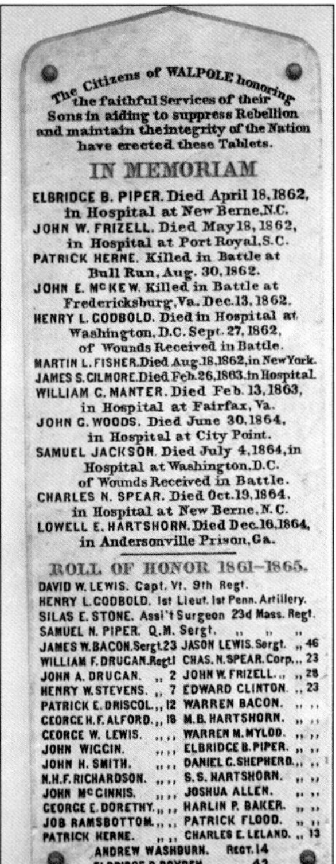

The committee for the marble tablets commemorating the Civil War soldiers reported, "119 names listed as Walpole's quota in the late war for the union. We recommend the names of all but bounty jumpers and deserters be placed on the tablets." The memorial lists the date and place of death of each soldier.

Walpole has never forgotten its citizens who served our country. The Civil War tablets are on the walls inside old Town Hall (seen here *c.* 1918), and prominently displayed on the lawn was the listing of the soldiers of World War I.

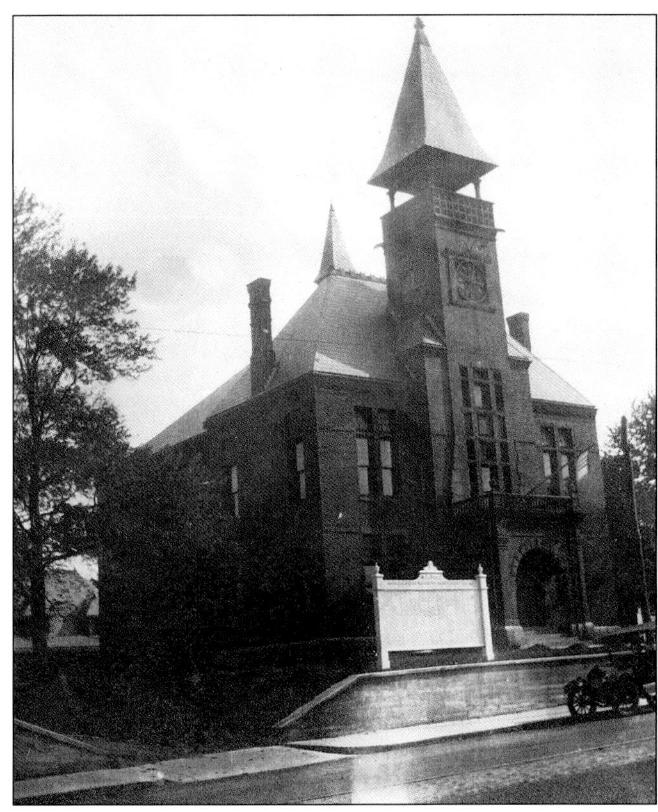

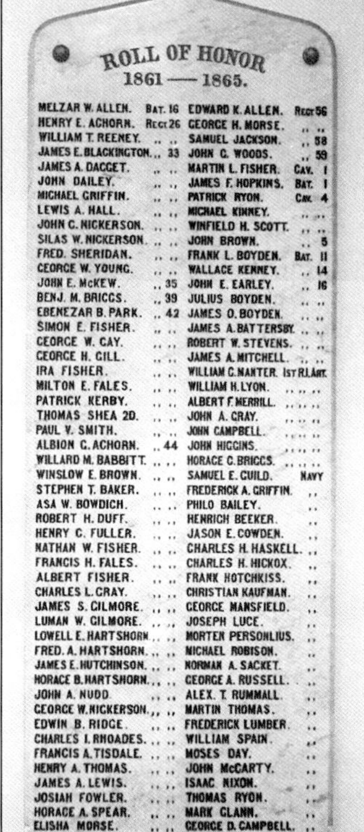

ROLL OF HONOR
1861 —— 1865.

MELZAR W. ALLEN.	BAT. 16	EDWARD K. ALLEN.	REGT 56
HENRY E. ACHORN.	REGT 26	GEORGE H. MORSE.	,, ,,
WILLIAM T. REENEY.	,, ,,	SAMUEL JACKSON.	,, 58
JAMES E. BLACKINGTON.	,, 33	JOHN G. WOODS.	,, 59
JAMES A. DAGGET.	,, ,,	MARTIN L. FISHER.	CAV. 1
JOHN DAILEY.	,, ,,	JAMES F. HOPKINS.	BAT. 1
MICHAEL GRIFFIN.	,, ,,	PATRICK RYON.	CAV. 4
LEWIS A. HALL.	,, ,,	MICHAEL KINNEY.	,, ,,
JOHN C. NICKERSON.	,, ,,	WINFIELD H. SCOTT.	,, ,,
SILAS W. NICKERSON.	,, ,,	JOHN BROWN.	,, 5
FRED. SHERIDAN.	,, ,,	FRANK L. BOYDEN.	BAT. 11
GEORGE W. YOUNG.	,, ,,	WALLACE KENNEY.	,, 14
JOHN E. McKEW.	,, 35	JOHN E. EARLEY.	,, 16
BENJ. M. BRIGGS.	,, 39	JULIUS BOYDEN.	,, ,,
EBENEZAR B. PARK.	,, 42	JAMES O. BOYDEN.	,, ,,
SIMON E. FISHER.	,, ,,	JAMES A. BATTERSBY.	,, ,,
GEORGE W. GAY.	,, ,,	ROBERT W. STEVENS.	,, ,,
GEORGE H. GILL.	,, ,,	JAMES A. MITCHELL.	,, ,,
IRA FISHER.	,, ,,	WILLIAM C. NANTER.	1ST R.I. ART.
MILTON E. FALES.	,, ,,	WILLIAM H. LYON.	,, ,, ,,
PATRICK KERBY.	,, ,,	ALBERT F. MERRILL.	,, ,, ,,
THOMAS SHEA 2D.	,, ,,	JOHN A. GRAY.	,, ,, ,,
PAUL V. SMITH.	,, ,,	JOHN CAMPBELL.	,, ,, ,,
ALBION G. ACHORN.	,, 44	JOHN HIGGINS.	,, ,, ,,
WILLARD M. BABBITT.	,, ,,	HORACE C. BRIGGS.	,, ,, ,,
WINSLOW E. BROWN.	,, ,,	SAMUEL E. GUILD.	NAVY
STEPHEN T. BAKER.	,, ,,	FREDERICK A. GRIFFIN.	,,
ASA W. BOWDICH.	,, ,,	PHILO BAILEY.	,,
ROBERT H. DUFF.	,, ,,	HENRICH BEEKER.	,,
HENRY C. FULLER.	,, ,,	JASON E. COWDEN.	,,
NATHAN W. FISHER.	,, ,,	CHARLES H. HASKELL.	,,
FRANCIS H. FALES.	,, ,,	CHARLES H. HICKOX.	,,
ALBERT FISHER.	,, ,,	FRANK HOTCHKISS.	,,
CHARLES L. GRAY.	,, ,,	CHRISTIAN KAUFMAN.	,,
JAMES S. GILMORE.	,, ,,	GEORGE MANSFIELD.	,,
LUMAN W. GILMORE.	,, ,,	JOSEPH LUCE.	,,
LOWELL E. HARTSHORN	,, ,,	MORTEN PERSONLIUS.	,,
FRED. A. HARTSHORN.	,, ,,	MICHAEL ROBISON.	,,
JAMES E. HUTCHINSON.	,, ,,	NORMAN A. SACKET.	,,
HORACE B. HARTSHORN.	,, ,,	GEORGE A. RUSSELL.	,,
JOHN A. NUDD.	,, ,,	ALEX. T. RUMMALL.	,,
GEORGE W. NICKERSON.	,, ,,	MARTIN THOMAS.	,,
EDWIN B. RIDGE.	,, ,,	FREDERICK LUMBER.	,,
CHARLES I. RHOADES.	,, ,,	WILLIAM SPAIN.	,,
FRANCIS A. TISDALE.	,, ,,	MOSES DAY.	,,
HENRY A. THOMAS.	,, ,,	JOHN McCARTY.	,,
JAMES A. LEWIS.	,, ,,	ISAAC NIXON.	,,
JOSIAH FOWLER.	,, ,,	THOMAS RYON.	,,
HORACE A. SPEAR.	,, ,,	MARK GLANN.	,,
ELISHA MORSE.	,, ,,	GEORGE D. CAMPBELL.	,,

The town meeting report of 1883 reads, "Voted to accept the report and recommendations of the committee. $200 would be appropriated for the payment for procuring and writing said tablets. Upon completion, tablets will be hung in the town hall." The pictured tablet lists the soldiers and the regiment or division in which they served.

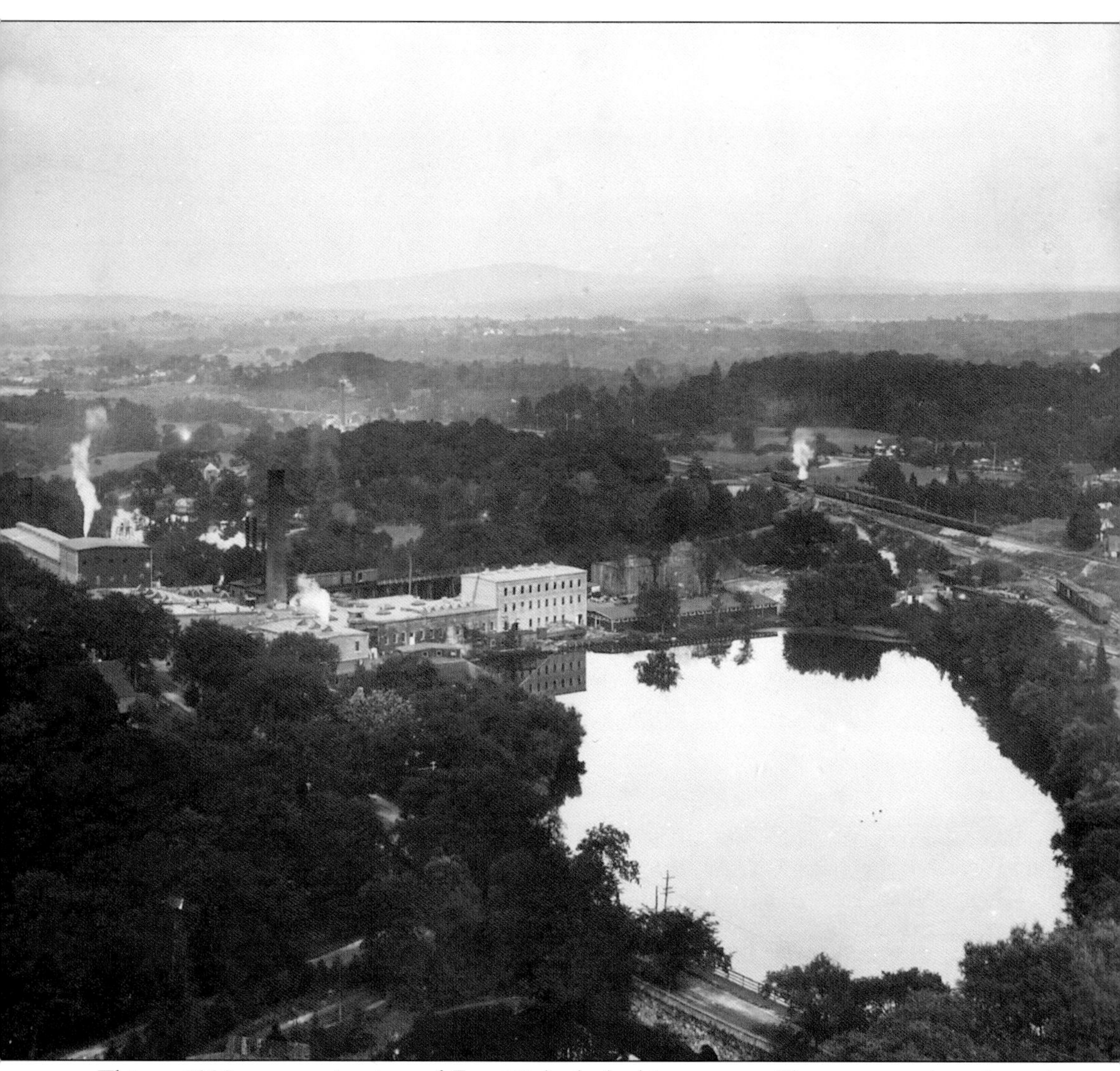

This *c.* 1900 panoramic view of East Walpole looking east to Sharon was taken from the 250-foot-high Bird and Co.'s smokestack (razed in 1994). The Hollingsworth and Vose Mill and pond occupy most of the left panel with just a glimpse of Washington Street as it crosses the twin-arched bridge. Bird Hall, with its newly added clock tower (1898), is visible at the left

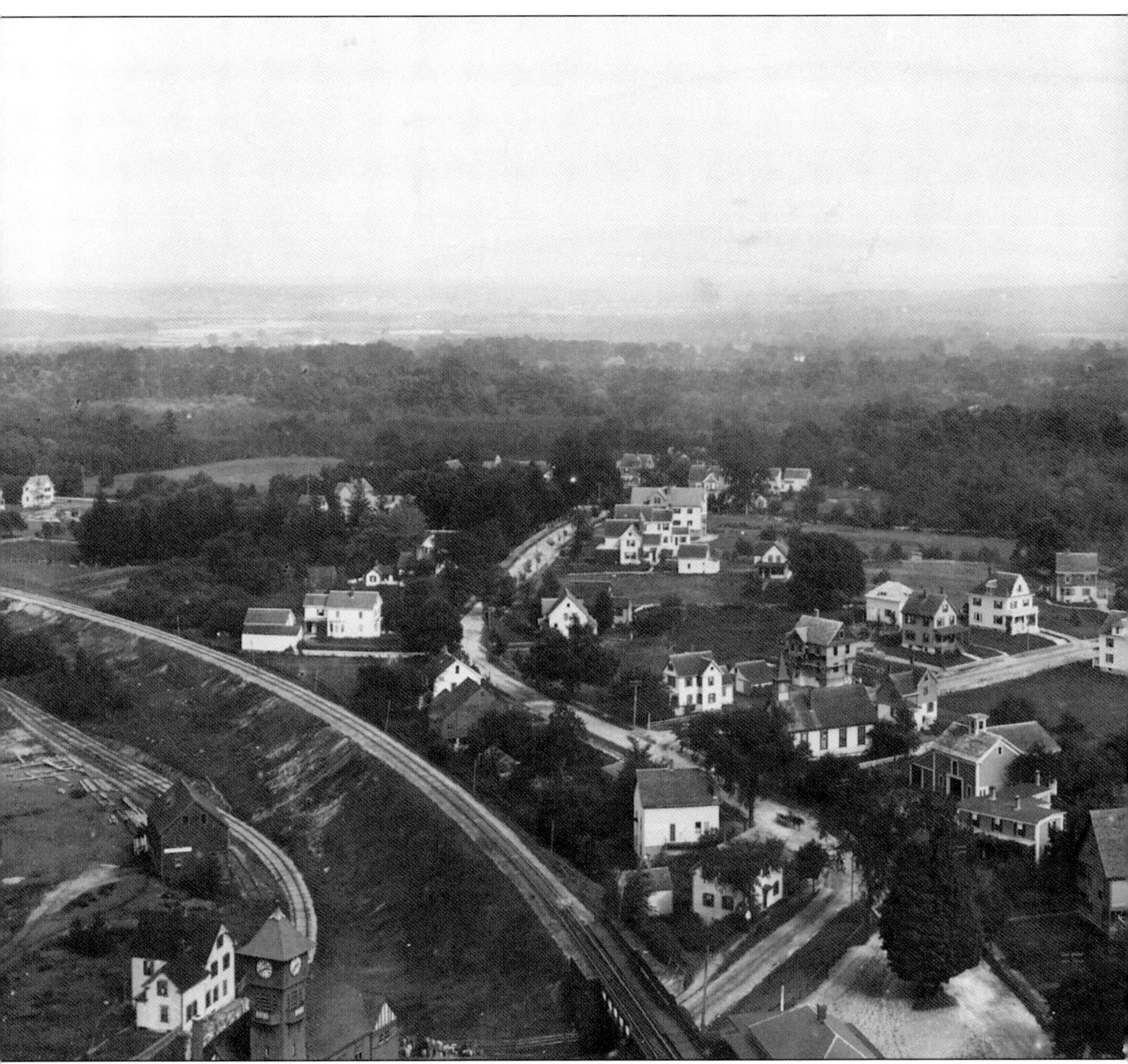

bottom edge of the right panel. The railroad tracks cross Chestnut Street ending at the train station's hip roof. In 1915, the Union Congregational Church moved to a new building on Rhoades Avenue. The vacant building became the Wednesday Club and later the branch library.

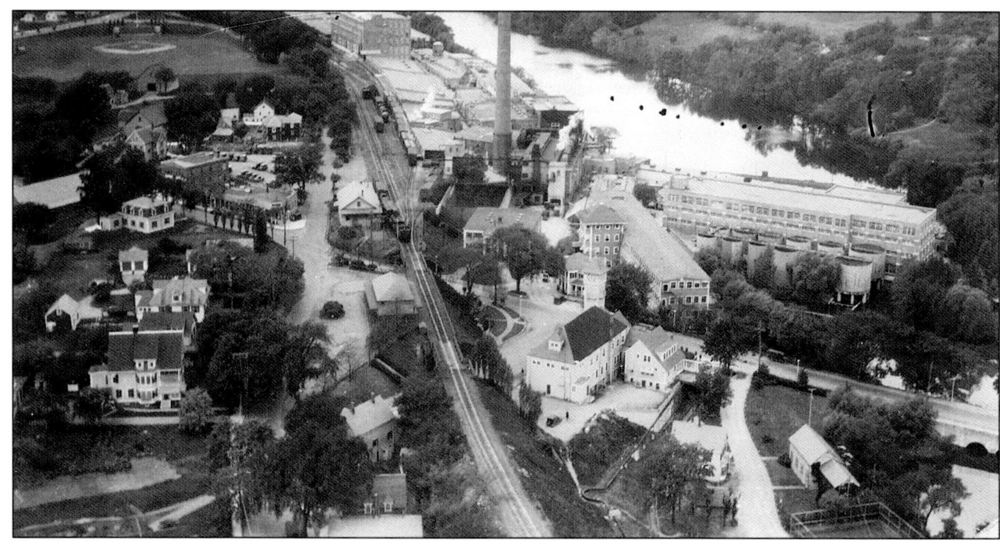

This is another panoramic view of East Walpole, looking toward Walpole Center. It was taken from a blimp in 1930. The many buildings of Bird and Son are to the right of the railroad tracks. Twelve large tanks hold water for paper making. At upper left is the Bird athletic field, the scene of many softball, baseball, and soccer games. In the late 1930s, Walpole High teams played their home games on this field. The open area in the lower left became the site of the new post office in 1940. Many of the trees in this photograph were destroyed by the 1938 hurricane.

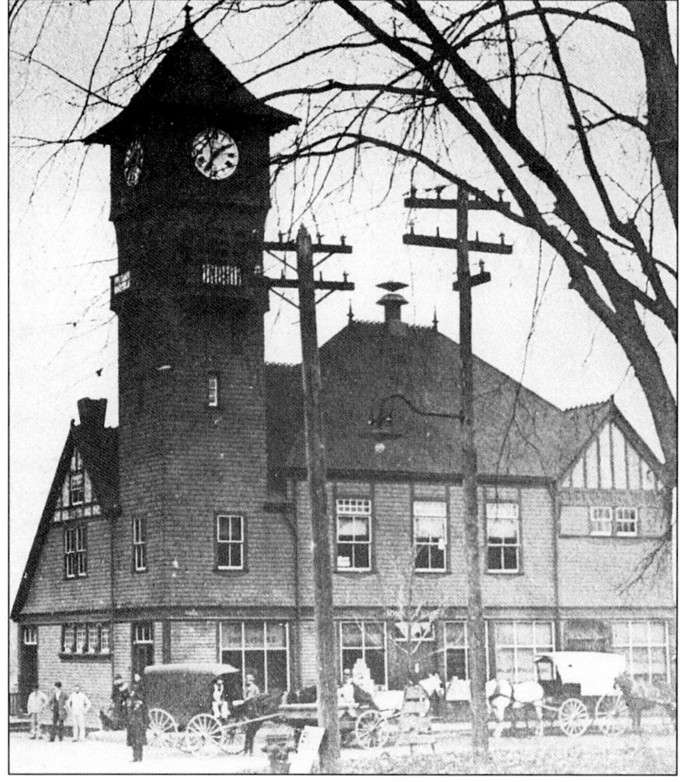

Bird Hall, the pride of East Walpole, was built in 1884 by Francis W. Bird for use by the community. The large second-floor hall was the scene of many lectures, banquets, plays, and "moving picture shows." It was also used for church services before St. Mary's Church was built. Postmaster John Freese operated a "department store" on the ground floor. The post office was located between "dry goods and groceries." In 1894, following the death of Mr. Bird, a fund to build a suitable memorial was established by residents and merchants. Bird heirs funded the 72-foot tower, and memorial funds were used to purchase an illuminated bell clock.

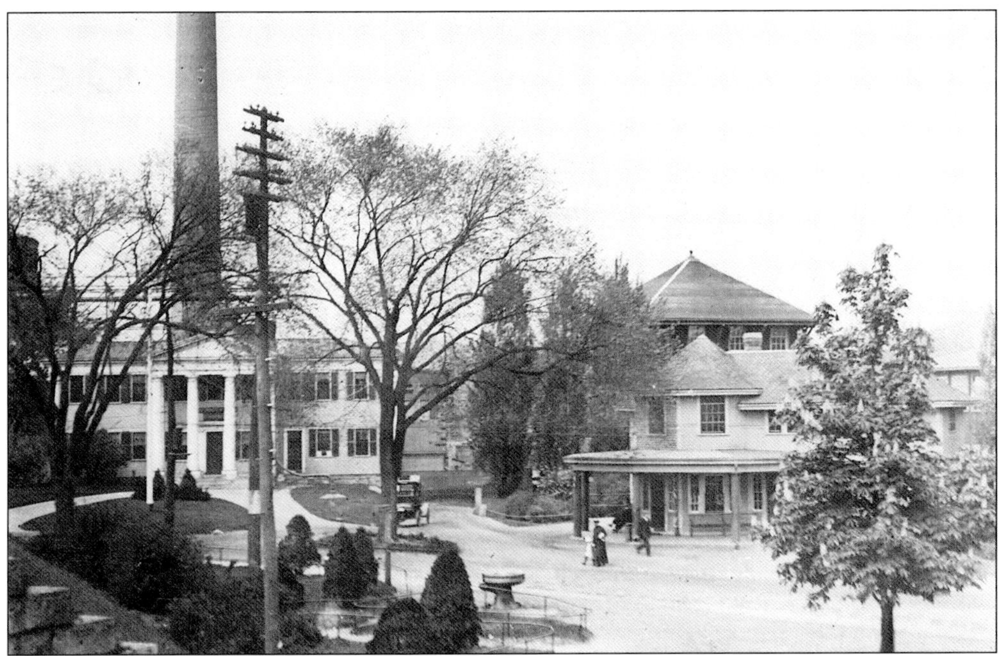

This undated photograph of Bird and Co. was taken before Washington Street was paved. The old Morse Tavern is gone, replaced with the triangle building. The stately chestnut tree was one of many elms and chestnuts planted around town in 1887 under the direction of the Improvement Society.

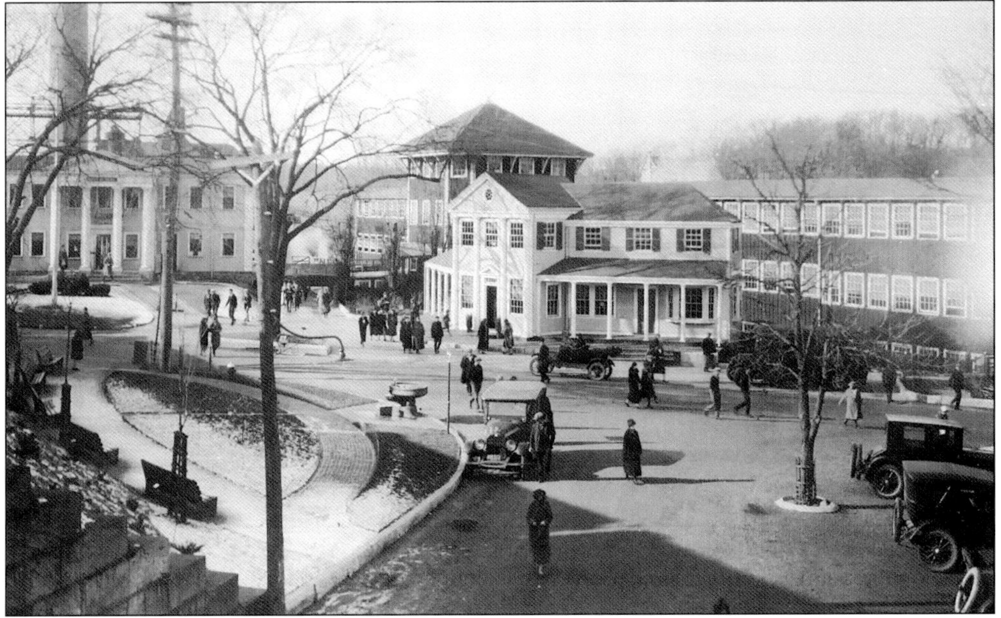

This scene occurred at the end of a work day at Bird and Son in East Walpole, c. 1920. The main office with its stately columns is at the left. The triangle building, housing the mill library, the employment office, and the hospital, can be seen at center. In the background is Box Shop #2. Washington and Chestnut Streets have been paved. A small park with a brick walkway and benches has been created around Miss Bird's fountain.

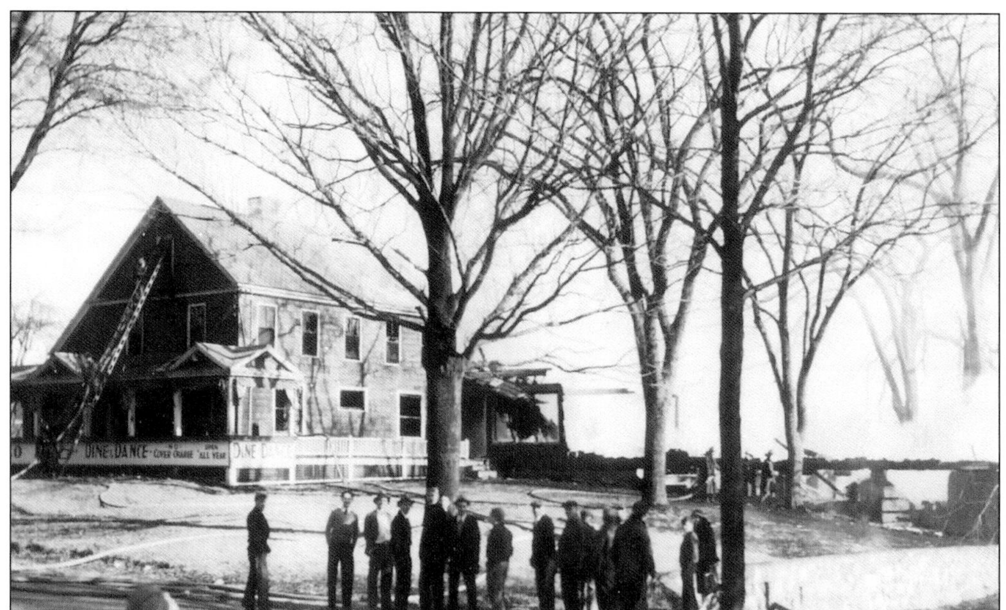

The Walpole Inn was located near the present site of Connolly's Garage on Main Street. The sign reads, "Dine & Dance No Cover Charge Open All Year." The Town Report of 1932 shows that a victualer's license was issued on May 27 to Salvatore Zimbaldi, d.b.a. Delmonico Inn, at this location. No license was issued in 1933. On Wednesday, January 18, 1933, a fire started at noon. Three alarms were sounded before the fire was brought under control at 6:15 p.m.

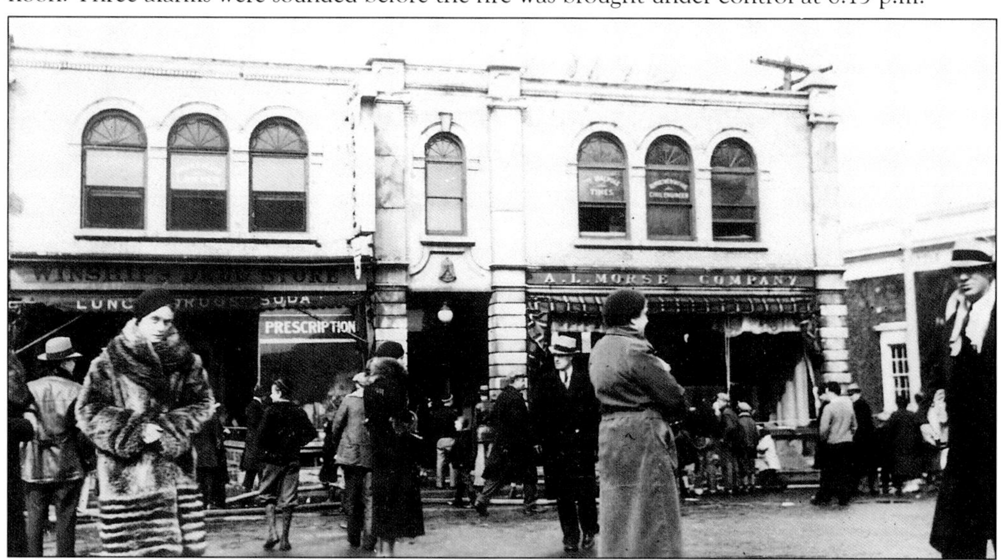

This view shows Walpole's Main Street, West Street, and the Glenwood Avenue intersection. The original structure at this site, *c.* 1829, was known as Bacon Hall. Reliance Lodge began meeting there in October 1881, when the lodge was founded. The building, owned by George E. Craig, became known as the IOOF Hall. A few years later the building burned down, and the Reliance Lodge bought the property and rebuilt the building. The new structure was dedicated as "Odd Fellows Hall" on December 12, 1901. A major modification was made in 1912 with the relocation of the hall to the back and the erection of a modern brick building in front with stores and offices. The present structure was built in 1935 by the Allen Construction Company.

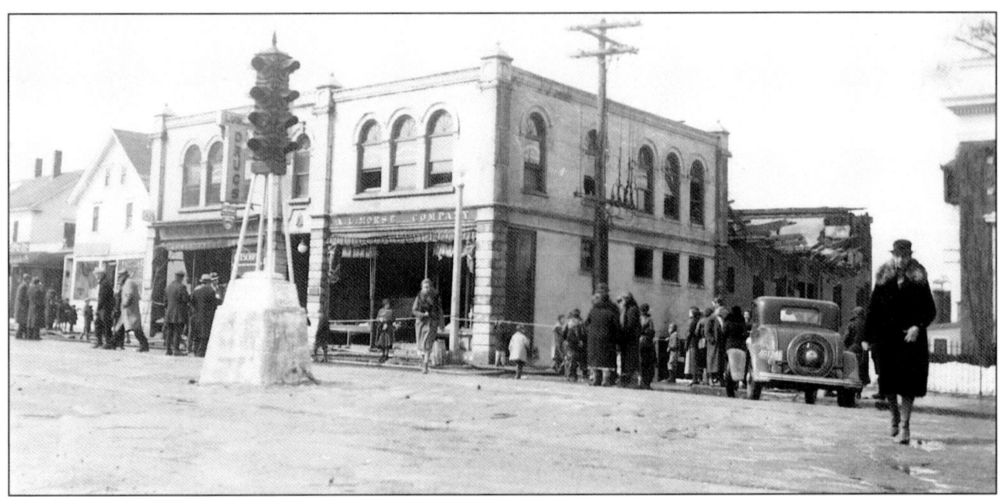

At 2:00 a.m. on Saturday, March 3, 1934, Police Sgt. Timothy Cullinane saw smoke billowing from the cellar windows of the Odd Fellows Building at the corner of West Street and Glenwood Avenue. Firemen quickly extinguished the fire in the cellar. Fire Chief Donnell made an inspection and found fire still smoldering within the upper floor partitions. The gas supply shut-off valve was not found before a small explosion of escaping gas occurred. The blaze reignited and gutted the interior of the building. An "all-out" was sounded at 8:00 a.m. Minor injuries were sustained by fireman William McDowell and Lieutenant Ralph Bassy. This photograph shows an intact facade, while a side view, seen below, reveals the extent of the damage.

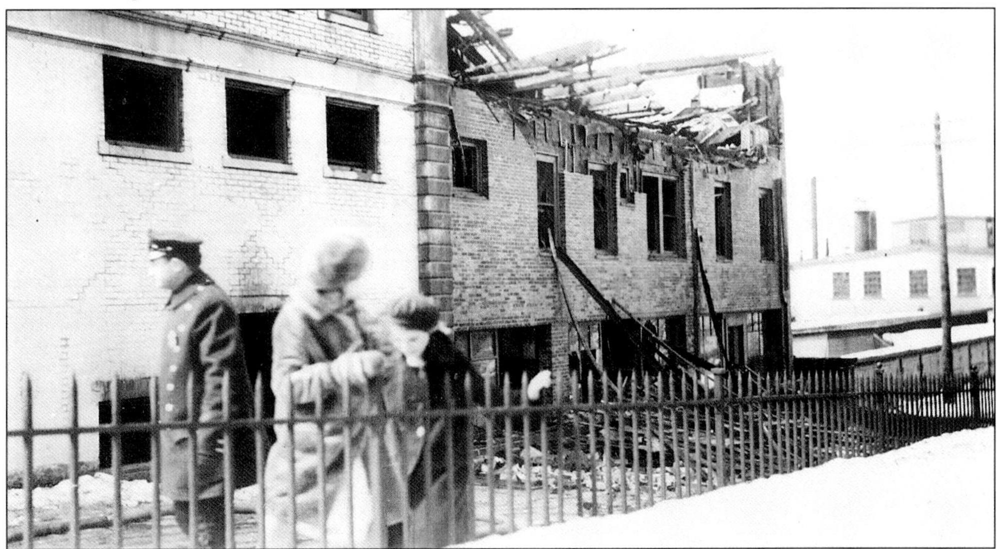

The damage to the Odd Fellows Building was easier to see from the Glenwood Avenue side. The iron fence marks the boundary line of Walpole Trust (now BankBoston) at the corner of Main Street. In the background is L.F. Fales Machine Shop. The Odd Fellows Building was owned by Reliance Lodge No. 137 of the IOOF. Tenants were Morse Dry Goods, Winship Drugs, the *Walpole Times*, dentist William Maguire, civil engineer Kenneth McIntyre, and lawyers George F. James and Richard H. Kannally. The large hall in the rear was a regular meeting place for 12 different groups and a social gathering place for wedding receptions, dances, lectures, and civic affairs. Losses totaled $120,000.

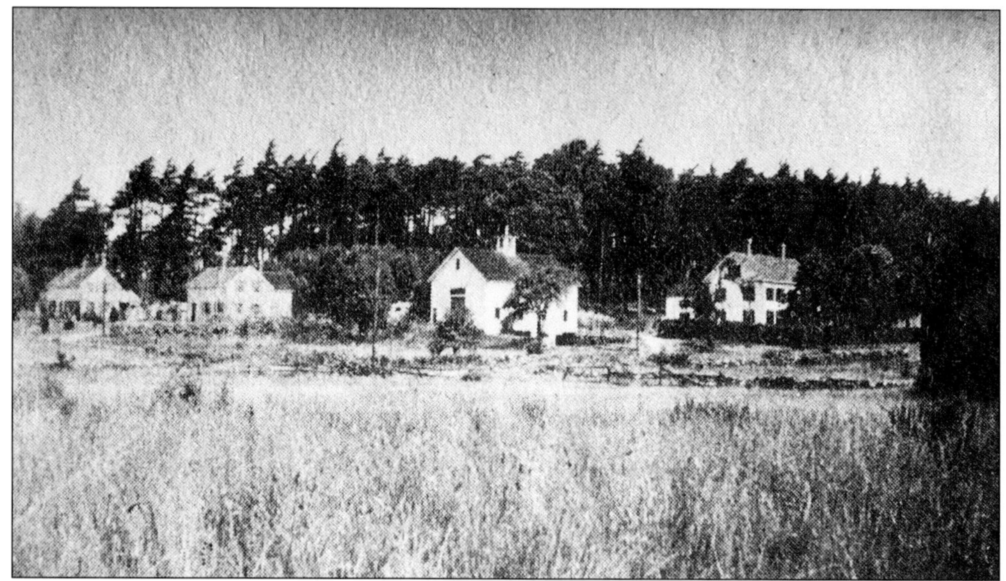

The Robbins Farm property dates to 1710, when the first homestead was built. The property stayed in the Robbins family until 1911, when it was given to the state department of charities. It became a home for young female state wards. By the time the program was suspended in 1934, five hundred girls had passed through. The Ballou family then rented the property. The main house, on the right side of the photograph, was located at the site of the present "stump dump." The barn was located on the present site of the VFW Hall. In the background is the grove of majestic pines that was leveled by the infamous hurricane of 1938.

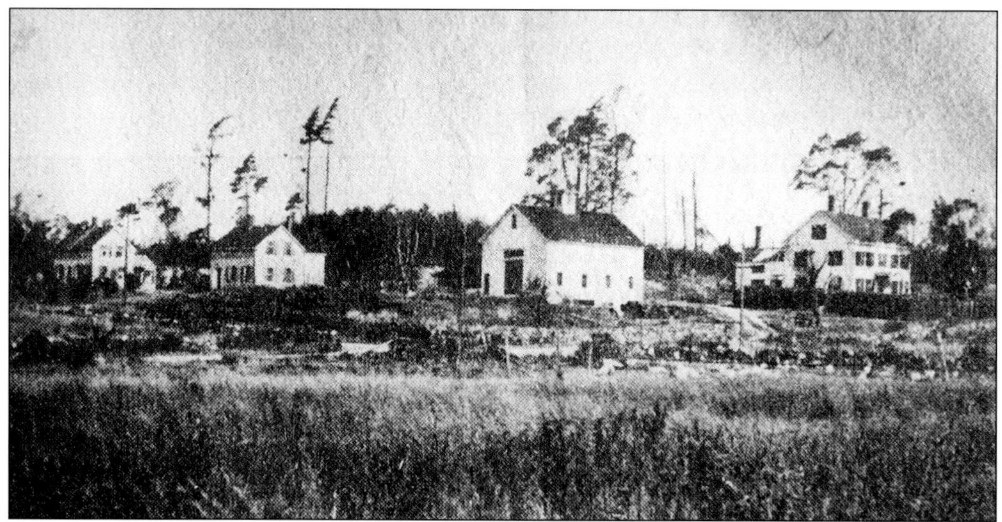

On Wednesday, September 21, 1938, New England was hit by a ferocious hurricane that left 685 dead and vast devastation. A wind gust at the Blue Hills Observatory measured 186 mph. Only one Walpole citizen died, Miss Marion Child, the sister of Mrs. Charles Bird. She was in an automobile that was hit by a falling tree on Nahatan Street in Norwood. This photograph shows the extent of the deforestation at Robbins Farm. The houses and barn, however, appear intact. The trunks of fallen pines were floated on Stetson Pond and later were cut into lumber at portable sawmills set up by the State. In 1949, the State gave the property to the Town to be used for the benefit of veterans. The property was used for housing and the VFW Hall.

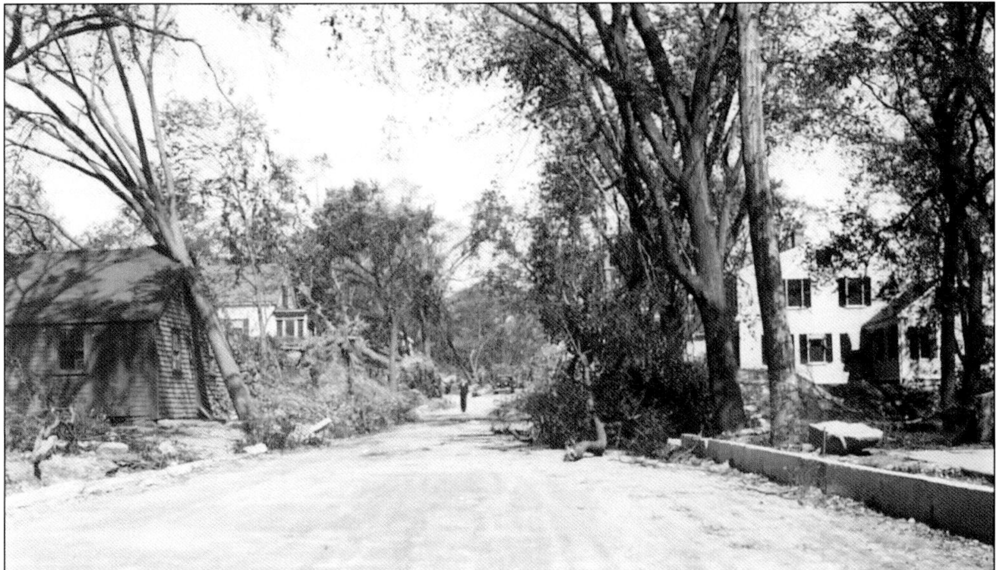
The aged Danom Forge blacksmith shop building supported a tall tree that succumbed to the hurricane's ill winds. The tree is long gone but the building still stands. The house at right is part of the Hollingsworth and Vose Company.

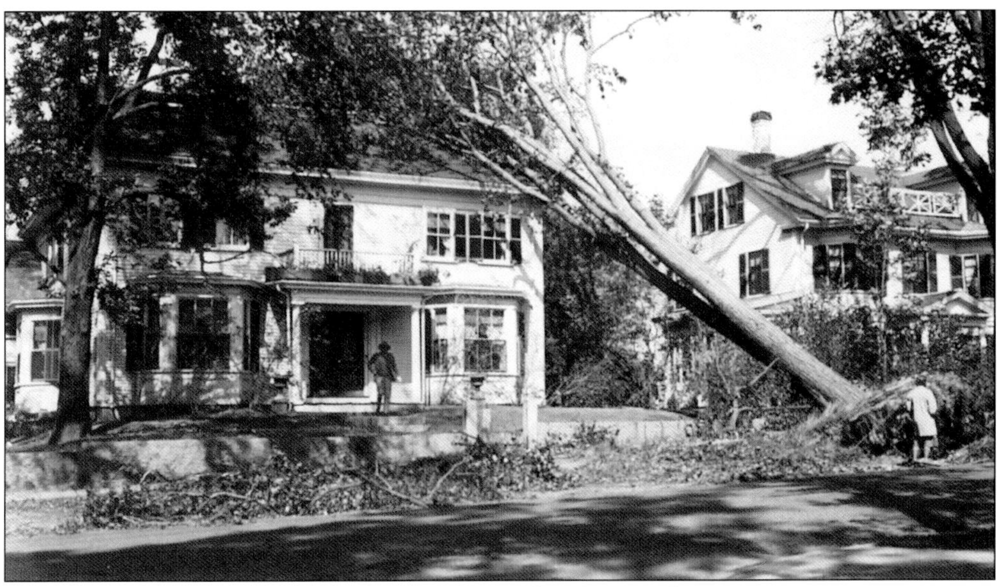
The Deacon Willard Lewis House is shown here after the 1938 hurricane.

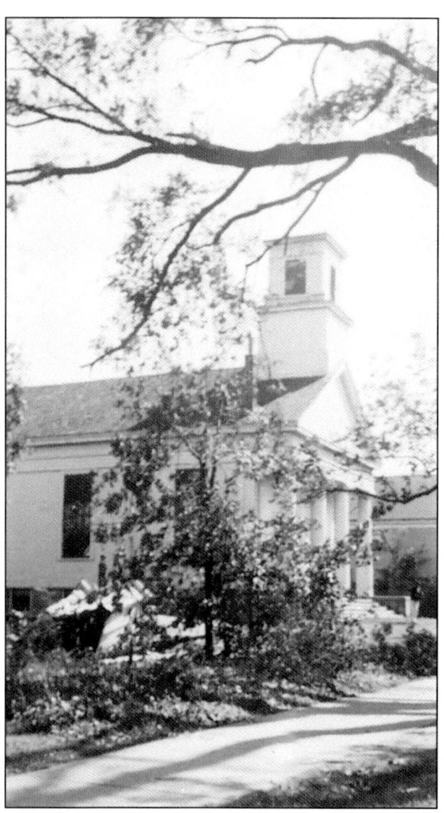

The skyline of many New England towns featured white church steeples that were no match for the hurricane's disrespectful wind. They fell by the hundreds. The steeples of Walpole's Orthodox Congregational Church on East Street and the Unitarian Church (pictured here) on Common Street both fell. Part of the steeple can be seen to the left of the small tree trunk.

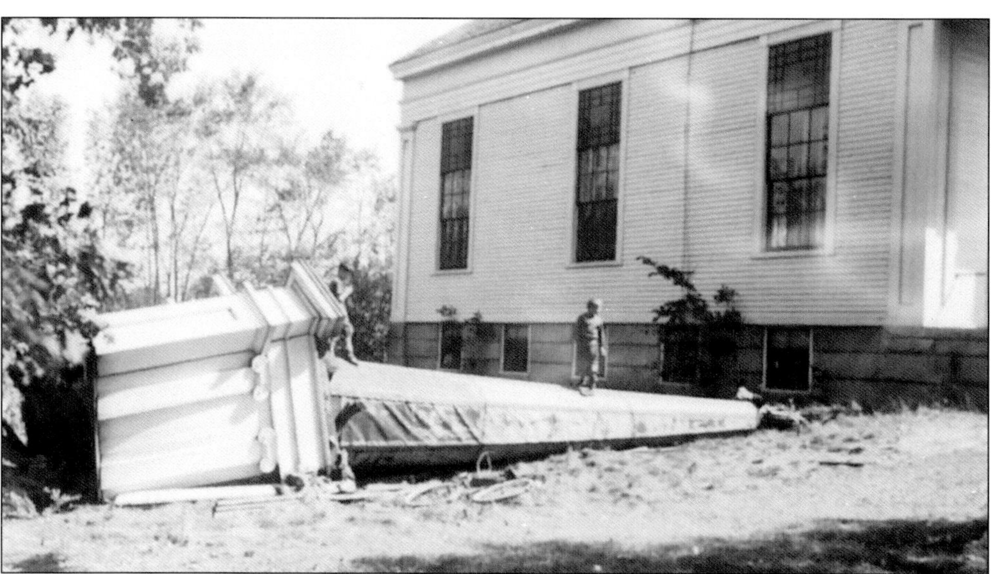

Boys will be boys! This closeup of the fallen Unitarian Church's spire suggests the diversions enjoyed by the younger set in the midst of the devastation suffered by their elders. The wrinkled appearance of the spire indicates evidence of copper sheathing. It was rumored that, within minutes of the toppling, two local looters were apprehended while trying to remove the valuable copper.

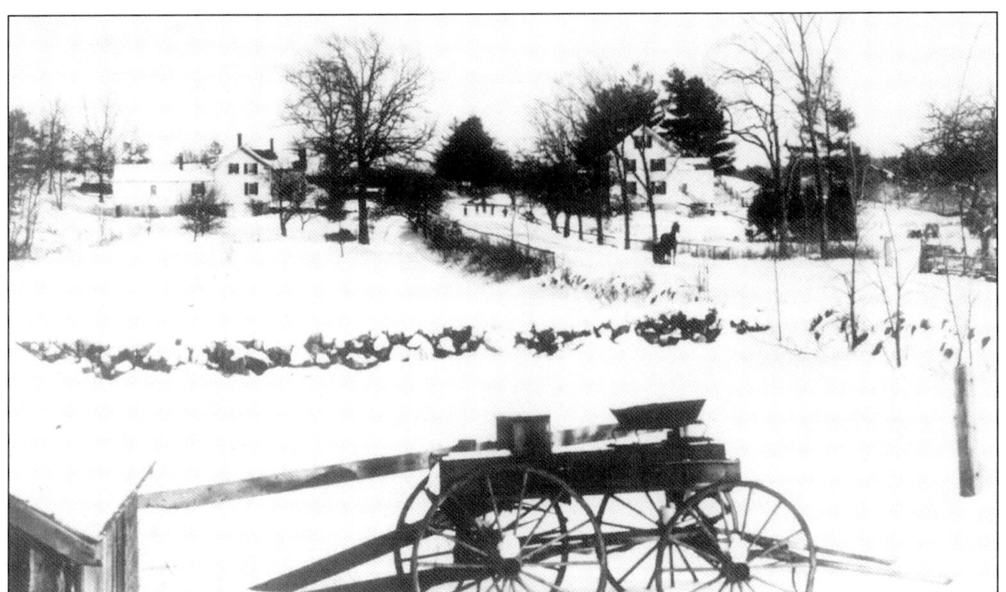

Looking east from Allen's Farm (Walpole Woodworkers today), there was little traffic on East Street (Route 27) when this photograph was taken on a snowy day in 1895. At that time Walpole Woodworkers, Allen's Pond, and the railroad bridge (top of picture) did not exist.

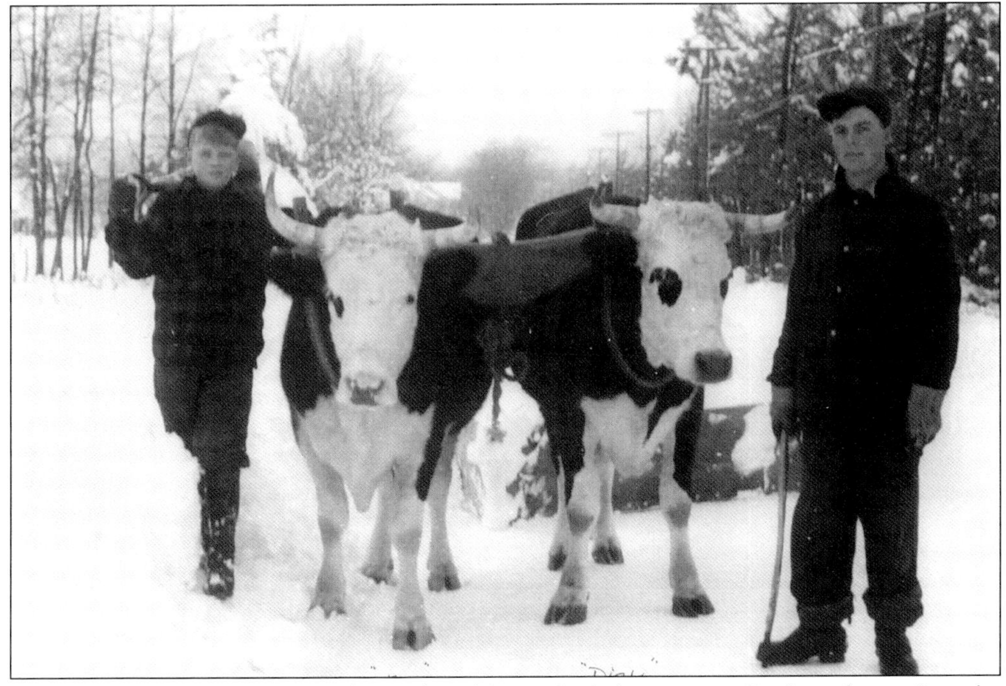

Leroy Jones (left), "Tom," "Dick," and Ted Jones (right) set out to "make a fortune" in the snow-plowing business during the very snowy winter of 1946–47.

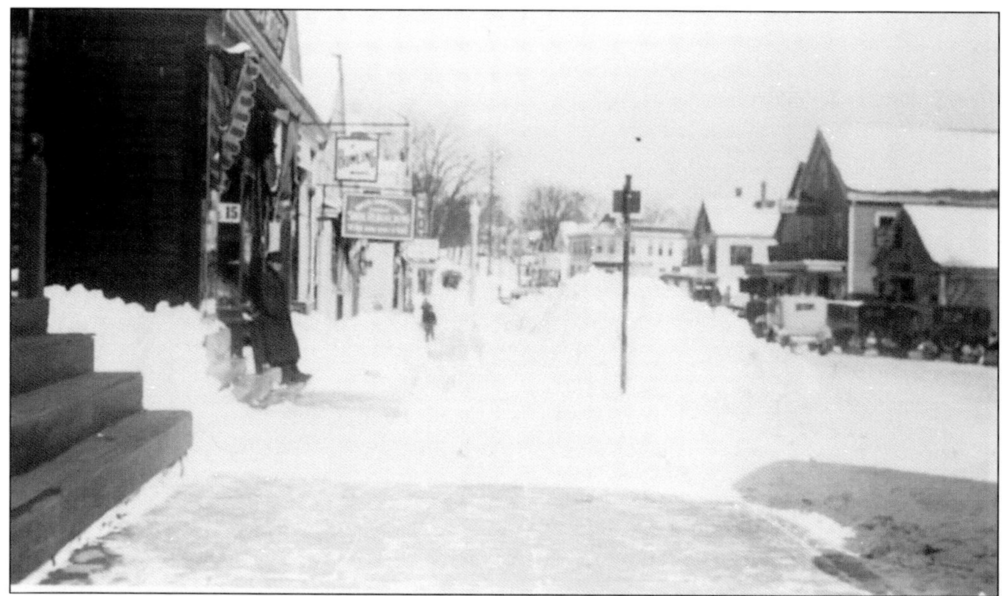

Occasionally the snow fall was heavy. This 1935 scene shows Main Street looking north. The "Bowling" sign points to the backyard location of T. Edward Kannally's alleys. Next door, Ernest Mannochio offers "expert shoe rebuilding while you wait." The sign with the vertical letters "ELIT" marks the location of the Elite Motion Picture Theater. At center is the only building still standing today, the Plimpton Block at the corner of Main and East Streets.

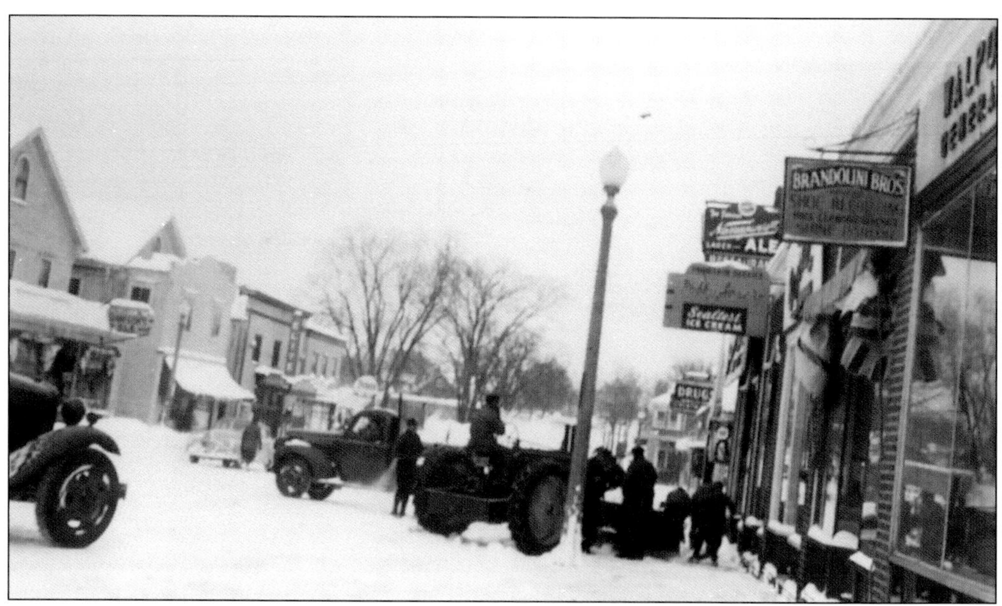

This image was taken on Sunday, January 18, 1948, as a snow removal crew was working overtime on the east side of Main Street. The signs, from left to right, identify Joe Ciannavei's Market, Paul Camelio's Package Store, Anselmo Franceschelli's Elite Movie Theater, Rollie Giandomenico's Tydol Gas Station, Haney's Drug Store, Sargent's Cafe, the Bobby Soxer Sandwich Shop, and the Brandolini Brothers Shoe Repair Store.

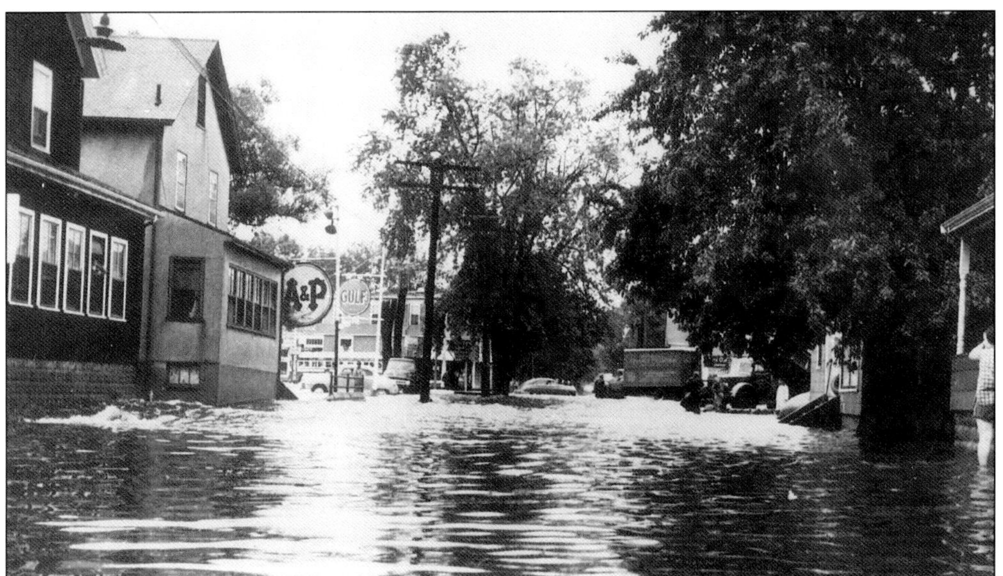

On Thursday, August 18, 1955, Hurricane Diane almost drowned Walpole. Three days of heavy rain swelled the Neponset River and its tributary brooks to flood levels. The dam at Diamond Pond broke, launching a torrent that cut a canyon through the new Diamond Street roadway. A mini tsunami wave engulfed Memorial Pond. The culvert under Main Street was inadequate for the flow. This view is of East Street looking eastward to the intersection of Main Street. Although resembling a picturesque Venetian Canal, the predominately Italian neighborhood including the Bornardi, Giandomenico, Giorgi, Paglari, Penza, and Saraca properties suffered heavy losses. The lack of traffic control allowed passing vehicles to produce waves, intensifying the damage.

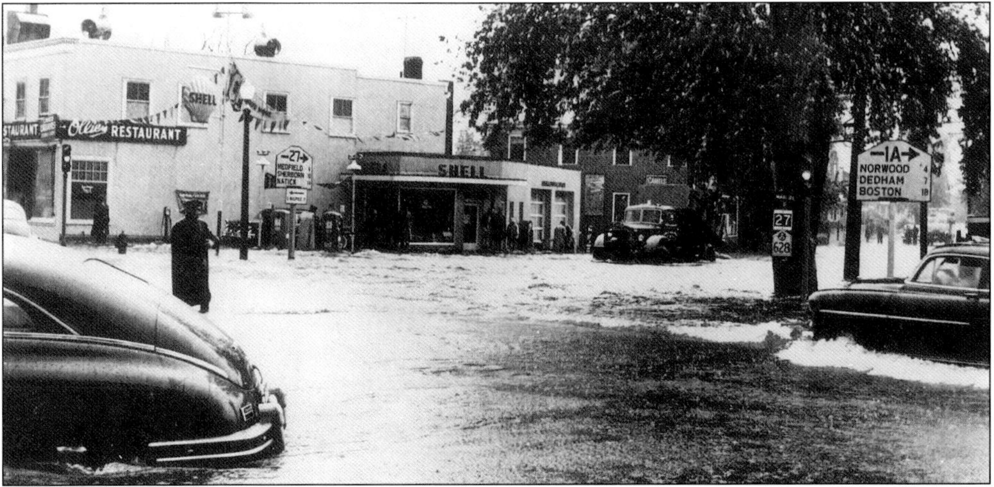

At the intersection of Main and East Streets, a 1949 Packard (left) lies stranded. Under the Route 27 sign is another sign identifying the road as Civil Defense Route 628. During the Cold War of the 1950s, a network of roads was designated alternate "escape" routes. Route 27, ironically, was an alternate to Route 128. At the height of the flooding, all roads to Walpole were blocked by washouts and other obstructions. The Shell Gas Station was operated by Danny Giandomenico. Ollie Hasting's Restaurant would later become Tee-T's under the proprietorship of Artelio Silvi and his sister, Mary Civita.

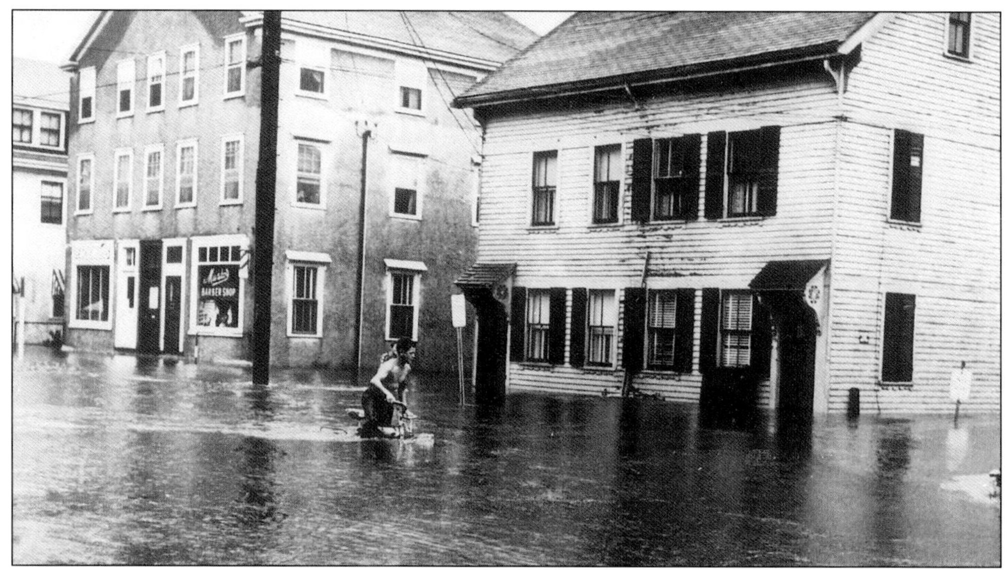

This image was taken on Friday, August 19, 1955, on East Street. At the far left is the Procaccini home and store, the present site of Hoops and Needles. The second structure contained Aldo Pellini's Tailor Shop (now Gene Federico's Walpole Music Studio) and Tony Musto's Barbershop. The house on the right is no longer standing. The unidentified muscular lad on the amphibious bicycle serves as a benchmark for water depth while proving that boys will be boys.

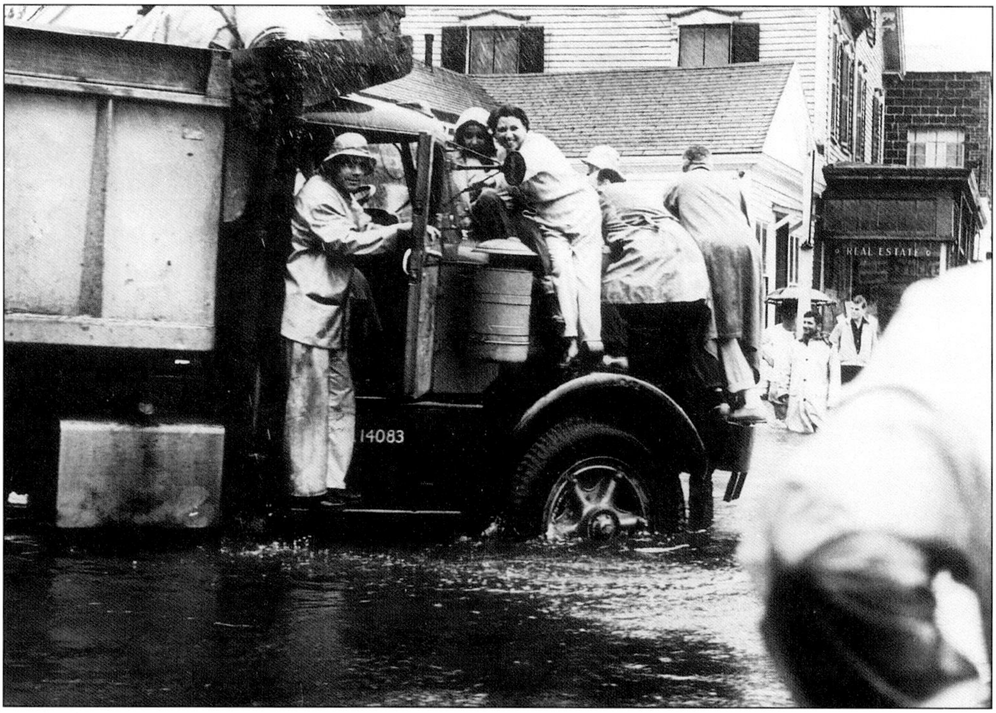

Walpole DPW to the rescue! The Musto family, Joey, Frances, and Tony, are moved to higher ground. The tour guide resembles Jim Clerici. Holding the delicate umbrella is Dom Rignanese, proprietor of the coffee shop obscured by the rescue truck.

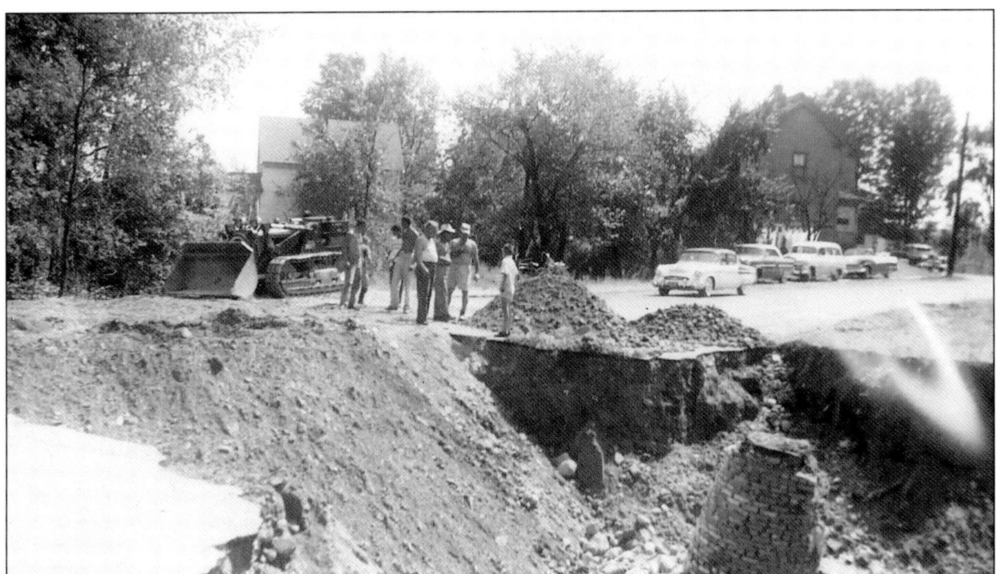

This image was taken on Saturday, August 27, 1955, after the floods had subsided. New Diamond Street is undergoing a fill-in of the 30-foot ravine gouged out by the torrent from Diamond Pond.

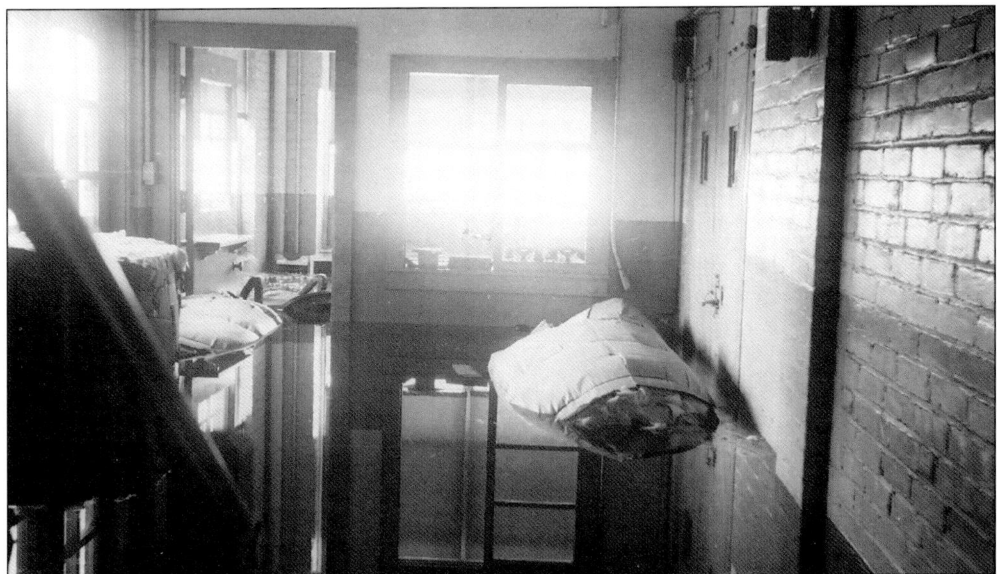

Walpole industries were born as by-products of the Colonial "Water-Power Privileges." Their locations by the waterways gave easy access to the power provided by moving waters. By 1955, long after waterpower had become obsolete, the riverside locations lost value and became expensive liabilities. Hurricane Diane transformed the Neponset River from a scenic feature to a swollen menace. The Kendall Mills plant on West Street reported a $20,000 loss. The value of lost wages during the flood was not included in Kendall's claim.

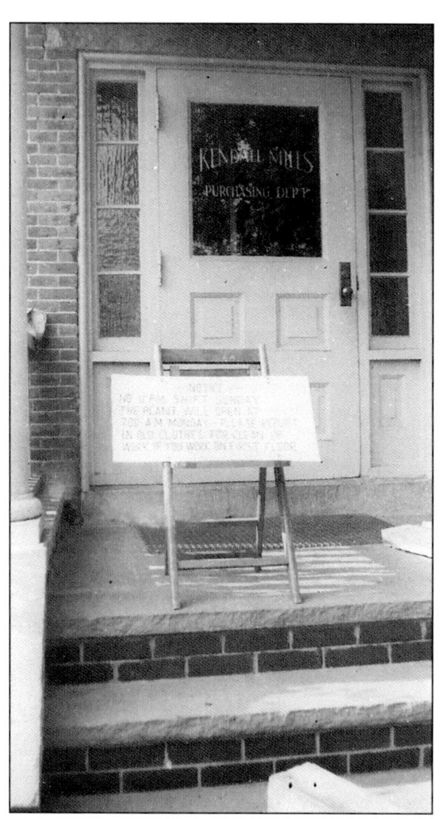

This image, taken on Sunday, August 28, 1955, shows a sign at the Kendall Company's front door. It reads: "Notice—No 11.00 p.m. Shift Sunday. The Plant Will Open at 7:00 a.m. Monday—Please Report in Old Clothes for Clean-up Work if You Work on First Floor."

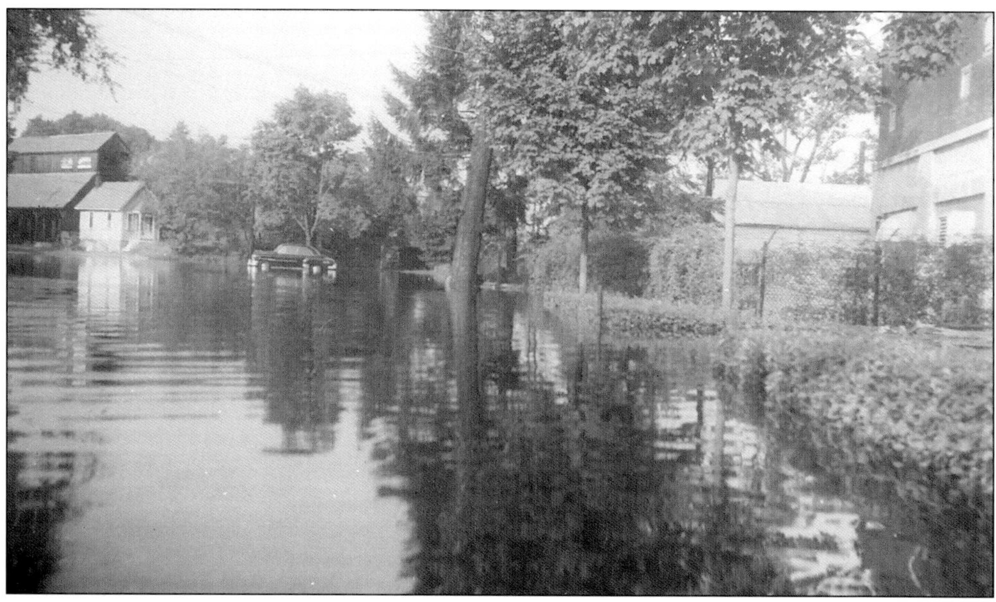

This Friday, August 19, 1955 photograph shows West Street with the Frank Fisher Coal Company (at left).

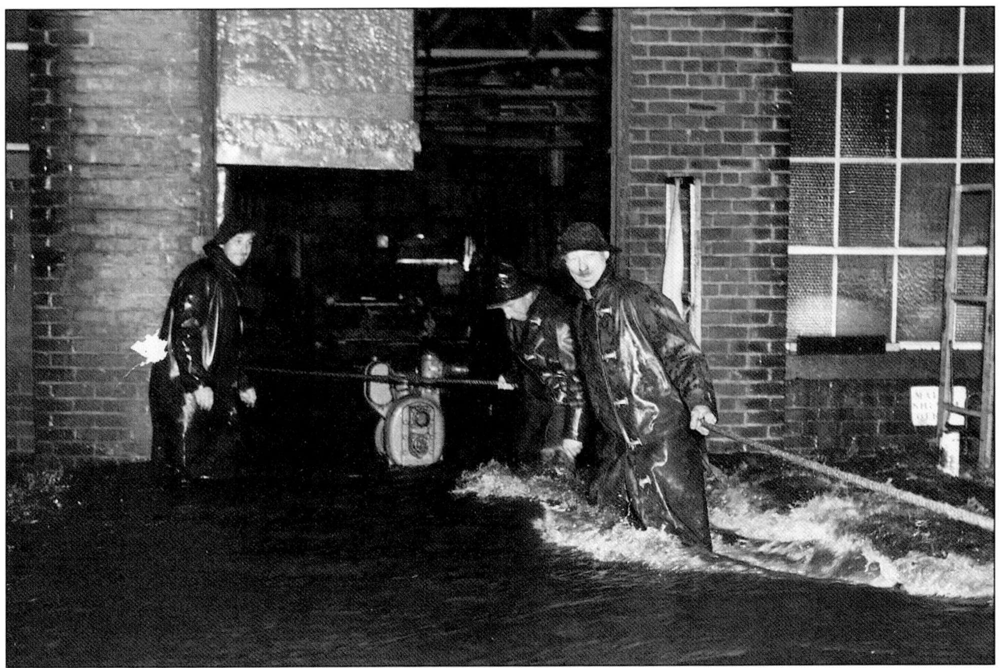

A crew at Bird's Floor Covering Plant clings to lifelines in a vain attempt to protect property while the rushing floodwaters hinder their progress.

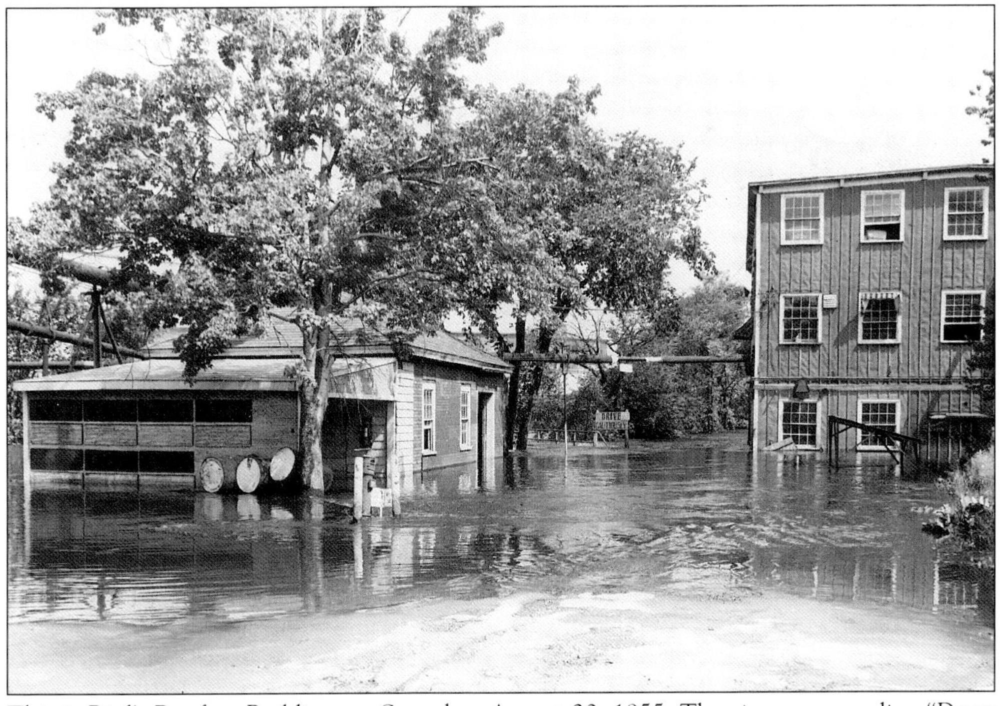

This is Bird's Roofing Building on Saturday, August 20, 1955. The sign commanding "DRIVE CAUTIOUSLY" is adjacent to the bridge over the Neponset River.

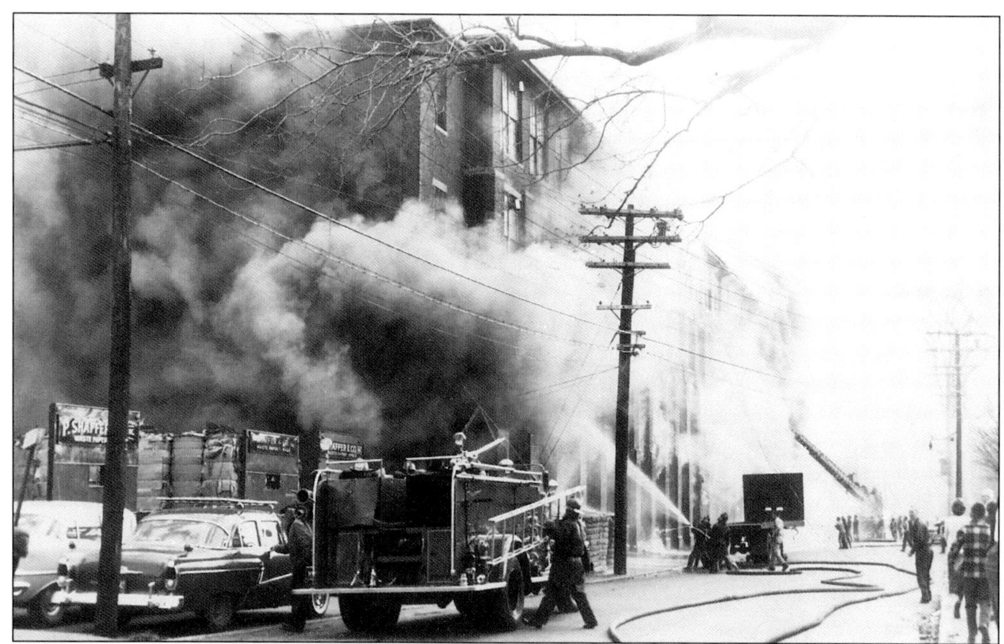

At 1:59 p.m. on Tuesday, October 29, 1957, a fire alarm sounded. The P. Schaffer Co. waste paper and rag reclamation plant on South Street was the scene of a fire. The building was built in 1910 as the Walpole Rubber Company (it later became the Multibestos Plant). The *Walpole Times* described the fire as the town's "closest approach to a major tragedy since the Odd Fellows blaze in 1934." One hundred fifty firemen, including those from seven surrounding towns, and 17 firetrucks fought the blaze. The high school football team left their nearby practice field to assist. The first firemen on the scene heard frantic screams from trapped workers.

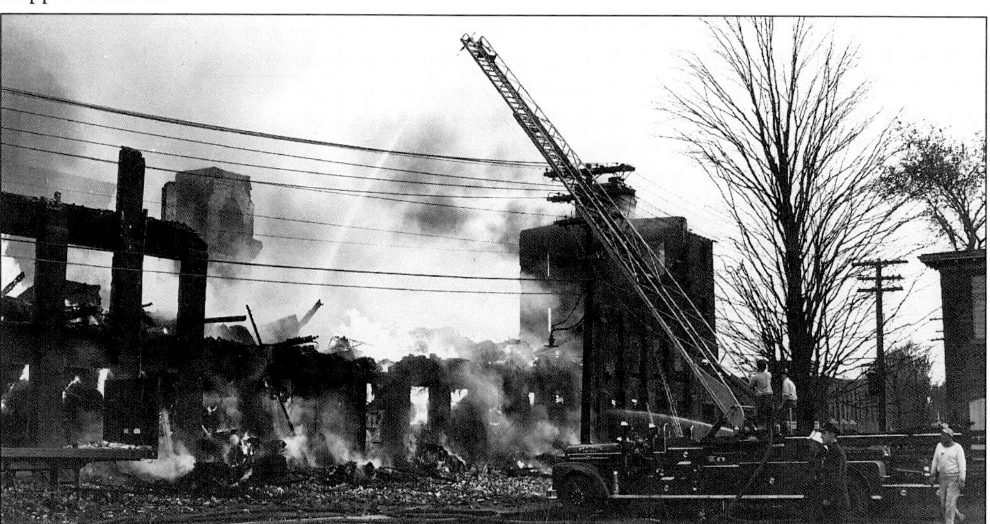

Fireman John Dalton entered the burning building and found Josephine Iagatta, Doris MacKinnon, and Violet Perrault. He helped them exit from a second-floor window. Firemen John Comfort, Ross Leper, and brothers Bob and Fred Mattson placed a roof ladder on a bale of waste paper and carried the ladies to safety. All were sent to the hospital and treated for smoke inhalation. In the picture a Westwood firetruck is directing a stream of water into the inferno.

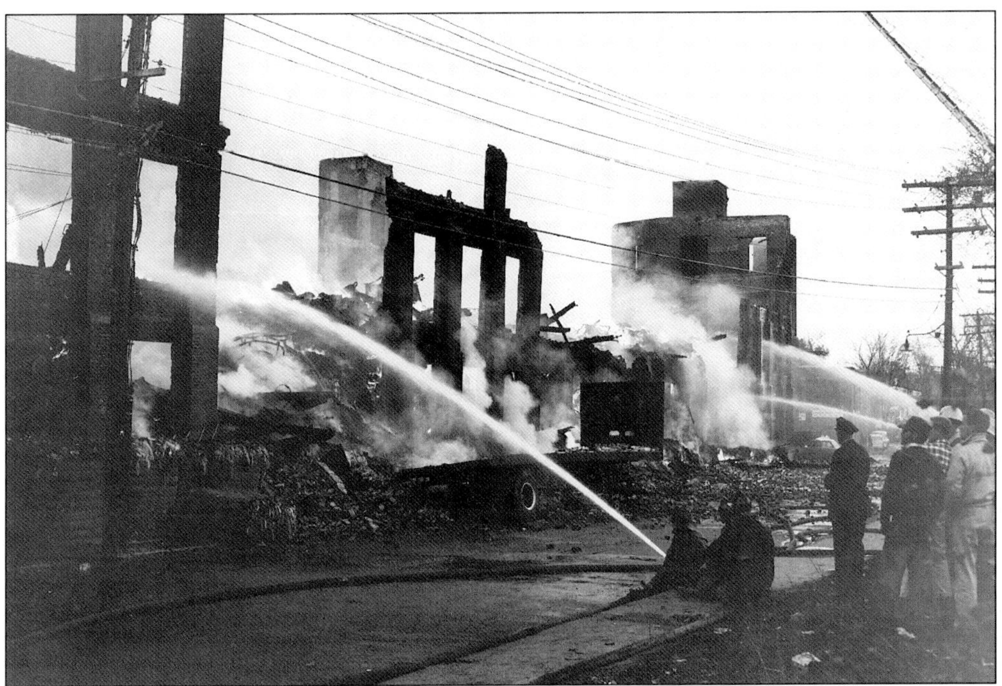

On Thursday, October 31, 1957, the fire at the Schaffer Company was still smoldering. Three firetrucks poured continuous streams of water onto the ruins.

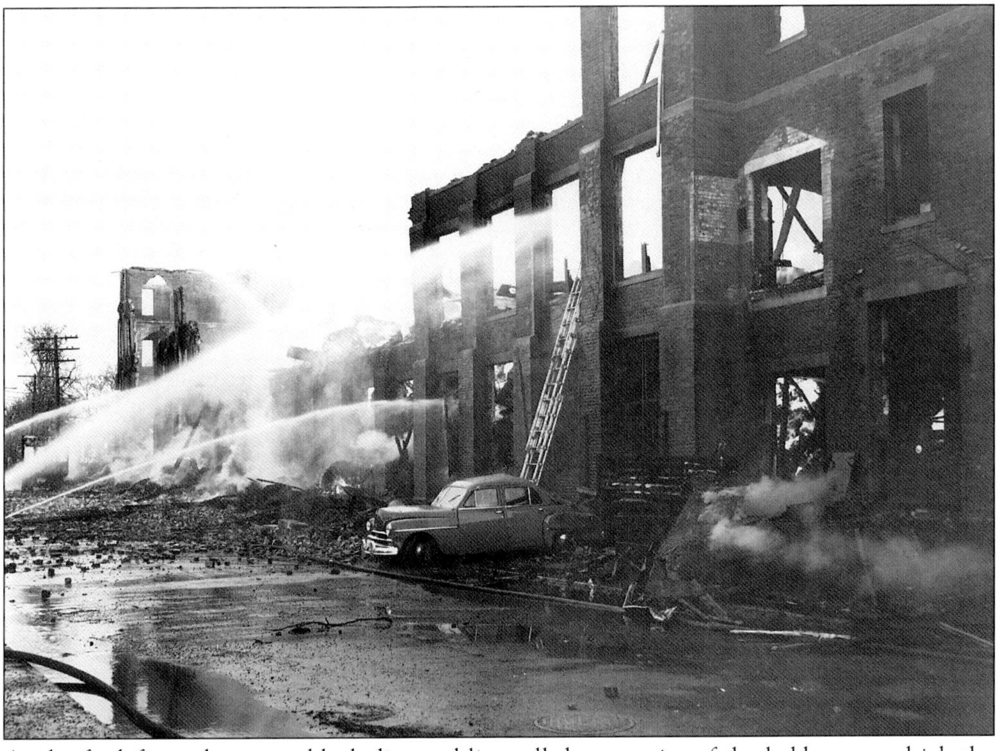

At the far left can be seen a black diagonal line, all that remains of the ladder over which the three women had been rescued.

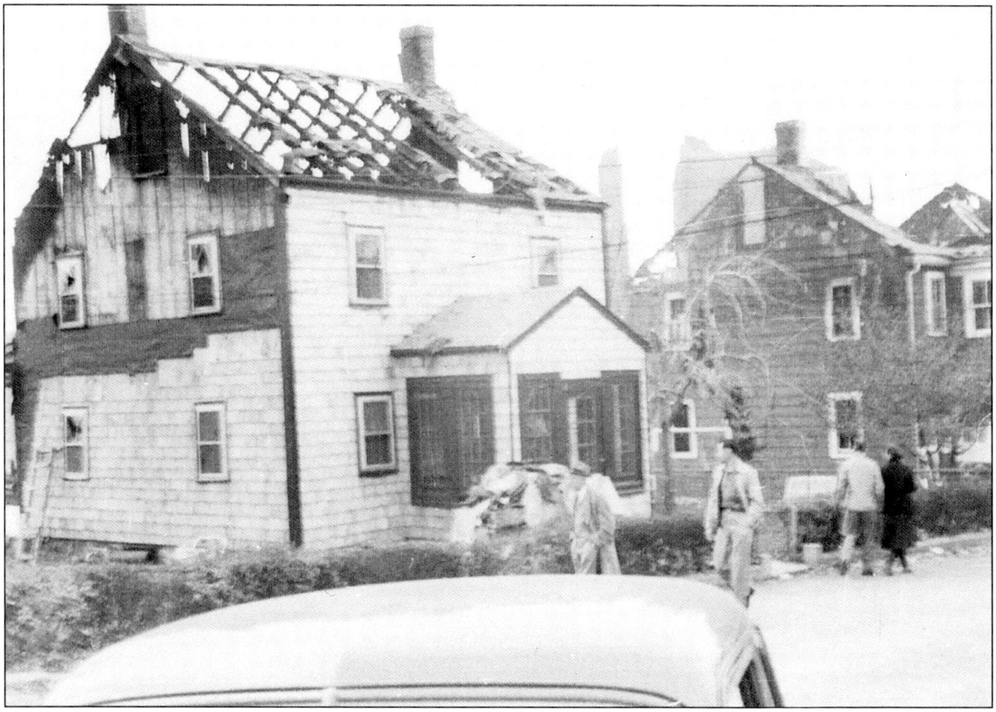

Around the corner on Gleason Court, two houses were destroyed by the intense heat of the Schaffer conflagration. The families of Michael Cashorali, William Loder, Daniel Iagatta, and Louis Santomarco were made homeless.

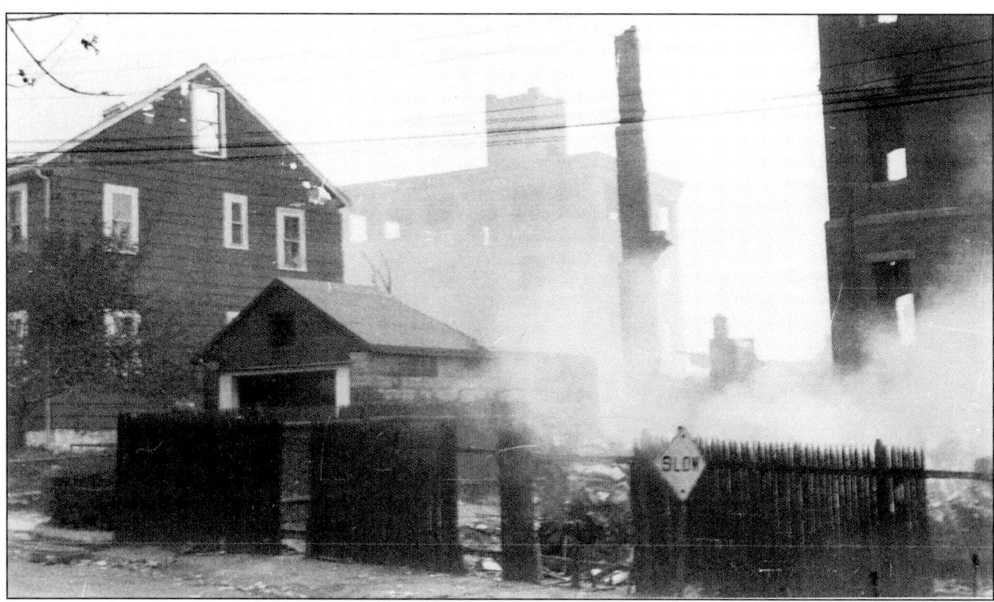

This view of the burned shell of the Schaffer Building was taken from the corner of South Street and Gleason Court.

Eight

Houses of Worship

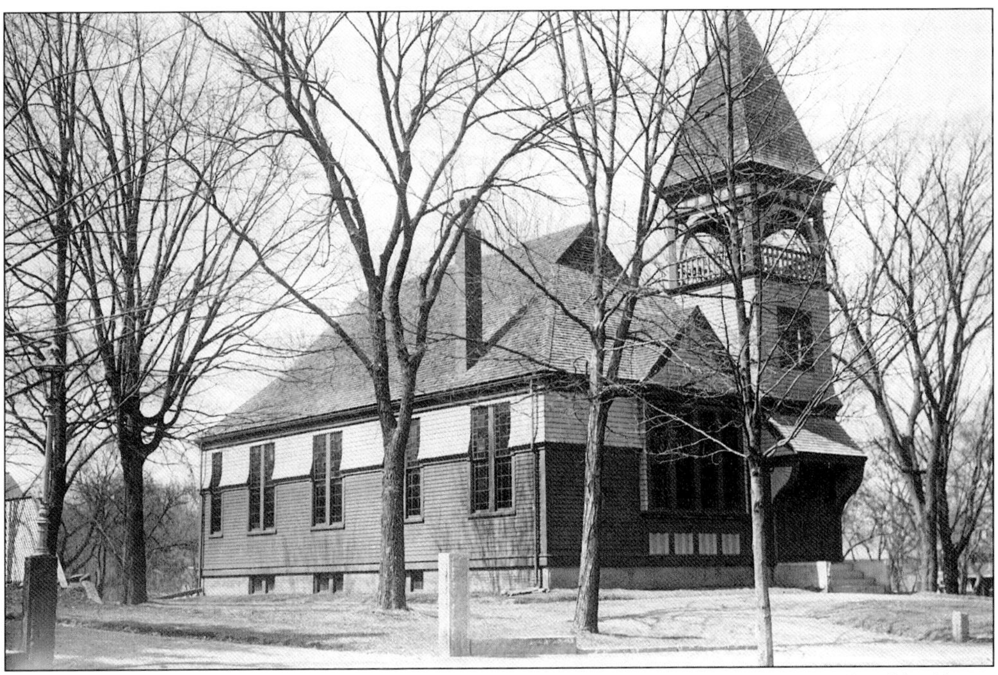

This is a 1916 picture of the Methodist Episcopal Church. The Center District School had been located on this Front Street site until it was destroyed by fire in 1884. Rev. John H. Vincent purchased the vacant lot for $1,000, and this church was built in 1886. Reverend Noon, the first pastor, and his 12-member congregation had held their services in a section of the hoopskirt factory (Main Street) referred to as the "Methodist Hall." Today the United Church rectory sits on the granite foundation of this church.

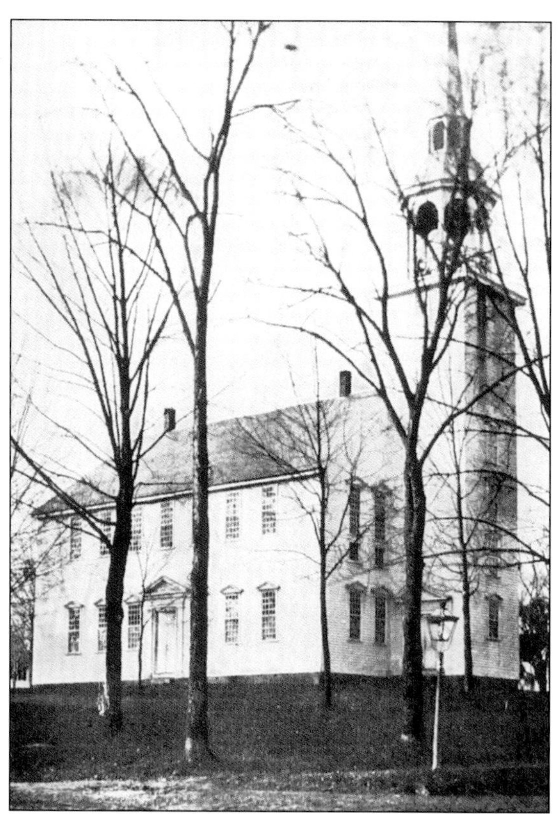

In November 1782, the Town voted to replace the First Meeting House. Under the supervision of Adam Blackman, the First Meeting House was razed and this new Second Meeting House was completed in 1783. In 1839, the meetinghouse was moved to 30 Common Street, where it remained until 1939, when it was demolished to make room for the new United Church. The large stone cross on Walpole Common now marks the site of the First Meeting House. A state law enacted in 1833 severed the connection between church and commonwealth, thus ending 109 years of "Welfare" support by public taxation.

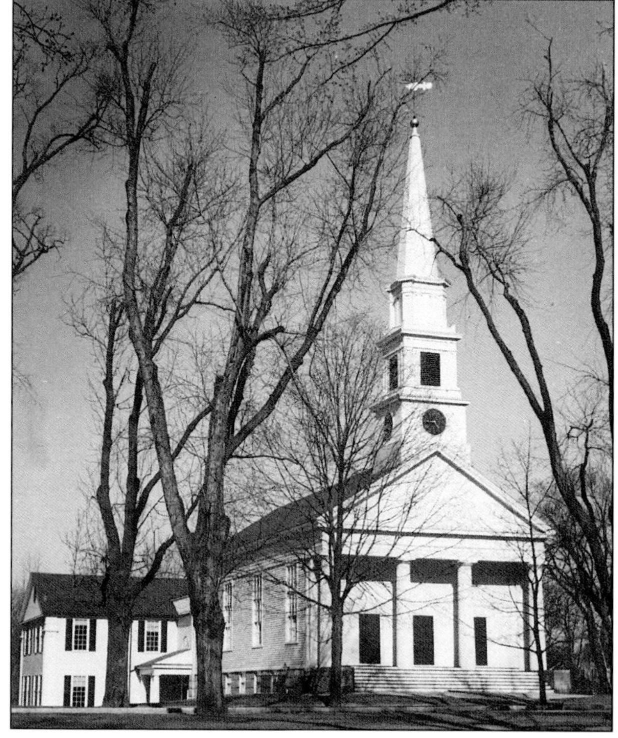

The Methodists, Unitarians, and the First Parish Church Congregational merged in 1927 to form the United Church in Walpole. Located on Common Street, some timbers in this structure date to the 1726 meetinghouse. In the chapel are stained-glass panels that were originally part of the Methodist Episcopal Church. Located on the back wall of the church, just below the balcony, is a large clock from the East Street Orthodox Congregational Church. The steeple was restored after suffering damage in the 1938 hurricane.

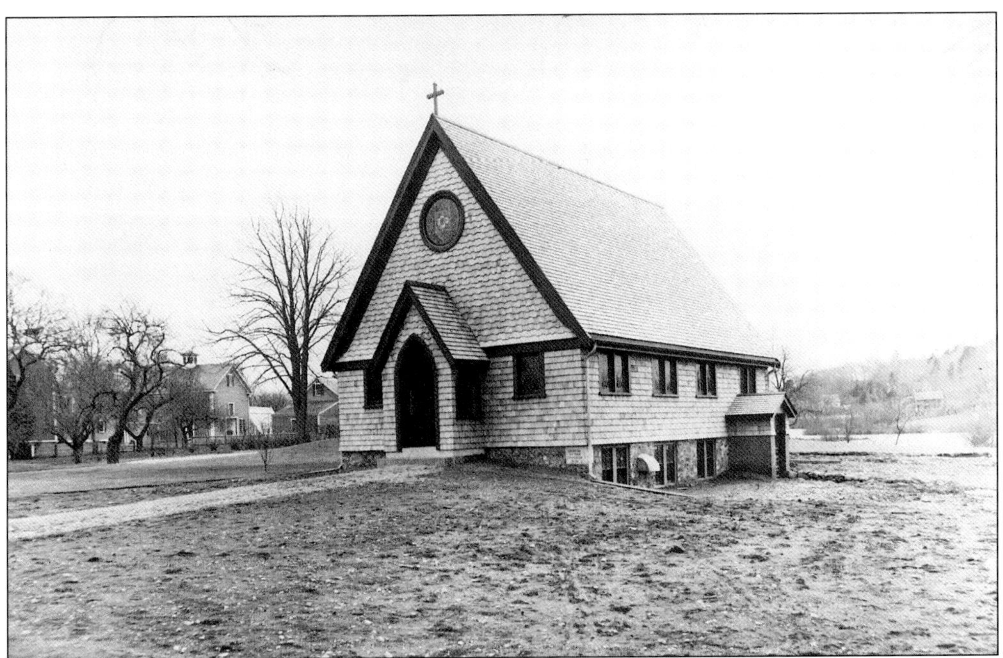

The Epiphany Episcopal Church was originally organized as St. Mark's Episcopal Church. Rev. Albert E. George, the first pastor, held services in Bacon Hall (the Odd Fellows Building). The present church (62 Front Street) was built in 1902 during the pastorate of Rev. William T. Dakin. In later years the weight of the roof caused the walls to buckle, and external buttresses were added.

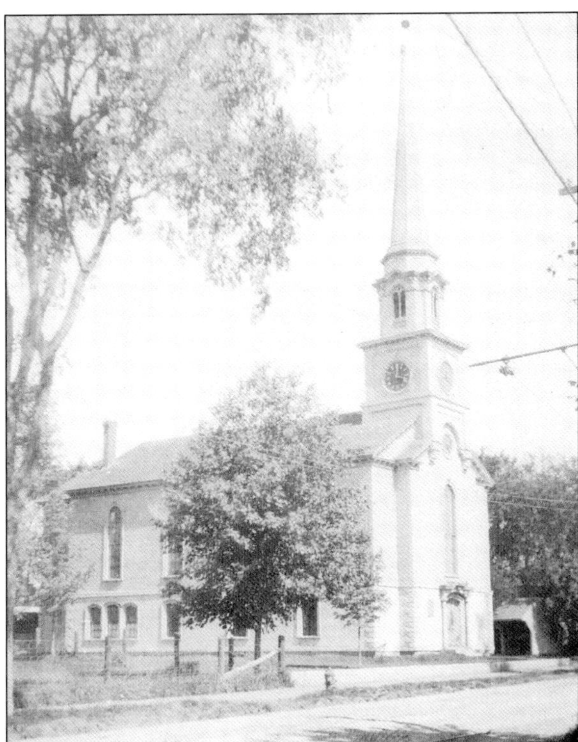

Dissatisfied with the teachings of the church, 82 members of the congregation presented a petition to dissolve their connection with the First Church. In November 1826, this group formed the Orthodox Congregational Society at the home of Catherine Allen. Two church bells rang on a September Sunday in 1827 at the dedication of the new church on East Street. The church was razed after being extensively damaged by the 1938 hurricane. Gallo's Flowers is on the site today.

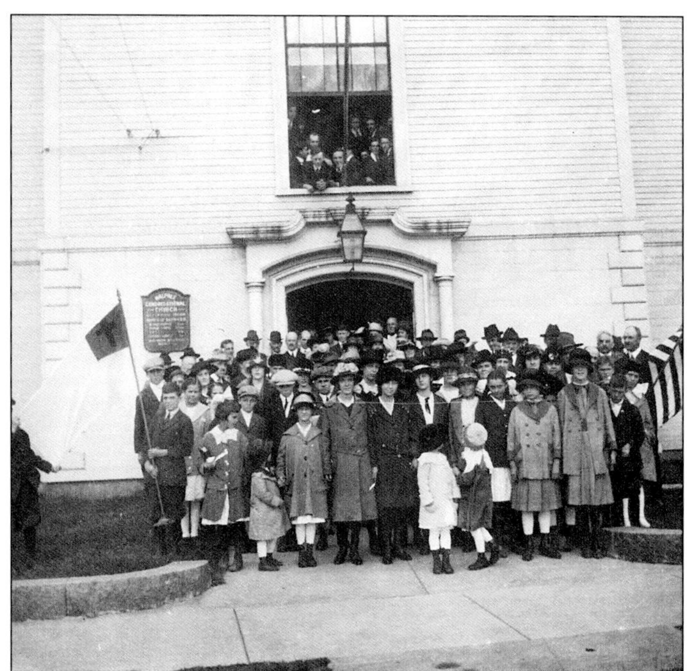

The Armistice has been signed and World War I has finally come to a close. Happy members of the Orthodox Congregational Church gather in front of their church on East Street in 1918.

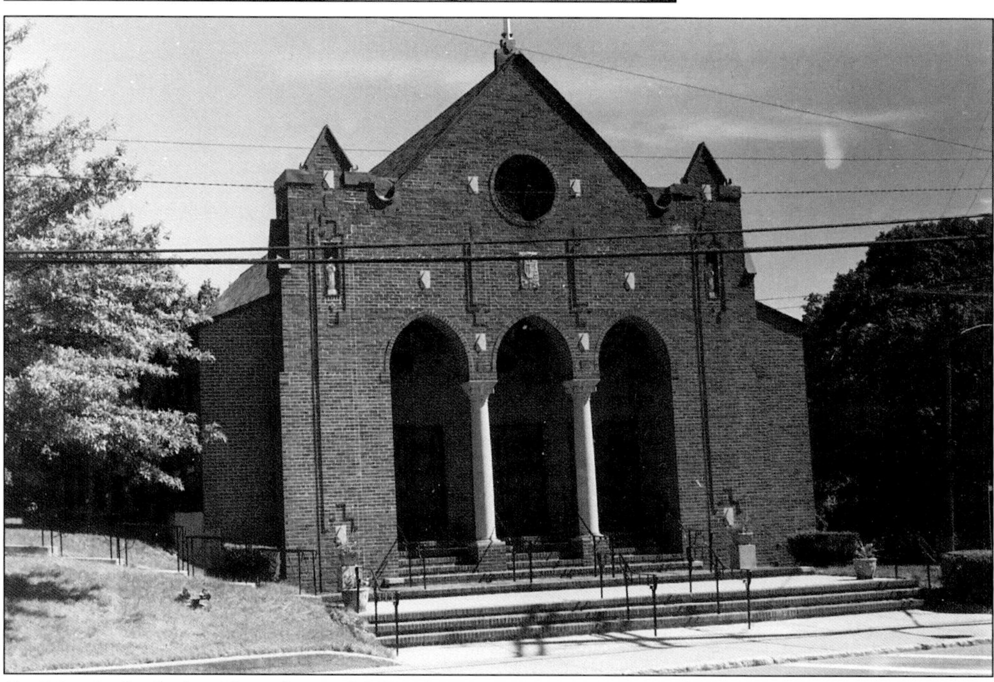

St. Mary's Catholic Church at 176 Washington Street, East Walpole, was dedicated in 1927. Catholics of East Walpole attended Mass at St. Francis Church until 1919, when Charles S. Bird granted Father Timothy Fahey the use of Bird Hall. Masses were held there until 1926. Mr. Bird also offered a piece of land for the construction of a church (it was rumored that the offer included a restriction that the church not be constructed of masonry). Father Fahey rejected the offer and had St. Mary's "Chapel" built on the present site. In 1931, St. Mary's became a separate parish.

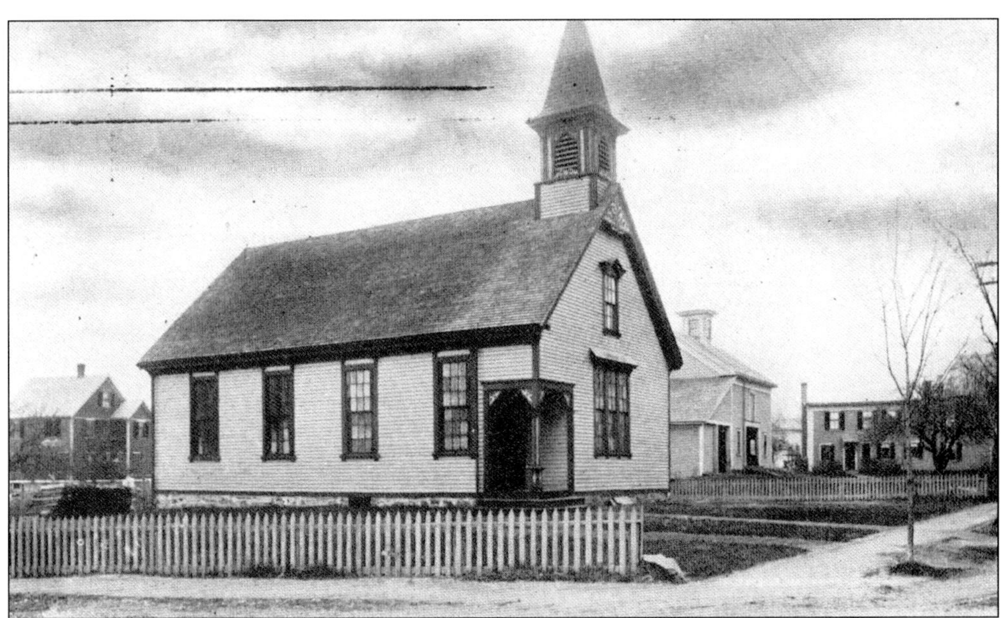

In 1877, a Congregational Society was formed in East Walpole. Services were held in F.W. Bird's hall on the second story of the old Morse Tavern. Their first meetinghouse (pictured here in 1915), located on Union Street and Walcott Avenue, was built by Frank Smith of Franklin for over $2,000 on land given by Deacon William Rhoads. In later years this old church became the home of the Wednesday Club and then the East Walpole Branch of the Walpole Public Library.

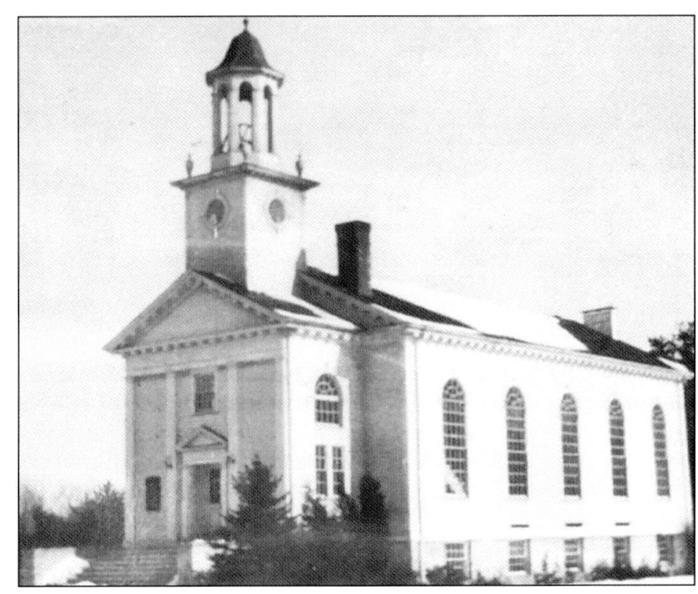

The Union Congregational Church, located on Rhoades Avenue, East Walpole, was built in 1915 on land donated by Charles Sumner Bird. This new church replaced the smaller church located at the corner of Union Street and Walcott Avenue. Because it is located next to Bird Park, it is sometimes referred to as "the Church in the Park."

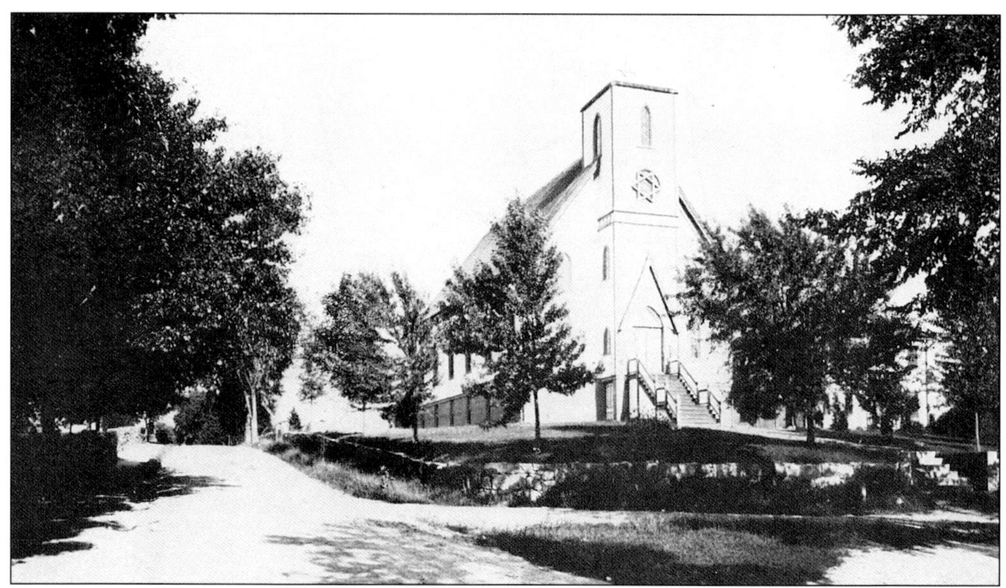

By 1863, the missions of Walpole, Foxboro, and Wrentham were part of the North Attleboro parish. They were attended by Father Philip Gillick of Greenville, Rhode Island, the first priest to minister to Walpole's Catholics with permanency and continuity. Saint Francis Catholic Church (shown here), located on East and Diamond Streets, was completed in 1879. Masses had previously been celebrated in private homes. In 1911, the wooden church building was moved to the rear of the property. Services continued here while the Blessed Sacrament Church was under construction. The old church was dismantled in 1922. The first pastor, Father Francis Gouese, died in 1901 at the age of 84 and was buried on the church grounds in the shade of his favorite maple tree.

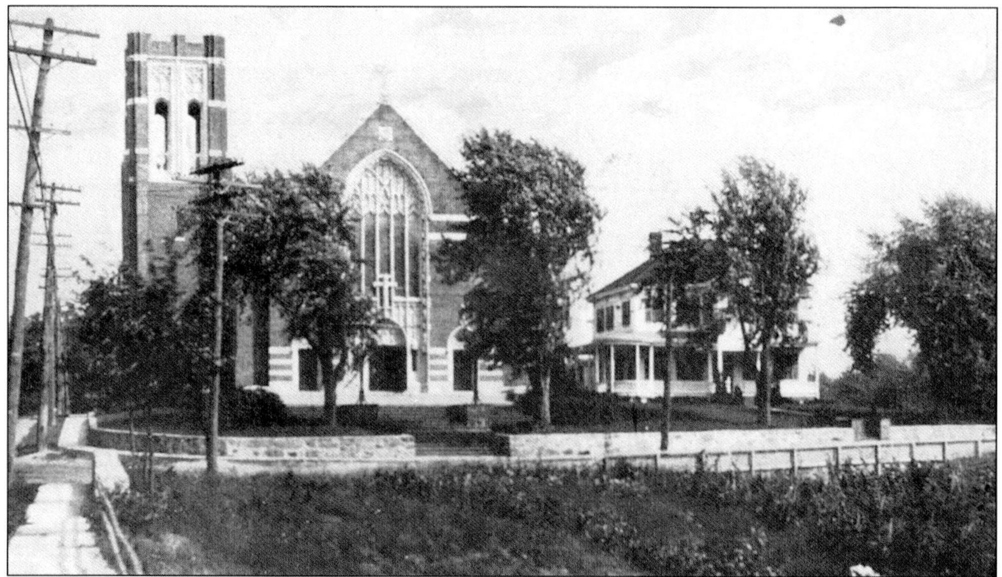

Blessed Sacrament Church, built under the direction of architect Matthew Sullivan, replaced the earlier wooden Saint Francis Church. Masses were first held in 1913. John Kirchmayer, an immigrant woodcarver from Oberamergau, Germany, carved the large ornate Apostolic entrance doors and many of the church's interior details.

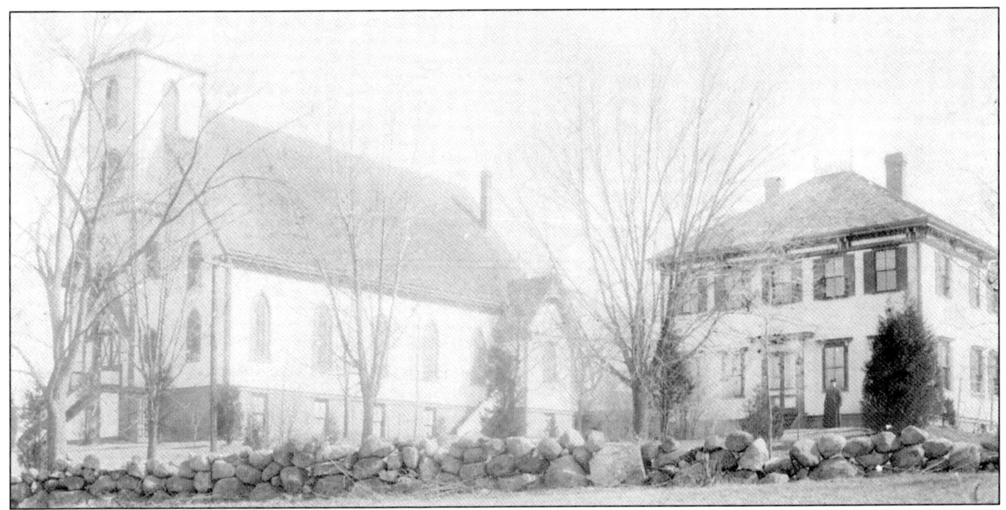

Father Francis Gouese, pastor of Saint Francis Church from 1872 to 1901, is shown here on the front lawn of the church's Diamond Street rectory in the late 1800s. The rectory has undergone many changes over the years, but the two front offices remain almost original. In the church's early days, one office was used as a weekday morning chapel during the cold winter months. Father Gouese's first rectory was a house on Kendall Street that later became the home of Henry Caldwell.

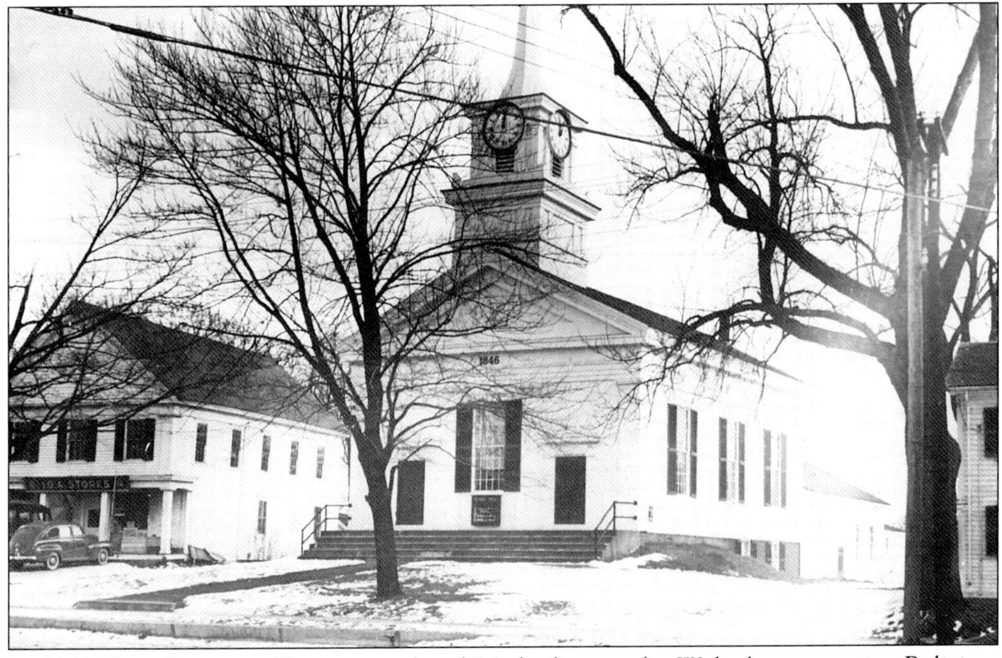

In 1818, Rev. Benjamin Haines introduced Methodism to the Walpole community. Religious meetings were held in private homes until 1830, when a small wooded church was built on Water Street in South Walpole. The new and larger United Methodist Church (shown here) was built on nearby Washington Street and dedicated on September 24, 1846. At the suggestion of Harvey Boyden in 1876, a neighborhood group comprised of church members and area residents contributed funds to purchase a "village clock" for the church steeple. In the early 1960s, the market at left was taken down to make room for the church's new educational wing.

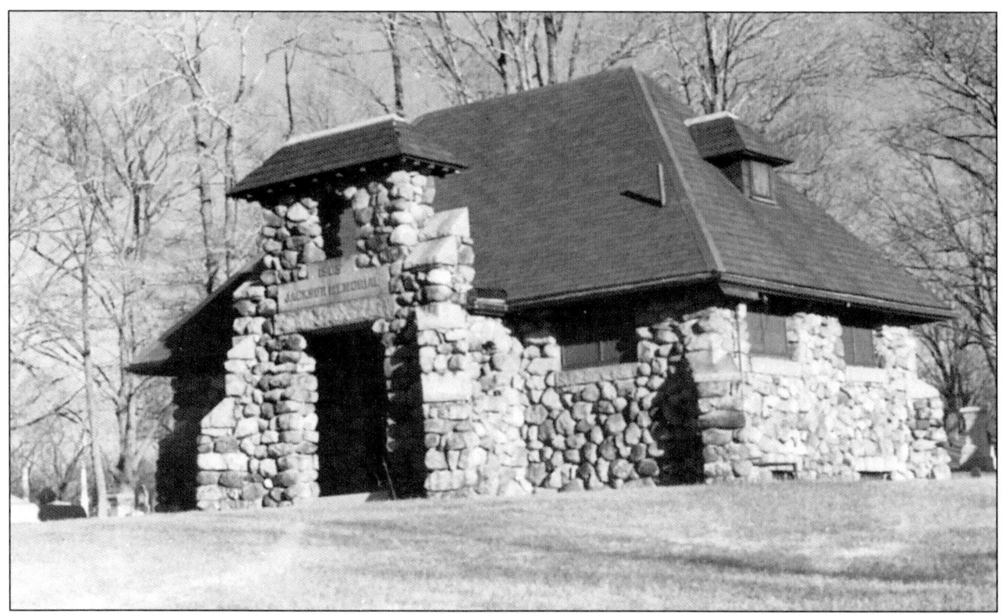

Sitting on top of a knoll, in the Terrace Hill Cemetery, is Jackson Memorial Chapel. Alfred L. Jackson built the chapel in 1905 as a memorial to his family. The fieldstone chapel seats 40 and is heated by a fireplace. Originally Terrace Hill was privately owned. Dwindling finances forced the trustees to relinquish its ownership to the town.

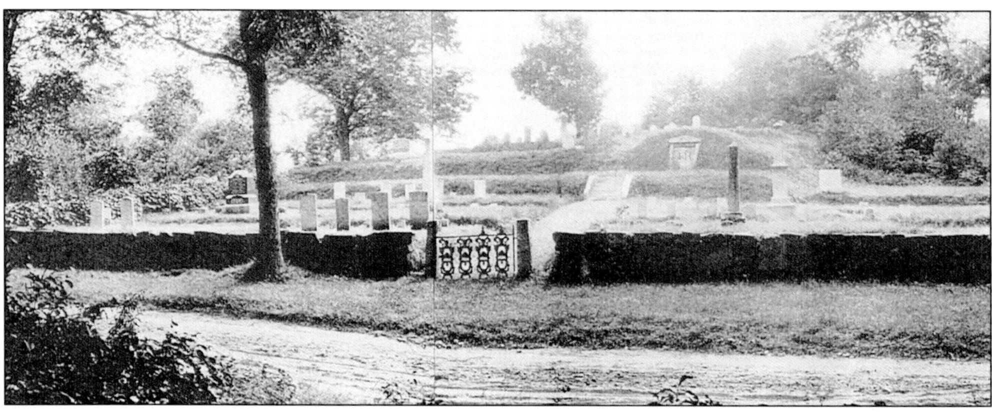

Rest in peace our forefathers.Your long hours, hard work, and dedication through the years have made Walpole the town it is today.
(The Guild Cemetery on Old Post Road is pictured here.)